CW01522135

The Logic of Chinese Politics

The Logic of Chinese Politics

Cores, Peripheries and Peaceful Rising

Sabrina Ching Yuen Luk

Associate Professor, Kunming University of Science and Technology, China

Peter W. Preston

Emeritus Professor of Political Sociology, University of Birmingham, UK

Cheltenham, UK • Northampton, MA, USA

Published by
Edward Elgar Publishing Limited
The Lypiatts
15 Lansdown Road
Cheltenham
Glos GL50 2JA
UK

Edward Elgar Publishing, Inc.
William Pratt House
9 Dewey Court
Northampton
Massachusetts 01060
USA

A catalogue record for this book
is available from the British Library

Library of Congress Control Number: 2016938590

This book is available electronically in the **Elgar**online
Social and Political Science subject collection
DOI 10.4337/9781784711276

ISBN 978 1 78471 125 2 (cased)
ISBN 978 1 78471 127 6 (eBook)

Typeset by Columns Design XML Ltd, Reading
Printed and bound in Great Britain by TJ International Ltd, Padstow

Contents

Preface

Since the 2008 Beijing Olympics, which presented to a global audience the face of contemporary China, the legatee of centuries of civilization, the beneficiary of recent decades of disciplined hard work and now orderly, prosperous and optimistic about the future, there has been a burgeoning literature of commentary on China. Many writers have contributed to this body of work and whilst the questions at issue shift and change with passing events, all revolve one way or another around the matter of the trajectory of development in China; its character, direction and possible wider consequences. In all this debate there are two familiar strands of more narrowly politically oriented work. On the one hand, Washington boosters, those who take the historical example of the USA for granted, a standard against which others, in this case China, can be judged; and on the other hand, China boosters, those who respond to foreign criticism by celebrating the long history, culture and present achievements of contemporary China, again in contrast to other countries, those with shorter, and implicitly less distinguished, histories. Yet both these approaches are foolish and unpersuasive as passing political judgements are allowed to confuse scholarly analysis. In contrast, in this short book we turn our attention to the internal dynamics of politics in China. Offering neither partisan-boosting nor criticism, we root our discussion in those traditions of scholarship with which we are familiar – the text is thus interpretive/critical and we deploy ideas dialogically offering our best efforts to reflexively grasp local logics. In particular we use the resources of historical institutionalism and related notions of culture criticism, as overall our aim is to report simply and directly how the political system works.

****

Formally, that is, in terms of theoretical approaches, we reject those which are informed by modernization/globalization theory as neither their evolutionism nor America-centredness are helpful. A familiar strand of work cast in these terms looks at China through the 'comparative lens of Leninist systems' but such approaches are doomed to fail as the party-state system is read in terms of the loaded concepts of authoritarianism and political transitions – in its crude and familiar forms such analyses read the world from the perspective of the Washington policy community, and this may be fine, if you are a member, but non-members should not confuse such work with scholarship. And in a similar vein we reject the analogous arguments which claim to be rooted in a distinctive East Asian reality and which offer counter-assertions invoking Confucianism or family types in order to speak about fundamentally hierarchical, paternalistic and moral polities. Here, one particular variant sees Chinese scholars invoking the example of Singapore, taking the self-aggrandizing claims of that country's government at face value and neglecting the wealth of available scholarship which tells a more critical tale of the enduring success of a trading port lodged deeply in the structures of the modern world. In brief, China-boosting is just as foolish as Washington-boosting. Then, third, more prosaically, we reject popular journalistic talk about the failure of the People's Republic of China for it is not collapsing, neither is it threatening, nor, contrariwise, is it without its own spread of problems.

And, finally, in contrast to these approaches and their various anxieties, we embrace those theorists who look to the country's history in the long unfolding shift to the modern world – we look to its institutional structures, to the agents animating the various components and to the sets of ideas running through the machineries of politics and administration and thereafter the wider society. In short, a mix of historical institutionalism and culture criticism. Such approaches allow scholarship a better access to the logic of Chinese politics. Another way of putting this is to look to the history of scholarly commentary on the European Union: at first, dominated by international relations theorists, conversations were concerned with the question of the nature of the European Union but attempts at classificatory analysis were not fruitful and later political scientists and others became involved and turned instead to the question of how the system worked – its logic. And so, here, in this text, we follow that line; we deploy the machineries of historical institutionalism and culture criticism in order to uncover the logic of Chinese politics.

****

So, in brief, in this short book we endeavour to grasp the underlying logic of the political system of the People's Republic of China. The book also covers a range of hot topics in China, including Internet sovereignty, the 'One Belt, One Road' initiatives and the South China Sea issue along with the problems of the elderly empty nesters and left-behind children.

We hope the book will provide the most relevant and up-to-date information to a broad audience of students, researchers, scholars, professionals, irrespective of discipline, and people with an interest in knowing about China or Chinese politics. We have deployed a mixture of historical institutionalist and culture critical analysis in order to grasp the way in which the system works. We are concerned to spell out the record of the polity; to take note of its beginnings, the historical context within which it was formed, to note the players, the agents whose efforts animate the story, to note the institutional structures which have been created, both ordering and facilitating the work of active agents, to note the policy lines that have been developed and put to work, sketching consequences, intended and unintended, calling attention thereby to the mundane realms of ordinary life, and to note thereafter the overall trajectory of the country and indicate possible future lines of direction.

Acknowledgements

In this short book we have been concerned to offer a straightforward characterization of the way in which politics works in China. We hope this book conveys some of our enthusiasm for understanding Chinese politics through a different and independent perspective and that it might inspire others to continue to do work in this area of research. We also hope that friends in China and elsewhere will find that what we have written is fair and realistic.

Many thanks are due to friends and colleagues in China, Hong Kong and England.

Abbreviations

ACWF	All-China Women's Federation
ADB	Asian Development Bank
AIIB	Asian Infrastructure Investment Bank
APCs	Agricultural Producers' Cooperatives
APEC	Asia-Pacific Economic Cooperation
ASEAN	The Association of Southeast Asian Nations
ASEM	The Asia–Europe Meeting
CCP	Chinese Communist Party
CMS	Cooperative Medical System
EGDI	E-government Development Index
GDP	Gross Domestic Product
GIS	Government Insurance Scheme
GLF	Great Leap Forward
GOP	Government Online Project
ICT	Information and communication technology
IMF	International Monetary Fund
IT	Information Technology
KMT	Kuomintang
LIS	Labour Insurance Scheme
MCA	Ministry of Civil Affairs
NATO	North Atlantic Treaty Organization
NPC	National People's Congress
PLA	People's Liberation Army
PRC	People's Republic of China
ROC	Republic of China
SAR	Special Administrative Region
SARS	Severe Acute Respiratory Syndrome
SCAP	Supreme Commander Allied Powers
SEZs	Special Economic Zones
SID	Supplier-induced-demand
SOEs	State-owned enterprises
TPP	Trans-Pacific Partnership
TVEs	Township and Village Enterprises
UN	United Nations

USA	United States of America
USSR	Union of Soviet Socialist Republics
VPNs	Virtual Private Networks
WTO	World Trade Organization

1. China and the modern world

The shift to the modern world took its initial form in Europe, where a unique constellation of economic, social, cultural and political processes ushered into being the world of natural science, industry, states, nations and mass societies. The form of life was dynamic, evidencing both domestic intensification and global expansion, and when the representatives of this culture, in particular traders, reached China, the demands of this insurgent culture slowly undermined the long-established, agrarian-based bureaucratic feudal system centred upon the emperor. The collapse of the system was slow, and European powers were crucial players with their insistent demands for free trade. The Chinese elite's eventual choice of some variant form of modernity was signalled by the 1911 Revolution, but in the event the revolution was beset by problems: there were internal divisions, a continuing foreign presence and finally civil war and outright foreign military invasion. The elite's embrace of modernity only found effective form in the 1949 Revolution, and the long process of collapse and recovery is now available in contemporary nationalist terms as the century of humiliation, a notion that unpacks to call attention to foreign aggressions and domestic failings and draws the lesson of the importance of national development – altogether, an era which, more positively, ended with the creation of New China.

It is the nature of the shift to the modern world that informs the logic of politics in China. The argument presented here will contextualize contemporary Chinese politics in this fashion, granting that the present is the out-turn of events in the past and turning to spell out institutional forms (the party-state), politico-cultural understandings (the national past, collective memory and the realms of everyday life) and patterns of policy action (ideas-in-practice). Together, these are the frameworks of contemporary debates amongst political players in China.

****

The notion of the shift to the modern world encompasses a number of elements. The modern world revolves around the rise of natural science based industry, the creation of a system of states, the invention of nations and the rise of mass popular politics. The shift to the modern world

1

entails complex social change, and the process is open-ended; it is not a one-time event, and its dynamics continue to run, and whilst its broad future development is clear, its particular detailed character is not determined in advance. The process began in Europe. It was the result of a fortuitous set of circumstances, and Europe was remade from the inside, and later the rest of the world was variously remade. In the nineteenth and early twentieth centuries these processes assumed the form of the creation of state-empire systems, followed later by system dissolution and the creation of new states. But these processes were not mechanical, and each episode of domestic change was discrete, just as each episode of external expansion was also discrete; so particular logics of change must be deciphered, as each country's shift to the modern world is unique.

In respect of China, the task of deciphering these logics of change is crucial as these long and unfolding historical processes underpin and give shape to the current politics. The past both shapes the present and offers the cultural resources whereby both past and present can be reflexively understood. This means that characterizations cast in the terms of outsiders will only have limited reach; it is the internal logic that must be grasped. So the research process is dialogic as sets of ideas are put to use, replies made and new material presented and new formulations advanced. The research process is also reiterative and open-ended, debates are renewed and reworked and rarely definitively settled. In this text, using the materials of historical institutionalism, the concern is to offer a simple, short, realistic characterization of the domestic logic of contemporary politics in China.

HISTORICAL INSTITUTIONALISM AND CULTURE CRITICAL WORK: AN APPROACH TO POLITICAL ANALYSIS

Scholars have produced a number of ways of approaching generic political analysis:[1] political philosophy (reflection upon abstract concepts); political history (records and reflections upon political events); political institutions (characterization and discussion of formal systems of political organization); political ideology (formal and informal programmes of parties and other agents); and, in contrast, political behaviourism (measuring aspects of political behaviour and subjecting the resultant data sets to statistical analysis, thus, parties, elections and voting patterns).

Each offers some valuable material, and each set of resources can be put to work and offer some insight into the nature of political life. However this text will use the strategies of historical institutionalist analysis[2] and culture critical work. The approach draws on elements of all the above and allows analysts to uncover the ways in which institutional machineries and ideas (organizational forms plus associated habits of thought plus ways of working plus strategies of legitimation within wider publics) have developed over time. Such institutional machineries are understood to be contingent creations, and they serve to order political life in particular ways, but they are not fixed, they are part of a deeper dynamic. As structural conditions shape the behaviour of agents, and the behaviour of agents in turn impacts structural dynamics, then the ways in which agents read their structural circumstances find expression in institutional machineries. And as structural circumstances change, so agents respond and thus institutions are reworked. The process is open-ended, but it is not without overall shape, and this is determined by the ongoing unfolding shift to the modern world, driven by the demands of natural science based industrial capitalism, states (and wider state systems), nations and popular politics.

Historical Institutionalism

Historical institutionalism has developed a particular repertoire of strategies of enquiry:

- case studies of particular countries (or parts of countries);
- historical studies of long-term patterns (of continuity and change);
- comparative analysis of the ways in which different countries have tackled the demands of the modern world;
- interpretation of patterns of understanding of key groups.

Historical institutionalism has developed a particular intellectual vocabulary:

- path dependency – institutions tend to run along lines set by the past;
- episodes of change – disturbances (external or internal) create crises and provoke change;
- punctuated equilibrium – societies work but are not static, that is, they are generally stable but liable to relatively abrupt change.

Culture Critical Work

Culture critical analysis has developed around a small number of central concerns:

- language – unpacking the relationship of human language and human practice;
- ideology – unpacking the social class-inflected nature of ordinary language;
- discourse – unpacking the routinization of ways of understanding and acting.

Culture critical analysis has developed a number of specialist intellectual vocabularies:

- hermeneutic elucidation of texts;
- anthropological/sociological elucidation of the ideas informing social practices;
- critical discussion of contemporary cultural practices (text analogues).

Together, these strategies of enquiry and their related concepts allow scholarly analysts to track the long-term historical development trajectories of countries, to uncover their changing institutional forms, to consider changing ways of understanding and to detail present politico-cultural circumstances. The ensemble of concepts points not to a collection of methods, rather a way of thinking.[3] Contemporary political and policy debates amongst elites and masses can thus be understood to be rooted in the unfolding development of the countries themselves, and, of course, it is within the framework of inherited institutions and inherited culture that the resources necessary to guide further change will be found.

THE LONG HISTORY OF CHINA RECALLED

The shift to the modern world in China was triggered by the demands of foreign traders in the nineteenth century, and their behaviour was aggressive, involved routine recourse to violence and was justified in terms of ideologies claiming beneficial results from trade.[4] These were the earliest agents that drew China into the nineteenth century global system of state-empires; however, China had existed for much longer, and one familiar way of grasping the history is to speak in terms of dynasties, but this is just one way of thinking about the country, its history and ways of living.

Grasping the Outlines of China

There are numerous ways of grasping the historical trajectory of a country, the mix of past, present and implied future:

- *China as a culture* – the history is presented in terms of a sequence of dynasties running back two thousand years;
- *China as a geographical term* – home to a number of polities over that same period with internal patterns and external borders shifting and changing;
- *China as a race-nation* – a nationalist tale mixing claims about race, racial origins, dynasties, foreign aggression, humiliation[5] and contemporary success;
- *China in the eyes of hostile foreigners* – critical tales specifying varieties of imminent economic and political failure;[6]
- *China as a dynamic modern polity* – with a domestic pattern of power and a definite place within the international system, the whole represented in public discourse in terms of a national past, the whole accessible to historical social scientific analysis.[7]

It is this last noted China that will be discussed here; in particular, its unfolding historical trajectory as it shifts into the modern world, a world which is itself continually changing its nature, an ongoing collective project.

Pre-modern or Traditional[8] China

After the modern world had arrived in the guise of foreign traders and related empire builders, soldiers, missionaries and so on, and had precipitated change, sometimes serving trade (hence the Treaty Port System), sometimes generating social problems (opium sales and growing addiction), and in other places precipitating unforeseen and unforeseeable chaos (Taiping Rebellion), Chinese reformers in the late nineteenth century borrowed terms from Japan in order to grasp the nature of the modern world, the world that had presented itself in the guise of rapacious demands from foreigners for trading rights, hence the concepts of nation and state and democracy. A clutch of other terms entered elite discourse around this time, later feeding into elite and popular practice, thus race. In brief, around the turn of the twentieth century, an idea of China as a nation, rooted in a distinct race, with its own state and the overall goal of democracy, began to take root.[9]

Today's China is therefore a recent construction, and the claims of nationalists to the effect that China – in these senses – is rooted in the long, distant past are quite false. The same argument, of course, is true of European and American polities; indeed, in general, social scientists offer quite different understandings of national identities from those offered by nationalists.[10] So, prior to the arrival of the modern world and the early moves to reconstruct the country, China, as we would now say, operated quite differently.

Pre-modern (traditional)[11] China operated as:

- a cultural sphere – those people who could read and write the Chinese script, those people who were conversant with classical texts and those people who were educated in these matters;
- an economic trading sphere – those people living in the mainland with its three macro-regions (northern around the Yellow River, eastern around the Yangtze River, and southern oriented towards the Pearl River), along with those people linked by trading networks, overland the Silk Road to the north and west, and by sea the trading networks along the coast plus those reaching down into the Nanyang;
- an international political sphere – those polities distinct from China which were nonetheless influenced by China, in particular, Korea, Japan and Vietnam, and worked within a definite relationship with China, tributary relationships or broadly the Sino-centric system;
- a social/cultural sphere – individual Chinese were embedded in the social world in terms of a number of spheres including family, kin groups, clan groups, place of origin and language groups, and then wider concerns were grasped via Buddhism, Taoism, Confucianism and the emperor system;
- a governance sphere – the imperial system of a core, plus provinces, examinations and a Confucian social hierarchy (emperor–scholars–soldiers–peasants–merchants).

These characteristics sum up the diversity of forms of life found in pre-modern China. The point here is that pre-modern China was a rich and diverse civilization, it functioned and its character was quite different from equivalent cultures in Europe. Its character today is in part a product of those historically accumulated characteristics; again, quite different from Europe.

Cores and Peripheries

The geographical extent of China understood as a polity has varied down the centuries. The territorial extent of the polity has waxed and waned, and at the present time, with the People's Republic of China (PRC), the country is near to its maximum historical size. China occupies a large geographical space, has a large population and has complex domestic politics. Institutionally the party-state system works as a hierarchy of descending/ascending cores and peripheries.[12] The unitary state unpacks as provinces, townships, villages and so on, so power is not spread evenly amongst geographical areas or populations. The capital city occupies the core position and thereafter there are distinct powerful subordinate cores and equally distinct subordinate peripheries. The pattern is changing somewhat as, in addition, government policy over recent years has favoured urbanization; thus cities are becoming increasingly powerful, economically, culturally and politically.

In the past, in pre-modern China, whilst there were powerful urban cores – economic, cultural and administrative – these tended to be closely integrated with peripheral agricultural areas. In pre-modern China cities did not display the distinctiveness associated with European cities of the same era.[13] China retained large areas of peasant farming, and as late as the turn of the twentieth century, the vast bulk of the population were farmers, living in rural areas. On this, Stockman comments that at the time of Mao's death only 20 per cent of the population lived in urban areas.[14]

In the present, in modern China, the crucial cores are cities, powerful economic, cultural and political centres. Today the linkages of these cities are not only domestic but also international, and there are three main sub-regions around Beijing, Shanghai and Guangzhou. The creation of this pattern can be detailed with nineteenth century patterns (reflecting the opening period of the shift to the modern world, thus, the impact of foreign traders and the creation of the 'Treaty Port System'), the early twentieth century patterns (reflecting the developments of the Nationalist era and the destruction of war), the early period of the Chinese Communist Party (CCP) where rural development was favoured, and then, finally, the current pattern, the creation of the period of reform and opening up, with large cities plus the accumulated impacts of CCP policy in respect of rural and urban development. Urban development is now, in the twenty-first century, a stated goal of the party-state, one aspect of the party's plans for the next stage of development.

THE IMPACT OF THE MODERN WORLD

Karl Marx and Frederick Engels wrote approvingly of the dynamism of capitalism, and they alluded to the experience of China, with capitalism battering down all Chinese walls and with this dynamism opening the way to progress capitalist style:[15]

> The bourgeoisie, by the rapid improvement of all instruments of production, by the immensely facilitated means of communication, draws all, even the most barbarian, nations into civilization. The cheap prices of its commodities are the heavy artillery with which it batters down all Chinese walls ... It compels all nations, on pain of extinction, to adopt the bourgeois mode of production; it compels them to introduce what it calls civilization into their midst, that is, to become bourgeois themselves.

The particular individual vehicles of these structural processes were traders. There had been early contacts from the mid-sixteenth century but the traders arrived in numbers in the nineteenth century. The British and French, in particular, sought trading rights and were not averse to using violence to advance their interests; nonetheless, recent commentators have argued that the Qing authorities had no clear idea who these people were or what they wanted.[16]

Foreign Traders, Domestic Problems and the Collapse of the Qing

Structural change requires that agents read and respond. Commentators suggest that the Qing failed to grasp the nature of the threat posed by foreign traders. China entered the modern world in a quite distinctive fashion, and the arrival of foreign traders signalled change; these traders were the early representatives of a form of life new to the Chinese elite, mercantile capitalism. European powers had been trading in the region for many years, thus the Portuguese established Malacca in 1511 and Macau in the mid-sixteenth century, and their activities fitted into established East Asian networks of trade, but later traders offered opportunities and made demands that the extant system could not accommodate. The key incoming players were the French and British, and other foreign groups also participated in the new mercantile capitalist trade.

China was the goal for both powers, and both approached from the south; the British traded at Canton in the Pearl River Delta, whilst the French traded from bases in Indo-China. The key players were the British, characterized by one scholar as a rapacious, violent and disreputable group,[17] and for many years they were a mystery to the authorities in Beijing, who could not understand who they were, why they were violent or what they wanted.[18] The British traded opium, the Qing authorities resisted, and the First Opium War followed. Hong Kong was established. A second trading base was established in Shanghai, and later the Second Opium War led to further bases being established. The Qing authorities had to address domestic problems, deal with aggressive traders and seek to understand the form of life which underpinned their activities, and the Qing authorities slowly failed. The 1861–95 Self-Strengthening Movement, the 1898 Hundred Days Reform and the later Boxer Rebellion all failed to stop the operation or extension of the Treaty Port System, as China was reduced to a quasi-colony of the Europeans, Americans and Japanese.[19]

The 1911 Revolution and Civil War

The scale of foreign depredations was clear by the last years of the nineteenth century. Qing era attempts at reform had not succeeded, and the Boxer Rebellion underscored the weakness of the authorities as scholars and political activists sought new ideas and new models. Japan was one model where the success of the Meiji Restoration was noted; ideas and information also flowed into China from Europe and America along with traders, settlers, missionaries, administrators and so on. All these available materials had to be read into Chinese culture, and new vocabularies were needed; thus state, nation, race, democracy and so on. These ideas fed into local debates, and one aspect was the notion of humiliation: that China had been brought low by its own weakness and the activities of foreigners.[20] But by now the Qing authorities had numerous opponents: regional, social class, popular and intellectual.[21] Moore[22] comments that by the time the Qing authorities realized the extent of required reforms it was already too late.

The 1911 Revolution began with a dispute about the control of railway infrastructure, where the Qing authorities sought to assert central control and local groups resisted. These disputes began in Wuhan in Hubei Province as local army personnel rebelled. The Qing authorities were repudiated and the rebellions spread until a provisional government was proclaimed in January 1912. The difficult task of creating a new political settlement was begun; that is, the proclaimed republic had to gather support from other regional elites and the mass of the population. The initial drive to create a republic ran from 1912 to 1913, and a double process followed: the republic government in the south was unable to assert its authority over the rest of the country and the Qing residues in the north could not sustain their position and gradually faded from the scene. In the period 1913–16 one key figure from the late Qing era – the soldier Yuan Shikai – assumed power, and the leaders of the republic acquiesced. Yuan then proclaimed himself emperor, but he died in 1916 and a political void opened. The failure of the republic left local forces in control of local areas, and the bulk of the country was controlled by warlords, some three hundred plus, with half a dozen major groups, and these groups fought numerous wars, some involving armies measured in the hundreds of thousands.[23] The result, predictably, was great confusion.

Chiang Kai Shek and the Nanjing Decade

The early death of Sun Yat Sen in 1925 saw power within his party shift to the military leader Chiang Kai Shek, who worked to unify the republican forces. He made an alliance with the Communist Party and opted to solve the problem of warlords via a mixture of military campaigns, co-option and bribery. And in 1926 he launched the Northern Expedition. Moving up from the south of China towards Shanghai and Nanjing, Chiang's armies were successful as warlords were defeated or fell in line. The Communist Party in Shanghai, anticipating his arrival, organized an uprising amongst their supporters in the industries of the city – workers – the closest the city had to a conventional Marxist proletariat, but Chiang did not support the efforts of his erstwhile allies; indeed, he took the opposite course as his troops along with the forces of local industrialists and city gangsters attacked and largely destroyed the Communist Party forces, actions that provoked the Chinese Civil War.

Over the next decade, the Nanjing Decade, running up to 1937, developments unfolded along three distinct trajectories. First, Chiang continued to move his forces northwards and, using the same techniques as before, organized a kind of unity for the country. The capital was based in Nanjing, the country was unified, and it began to put in place the apparatus of a modern state and to wind back the privileges of the foreigners. Then, second, Chiang began a series of military campaigns designed to extirpate the remnants of the Communist Party, and a number of campaigns were launched against communist rural base areas. In time the base area organized by Mao was overrun; the remnants fled in a long retreat over difficult ground in remote areas of China before eventually finding a form of sanctuary in the far north of the country. And then, third, in 1937 the Japanese invaded China and the human and material losses were severe; further chaos followed. The civil war resumed at the end of the Pacific War, and the CCP secured a rapid military victory. Mao declared the founding of the PRC, and the remnants of the nationalists fled to Taiwan.

Mid-century Warfare

The slow decay and eventual collapse of the Qing dynasty was followed not by the modern republic of the revolutionists' designs but instead by waves of violence as warlords fought numerous wars and nominally modern political parties/movements fought a civil war. A newly created state-empire launched a military invasion, and American and European powers were drawn into a Pacific War. This in turn was subsumed within the wider Second World War, which in turn was followed by the nascent, cold war inflected final phase of the civil war.[24] The results of all this for China were catastrophic, and the number of deaths can be put at around 30 million or so – add to that the injured, the material destruction and the reactions and memories of those, the majority, who survived.

These episodes are read into contemporary official politico-cultural understandings; different memories have been stressed at different times:

- Kuomintang (KMT) government ideas in the 1930s of legacies of national humiliation;
- the KMT's claims to a New China;
- the CCP's creation of the idea of 'the long march';
- the CCP's (nationalist) claim to have led national resistance to Japanese invaders;
- the CCP's (nationalist) embrace of national humiliation and anti-Japanese rhetoric.

The government of Xi Jinping celebrated the Seventieth Anniversary of the end of the Pacific War with a large military parade in Beijing, and thus the CCP laid claim to a central role in the military victory.

The PRC

The CCP came to political power in China in the wake of a series of wars including civil war, inter-state war and regional war, and finally world war. The consequences of these conflicts for China were severe in terms of casualties, material losses and social disorder. It is unsurprising that when the CCP came to wield political power that its first concerns were not dissimilar to those of more straightforwardly post-colonial regimes: security, order and development. Domestically, first the CCP had to deal with the remnants of the nationalist forces and their sympathizers amongst the population, landlord and business classes. At that time, 90 per cent of the population was rural, so landlords were particular targets. Estimates of the numbers killed often say around a million. Second, the

CCP had to construct its party-state apparatus and draw in the population, mobilizing and disciplining them to the CCP's politico-cultural project. And third, the CCP sought development, and the project was cast in local terms. The CCP leadership advanced an amalgam of ideas including Marxism–Leninism as a framework, hence, class, class conflict, progress, along with Chinese nationalism, here a celebration of country, culture and people, taken as evidenced during the war years plus a celebration of the vitality of the peasantry and the possibilities inherent in that energy.

The early period 1950–56 was successful: foreign interests were expelled, the country unified, and a reform programme begun; rural areas were reorganized, with landlords disposed and peasants given land; and urban areas were reorganized as private property was progressively curtailed. The development record was good, but inevitably there were problems. Early on the CCP invited criticism – the Hundred Flowers Campaign – but critical debate was quickly closed down in the Anti-Rightist Movement, and intellectuals and professions were demobilized, expertise rejected. The later 1958–60 Great Leap Forward (GLF) was an elite-sponsored attempt to skip stages of development, with mass mobilization as the key, but it failed and famine resulted.[25] Mao was sidelined and experts reasserted their ideas. Subsequently, Mao mobilized support amongst students and used them to attack the apparatus of the CCP. It was understood by participants as an attempt to remake culture, the ways in which people thought, hence the Cultural Revolution. The conflict continued until it began to threaten the army, the core of the state, at which point the revolution was halted; yet the elite-level political conflicts continued, and the death of Mao was crucial, for now elite-level power balances shifted as those closest to Mao were arrested and given a show trial as Deng Xiaoping took control.

The contemporary institutional system inherits this history plus the impacts of state-empire systems plus the more enduring cultural residues of pre-modern China. Today China is a dynamic modern polity, but it has a distinctive form: the country is geographically sub-continental, the party-state system is a distinctive double bureaucracy/hierarchy and the elite are committed to national development; in all, a variant developmental state.

Reform and Opening

The new leadership inaugurated a new programme, in effect learning from the experience of East Asia, and their approach was pragmatic. In the period 1978–84 reforms were carried out in agriculture and a number of Special Economic Zones (SEZs) were set up. In agriculture

the process was one of de-collectivization with the household responsibility system, and the results were dramatic; agricultural output rose
and levels of living improved. At the same time, rural industry was
encouraged, and it took the form of Township and Village Enterprises
(TVEs), low-level production oriented towards an open market that
soaked up surplus labour and generated a perhaps modest economic
surplus. In the period 1984–87 urban industry and finance were
reformed, but this proved to be more difficult to organize as the
economic and social make-up of a city was more complex than that of
a rural area. Individual enterprises were given more autonomy and
moved towards open-market operation – again, a process of liberalization. There were many issues to address: the notion of private ownership, issues of transferring ownership from state to reformed enterprises,
questions of financing and managing quasi-private enterprises, and
problems of building up liberal-type welfare operations. These experiments adopted one novel form, that is, SEZs, and five were created on
coastal sites. One was adjacent to Hong Kong in Shenzhen, and the area
prospered, so too the other SEZs. However, the country suffered the
stresses and strains of rapid change, and popular discontent was made
clear in June 1989.[26] Deng Xiaoping's 1992 Southern Tour was designed
to reaffirm the policy of reform, and a new policy was established, the
1992 programme of creating a socialist market economy. Further
sweeping reforms followed, and in 2001 the country joined the World
Trade Organization (WTO). This signalled the country's participation
within the global economic system, and a species of finally achieved
complete success was celebrated at the 2008 Beijing Olympics.[27]

The elite has pursued the goal of economic advance pragmatically and
single-mindedly, and the policy is now more than 30 years old and has
produced dramatic economic and social changes. Economic advance has
been headlong, and material levels of living have improved, but there
have been difficulties as inequality and corruption have grown, and there
are severe environmental problems. In this period the party-state system
has reformed and adapted,[28] and contrary to the expectations of un-
sympathetic foreign critics, it has not collapsed.

CHINA: INSTITUTIONAL FORMS AND
POLITICO-CULTURAL UNDERSTANDINGS

China entered the modern world via a long experience of quasi-colonial
rule. From the early nineteenth century through to the opening years of
the twentieth, the nature of Chinese politics – institutions and ideas – was

shaped by the exchange with foreigners, and the Qing regime was slow to react and in time was displaced. The earliest attempts at a coherent and effective response to the foreigner-carried demands of the modern world came with the Republican Revolution, but this failed and was followed by civil war, with the domestic situation made much worse by inter-state warfare. Matters were finally brought under domestic political control with the establishment of the PRC. A new political settlement was put in place,[29] a matter of institutional machineries and ways of understanding that together carried new domestic power relations, official ways of understanding, along with projects looking forward.

Standard Social Science Strategies of Analysis

Debates about the nature of politics in China are not new, as both domestic and foreign scholars have written extensively. In regard to recent, that is, modern-era work, two rough characterizations can be offered: domestic work is cast in terms of 'worrying about China',[30] whilst foreign material has been cast in terms of the resources of the social sciences, and in the post-Second World War period this last noted has been heavily influenced by work done by American scholars, itself shaped by the environment of cold war, and cast negatively in terms of the party-state.

Flemming Christiansen and Shirin Rai review analyses of the party-state:[31]

- the party-state is totalitarian and so the entire economic, social and political system is controlled by one ideologically motivated repressive party;
- the party-state system is dominated by an elite but elite control is fissured by continual manoeuvring for position and advantage, that is, the party-state is nominally well ordered but in fact is riven with factionalism and clientelism;[32]
- the party-state system is a complex bureaucracy and the system is essentially bureaucratic with decisions taken inside the system and handed down;
- the party-state system enshrines some fundamental traits of Chinese culture, in particular, the common social practices of hierarchy and obedience.

The first of these – totalitarianism – belongs to the less plausible habits of thought of the cold war. David Shambaugh[33] offers a sophisticated example of this conventional analysis. He reviews a number of major

American China scholars looking at post-1989 China, and the discussion is cast in terms of 'the comparative lens of Leninist systems'.[34] Such work has a deep expectation of uni-linear movement towards a liberal-democratic future, and in this perspective the PRC party-state might escape inevitable breakdown, but only via repression or muddling through, and its best chance is to become authoritarian and corporatist, maybe with some liberal-democratic aspects, like Singapore or Hong Kong.[35] The problem with this sort of analysis is clear: it is uni-linear (modernization/globalization), it is doubly un-reflexive (the USA is the unspoken ethico-political model and the unspoken context for the discussion) and it belongs to the cold war era (now over); but thereafter, to be clear, the author opts (sensibly) for atrophy and adaptation, thus the party-state system is losing support but is adapting.

It might be noted that these cold war style habits of thought are recognizable in contemporary American (or Western) commentary, with publicly voiced anxieties about PRC military expenditures, publicly voiced concerns about PRC's domestic human rights record (dissidents or death penalty or Tibet and so on), and publicly voiced China-related concerns for governance of the global economy (debates around the Trans-Pacific Partnership (TPP) or Asian Infrastructure Investment Bank (AIIB) or International Monetary Fund (IMF) rules), thus recently – summer 2015 – publicly voiced anxieties about the condition of the economy of China.

Then the second – factionalism and clientelism – may have been accurate during the civil war years when the CCP was under sustained pressure from the KMT and the mix of military and political policies was an urgent matter, that is, a wrong decision in the 1930s could have led to the party's demise, and it may have been accurate during the post-revolutionary period dominated by Mao Zedong, with elite level confusions around the Hundred Flowers episode or GLF or – paradigmatically – during the Cultural Revolution. One instance of the concern for factions and networks is offered by Tony Saich. The analysis looks from the outside and overlaps with the cold war habits noted above – thus:[36]

Personal power and relations with powerful individuals are decisive throughout the Chinese political system and society ... Thus the Chinese political leadership is riddled with networks of personal relationships and is dominated by patron–client ties ... This system ... lends itself easily to the formation of factions within the leadership ... This overdependence on personal relationships makes the Chinese political leadership extremely unstable.

However, more recently, whilst the post-Mao regimes have been analysed in similar fashion, the party has made efforts to regularize internal elite-level decision making, including elite cadre retirement and elite replenishment, and, of course, with Xi Jinping, it has launched an unprecedented purge of corrupt party members and officials within the state machine.

Thereafter, the last noted – fourth line – must carry some weight. It is a culturalist approach that appeals to the cultural resources of the Chinese, urging that as humans are social animals, they dwell in communities, shaped by rules handed down,[37] whilst cultures shift and change, they do so slowly.

Nonetheless, it is the third line – complex bureaucracy – that is the most appropriate line of commentary for present purposes. It is in line with the historical institutionalist approach taken in this text, so the party-state system is best conceived as a double bureaucracy: there is a state bureaucracy/hierarchy with a spread of familiar functions and, for its membership, familiar paths of career advancement; and there is a professional party/hierarchy with its own functions and paths of career advancement.[38] The two bureaucracies are intertwined, but they have their own views of the world. Picking up this line, a related strategy is offered by Zheng Yongnian,[39] whose work borrows elements of neo-institutionalism and neo-Marxism, thus institutions and ideas, and who offers a take on the domestic trajectory and logic of the polity, thus the CCP is the organizational spine around which debate revolves – it is an 'organizational emperor'.

Double Bureaucracy/Hierarchy – Institutions/Ideas

China is ordered via a party-state system. The party-state works as a double bureaucracy. Party and state are nominally separate but in practice intermingled, and commentators report that the party is the key player. Larus comments: 'State government and the party have overlapping memberships, and high-ranking government personnel are important CCP leaders.'[40] So, first, the party elite is reported to number around 2,500 and is organizationally centred on the Politburo and its Standing Committee;[41] second, the party is reported to have a membership of some 80 million[42] and an elaborate hierarchical structure that reaches down through numerous administrative levels producing around 825,000[43] committees of one sort or another, national, provincial, prefectural, municipality, township and village; and third, the machinery of the state comprises a number of organizations, thus the State Council, National People's Congress (NPC), Supreme People's Court, Central Military

Commission, plus the administrative civil service, plus provincial and local government.[44]

On the machinery of the party, Wang[45] reports that 'the salient characteristics of the party as an organization are that it is hierarchical, pyramidal, and centralist in nature' and so power is concentrated in the hands of party leaders who operate via the major organs of the party: the National Party Congress, the Central Committee, the Central Commission for Discipline Inspection, the Politburo and its Standing Committee, along with the General Secretary.

The National Party Congress, which convenes once every five years, is the largest meeting of party members, and its primary function is to elect a new Central Committee and a new Central Commission for Discipline Inspection. The Central Committee is, in theory, the supreme authority of the party when the National Party Congress is not in session, and its primary functions are (i) directing the work of the party; (ii) representing the party in its foreign relations; (iii) determining the members of the Central Military Commission; and (iv) electing the Politburo and its Standing Committee, and the General Secretary.[46]

However, the Politburo has 'the ultimate decision-making power concerning war, armed force, and national defence'[47] and its Standing Committee 'works as a kind of inner cabinet and groups together the country's most influential leaders';[48] its members meet regularly and frequently to discuss issues in different policy areas, and they also conduct fieldwork and observation nationwide, especially when there is an outbreak of crisis or a natural disaster.[49]

Leading Small Groups are set up by the Politburo and its Standing Committee in an ad hoc manner to address special and strategic issues, and they are 'supra-ministerial coordinating and consulting bodies formed to build consensus on some crucial and strategic issues when the existing bureaucracy is unable to do so'.[50] At present, in early 2016, President Xi Jinping is Head of four Leading Small Groups: (i) Leading Small Group on Comprehensively Deepening Reform; (ii) the Central Finance and Economics Leading Small Group; (iii) the Central Internet Security and Informatization Leading Group; and (iv) the Leading Group for Deepening National Defence and Military Reform.[51] The General Secretary 'is the highest-ranking official of the Party and heads the Politburo and the Standing Committee … [and is] responsible for convening the meetings of the Politburo and its Standing Committee and presides over the work of the Party Secretariat'.[52]

In addition to these bodies, the Central Commission for Discipline Inspection is important; its tasks are the '(i) maintenance of party morale and discipline; (ii) control over the performance of party organizations; and (iii) investigation of breaches of party discipline'.[53]

The major organs of the party are shown in Figure 1.1.

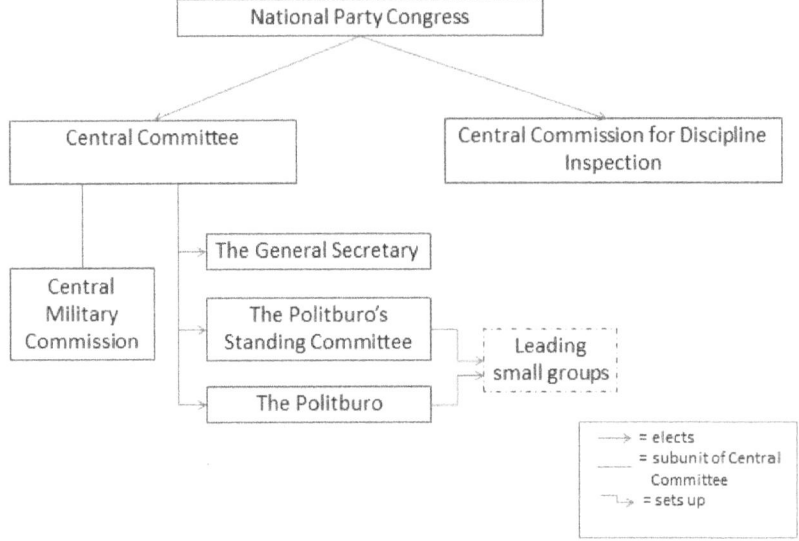

Figure 1.1   The major organs of the Chinese Communist Party

On the machinery of the state, Wang[54] reports that the state comprises a number of organizations, which includes the NPC and its Standing Committee, the State Council, the Central Military Commission, the Supreme People's Court and the Supreme People's Procurator, in addition to a huge bureaucracy.

The NPC, which is the highest organ of state power and the highest legislative body, elects the President and Vice President of the PRC and 'is empowered to amend the constitution, to make laws, and to supervise their enforcement',[55] and when the NPC is not in session, 'its Standing Committee serves as the executive body to act on behalf of the congress'.[56] And down the hierarchy, Local People's Congresses, established in provinces, municipalities, counties and townships, are the local organs of state power, and they are empowered to 'adopt and issue resolutions and examine and decide on plans for local economic and cultural development and for the development of public services'.[57]

The State Council is the highest executive body headed by the Premier, and its primary functions include (i) enacting administrative regulations and issuing decisions and orders in accordance with the Constitution;

(ii) formulating the tasks and responsibilities of ministries and commissions subordinate to it; and (iii) directing and administering such affairs as economy, national defence, education, and urban and rural development.[58]

The Central Military Commission, a subunit of the party's Central Committee, is the highest military command body, through which the party ensures control over the People's Liberation Army (PLA), and it is responsible to the NPC and its Standing Committee. Its primary function is 'to appoint and remove military personnel, especially the commanders of the seven military regions'.[59]

The Supreme People's Court, which is responsible to the NPC, is the highest judicial organ in the nation, and it 'supervises the administration of justice by the people's courts at various local levels and by the special people's courts'.[60] The Supreme People's Procuratorate is responsible to the NPC, and it 'directs the work of the people's procuratorates at various local levels and of the special people's procuratorates'.[61]

The state relies on bureaucrats to carry out the administrative and executive functions of the government. Larus comments: 'The size of China's bureaucracy is huge, with bureaucrats at every level of Chinese government ... There are ministries and commissions at the central government level, departments at the provincial level, divisions at the county level, and sections at the township levels.'[62]

The machinery of the state is shown in Figure 1.2.

The party organization is the dominant element, the state machine subordinate. Together they order a hierarchical system, and the party elite in Beijing sit atop this structure; and thereafter, party machinery and state machinery together reach down via provinces, cities, townships and villages into the broad population of China.

Organizational Emperor

The sum total of the activities of the machinery of the party have been recently summed up in terms of the notion of an organizational emperor,[63] and the system can be read in terms of institutions and culture. It is top-down, it does adjust and, lately, politically it has drawn in more participants, but it is not oriented towards the goal of liberal democracy, and critical voices and novel social groups are absorbed as the inherited system adjusts.

Zheng Yongnian[64] attends to the nature of the CCP and, rather than judge the party moralistically (authoritarian, despotic and so on[65]), or judge it in terms taken directly from European or American experience (where elections equal democracy and the future is understood in variants

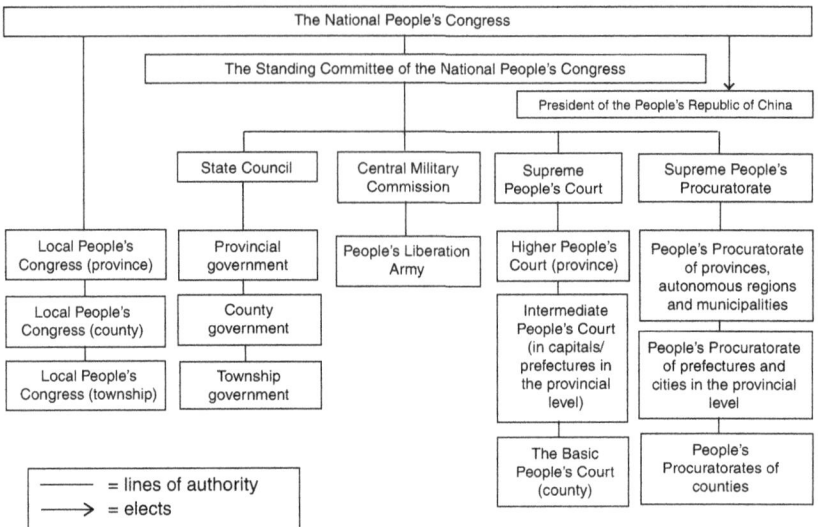

Figure 1.2   The state machinery of the People's Republic of China

of modernization/globalization), asks how does it work? Zheng picks up United States (US) referenced historical/sociological institutionalism (institutional structures of governance shift and change down through time in response to changing external and internal circumstances) along with strands of European Marxism and other contemporary French social criticism in order to make use of the notions of hegemony and discourse; thus institutions change down through time and the agents who animate these systems can only act in line with their understandings and thereafter deploy ideas in order to discipline/mobilize their populations.

Historical and sociological institutionalism opens up issues of under-standings and identities; it lets analysts get at how agents understand and act in given circumstances. The line of enquiry can be enriched by the neo-Marxism of Gramsci and the work of French theorists of power/society (Foucault/Bourdieu), as they variously let analysts get at ways in which elites run arguments within society. The key for the party is continuity and practical adjustment. The organizational emperor embraces the political system and so official obedience is required, but piecemeal change is available (change is within the system, not of the system itself). Using these resources, analysts can get at, first, intra-party and party-state relations and, second, party-state and society relations; that is, how the party orders its affairs and dominates the state and how thereafter the party-state machinery dominates society, together revealing how the CCP organizational emperor system works.[66]

Cast in these terms, the CCP is an institutional apparatus that combines historical resources (ways of understanding the machineries of governance inherited from dynastic days) with locally read imported ideas (European Marxism–Leninism) and that has been shaped by the particular historical experience of revolution/civil war; the upshot is a vanguardist Chinese party where the logic runs thus: the elite guides the party in state making and creates a party-state system which thereafter is wedded to the pursuit of development; the Chinese party-state is only a governance institution and so in that sense it is an organizational emperor. The CCP is not a party on a European or American model (that is, lodged in a competitive liberal-democratic party system of governance); rather, it is an organizational emperor: there is only one very complicated structure of governance, the party-state, and the core is the CCP.[67]

Zheng argues that the historical legacy of the emperor system offers resources for the present day. The emperor system was centralized, hierarchical and distant from the population, and it was sustained by ritual and occasional violence. The late nineteenth century added ideas of nation, race, state, party and party vanguard to debates about the polity.

There are two important features of the emperor system: first, it is hierarchical, and this was sustained by a stress on ideological conformity (official truths must be respected); and second, the emperor's power was limited as the core could make rules but all these had to be put into practice by subordinates in the centre and the provinces. Thereafter, in the late nineteenth and early twentieth centuries new ideas were imported and reworked – state, nation, democracy, development and so on – and all were picked up as ways to reorganize China so as to resist foreigners and join in the modern world. But the 1911 parliamentary system failed. The KMT and CCP both moved to the organizational emperor system: an elite-led party-state system oriented to mobilizing the population, either via the KMT system[68] or CCP system.[69] However, intra-party democracy in the CCP was weak. In the pre-reform revolutionary and civil war era the struggles amongst the party elite were ruthless and produced a 'winner takes all' style of politics,[70] but in the post-reform era attempts have been made to institutionalize intra-party politics and today power is more widely distributed. The system is hierarchical and geographically dispersed; there is a nested hierarchy of centres of power; and ritual obedience has to be shown to the CCP emperor, but thereafter individual- and institution-based factionalism is rife as factions manoeuvre for position in the party, in the state and in ideology;[71] only the disloyal are rejected.

Zheng[72] later discusses elite politics in more direct terms, that is, in terms of factions as they manoeuvre for position and advantage around (i) institutional bases (organizations or offices within the party-state machinery); (ii) policy/ideology (hence all the programmatic statements associated with particular leaders); and (iii) the issue of succession (positioning for change in the direction of the wind). So, with (iii) achieved, then (ii) and (i) are revised accordingly. The post-1949 political history can be read in these terms. The reform era, that is, post-1978, can be read in terms of three phases: first, the Deng Xiaoping era (1978–89); second, the Jiang Zemin era (1989–2002); and third, the Hu Jintao era (2002–12). In each there was a process of power concentration, then new policy and ideological gloss and slogans. Overall, there has been a slow process of intra-party reform, and the key issue of succession is now much more institutionalized (this was not the case in the Mao or Deng periods). And now the leader is Xi Jinping, and commentators note his extensive drive on corruption; and with the September 2015 military parade in Beijing, they also note that he has settled accounts with the important players of the military.

So there are two systems of governance, the party and state, and the relation between the two is crucial; however, the CCP is 'the pillar of the Chinese state'.[73] Under Mao a central system was created: 'A party-centred political hierarchy was formed: the Party made all decisions over state affairs and the power of the Party at different levels was centralized in the hand of Party secretaries there, and nationwide, all ultimate power was centralized in the hands of Mao Zedong.'[74]

After Mao, the paramount leader, Deng Xiaoping, advocated reforms, both economic and political, so there was a discourse of political reform, but the 1989 Tiananmen events stopped these conversations: 'Instead, how to strengthen the domination of the Party over the government is at the centre of reform discourse.'[75]

Now the party has a number of important mechanisms. First, the nomenklatura system, whereby the CCP elite controls appointments to very many important posts within the party and the state:[76] appointments, promotions/relocations, dismissals and retirements. Second, the Central Leading Small Groups, which are party-controlled cross-ministry groups that determine general policy, whilst related State Council Small Groups attend to matters of administration,[77] and, at lower levels of the hierarchy, there are many similar groups. Third, the Party Core Groups[78] that oversee work in all government agencies. And, finally, Party Schools[79] ensure that CCP cadres understand their role. Together these organizations allow the party to control the state.[80] Thereafter, the party-state asserts power over society. In the pre-reform era all this was very centralized, but in the post-reform era there have been changes, with decentralization within the party-state (centre and provinces) and decentralization between the party-state and the wider society by allowing more social groups to form and act.[81] The party thus secures hegemonic power. The ideas of the party are spread widely through the party-state and through wider society; it is a mix of control plus co-option plus greater tolerance plus nationalism.

All that said, the CCP will change and adapt, as it has in the past,[82] but the goals built into the CCP apparatus do not point towards a European- or American-style competitive liberal party system. It is true that the CCP has reformed internally and has reformed its involvement with wider society, but it has not moved towards a European or American competitive party system.[83] The CCP is an organizational emperor and the party is the core of the Chinese political system. It will adjust but not change its core identity[84] – reforms, yes, and accumulative, drawing in more people and regularizing the procedures inherited from revolution/civil war days, but the core of the emperor system is a commitment to continuity.

****

So, overall, the key to the future lies within elite party circles and the associated policy community. The machinery of governance is centred on Beijing. It is organized via the double bureaucracy/hierarchy of the party-state system, animated by the machinery of the party[85] and legitimated today in terms which call attention both to material advances within the country and an ideology of Chinese nationalism. The party remains the key locus of political life.[86] It has around 80 million members. In recent years Xi Jinping has emphasized the importance of the anti-corruption drive and there has been a stress on nationalism, and both find expression in the official media and in social media. The anti-corruption drive has been pursued with great vigour. The related nationalism is often hostile towards the USA and typically virulently anti-Japanese.[87] Commentators suggest that all this implies that Xi Jinping's government is, in a sense, conservative, that is, committed to the rule of the party and the continuing international rise of China.[88]

THE PRC IN THE TWENTY-FIRST CENTURY: ACHIEVEMENTS AND CONTEMPORARY ISSUES

All this material may seem remote from contemporary politics, but historical institutionalism looks at the ways in which the past runs into the present day, not merely institutional forms but also sets of ideas – institutional practices and sets of ideas shape political life.

Reforming the State-Socialist System

The state-socialist system sought to embrace all aspects of the lives of its citizens, drawing them into productive work, social exchanges and the government of the country via local party and state representatives. It was an ambitious programme, and there was much scope for flexibility in the translation of theory into practice; or, to put it another way, the historical trajectory of the country shaped internal organization, and explicit directions from the state were but one aspect of the mix, ideological convictions on the part of the elite being, in turn, one element of that particular mix. That said, a party-state system was created. Once in place, thereafter, in pursuit of reform, disentangling all these elements in pursuit of a programme of liberalization was never going to be easy: it required the creation of a marketplace (law, regulators, firms and consumers); it required the creation of social welfare systems (health, schooling, housing, accessed now as citizens); it required the reordering of society (the ideologically motivated reconstruction of inherited or traditional patterns of social action was relaxed, old forms allowed to resurface and new marketplace-oriented interactions allowed, in sum, Chinese tradition plus new individualism); and it also involved formal political reforms, so the state-party apparatus adjusts, new categories of members are recruited, administrative structures are reformed and public legitimation shifts from ideological exhortation rooted in the experience of war and revolution towards practical achievement, that is, material advance, plus a reasserted nationalism. Problems remain with corruption amongst the elite, official and corporate sectors. Problems remain with administrative reforms. Problems have emerged with nationalism, which the elite find useful but which can also assume virulent anti-foreigner forms, in particular amongst Internet users where it appears to be an aggressive nationalism rather than a celebration of place and people.[89] Notwithstanding these problems, there has been much success.

Adopting the Model of the Developmental State

The reform programme inaugurated cautiously in the late 1970s and early 1980s is usually associated with the leadership of Deng Xiaoping, and whilst the initial impetus to reform may have been domestic, that is, an elite level rejection of the voluntaristic politics of the Cultural Revolution, the overall model of reform, the recipe, so to say, was found in the record of the countries of the wider East Asian region, a set of experiences summed in terms of the notion of the developmental state. The term identified a novel strategy of governing the economy, one where the key decision-making group consisted of elite-level officials, supported thereafter by business leaders and politicians, with the triangle of power holders united in the pursuit of national development, that is, carving out a larger space within the global economy and distributing the benefits widely throughout the population within the territory that they controlled. The contrast is with the goals written into then current ideas of liberal markets and modernization, which cast the state as a neutral rule-maker whose job was to facilitate the piecemeal accumulative growth of a global rule-based and self-regulating marketplace. The latter project-cum-economic space was dominated at the time by the USA, but the debate between the goals of national development or liberal market development goes back to Europe in the late nineteenth century, when theorists argued that late developers needed a powerful, nationally oriented state in order to compete with the dominant British free-traders. All these debates have run on for decades, and in this text they can be revisited later – in chapters 4 and 5 – as events, along with newer debates, have unfolded in East Asia.[90]

The reform programme has produced dramatic results, and hundreds of millions have seen their levels of living significantly improved. The keys to this record have been the cities adjacent or linked to the coast: the Pearl River area, the Yangtze River area and the Yellow River area; all these areas have created a powerful manufacturing export machine, and the country enjoys trade surpluses with the European Union, the USA and others in the Global South. The Beijing authorities have come under pressure from their various trading partners to curb these surpluses, but they persist. More generally, the authorities in Beijing face four inter-linked tasks: first, replicating the coastal success story in the western or inland parts of China; second, upgrading the economy so that it operates in higher-value-added manufacturing, an aspect of escaping the 'middle income trap'; third, upgrading the financial system and also internation-alizing the currency; and fourth, reorienting the economy from exports and infrastructure towards private consumption. These, it might be noted, are problems consequent upon success; thus the economic record is marvellous and standard agency data record the success. As noted above, hundreds of millions have seen their levels of living raised, with rough estimates suggesting that around 300 million now count as middle class citizens.

Yet, there are also many problems. There is corruption amongst elite cadres/officials, lower-level officials and corporate sectors; over-investment in infrastructure; wasteful duplication as provinces and cities compete for infrastructure projects; environmental degradation; a weak rule of law (which finds expression in part in mass incidents or rightful resistance[91]); and there is inequality between coastal and western or inland China, which feeds inward migration to the cities and, in turn, creates problems, thus the growth of 'villages-in-the-city', homes to communities of migrants.[92]

Collective Memory and the National Past

The idea of collective memory was presented by the scholar Maurice Halbwachs,[93] and it points to the ways in which individuals located within groups turn events into memory and pass these memories down to succeeding generations. Collective memory can be carried in families, communities, organizations and so on, and these resources serve to lodge people within the flow of time and are part of the wider stock of ideas carried within a culture, and thus they are available to interpret novel experiences. Halbwachs points to the dispersed nature of collective memory. It is dispersed through the social world in general. However, there are other aspects to this matter, in particular, the role of the state, and here a related idea can be presented, developed by the scholar Agnes Heller.[94] Heller points to the way in which the production of memory is located within a definite social world: a social world shaped by the demands of modernity, a social world shaped by the modern bureaucratic rational state and a social world shaped by differences in social class. The diversity is brought into some sort of focus via the promulgation by the state of an idea of the nation: who its people are, where they have come from and where ideally they are going. This set of ideas can be summed as 'the national past'; it is always provisional, always contested, and like collective memory, it is always in the process of construction and reconstruction.

China's route to the modern world was chaotic and violent.[95] The long-established pre-modern empire of the Qing was undermined over the period of the nineteenth century by European, American and Japanese traders; traders who helped establish a species of colonial rule over parts of the country. There were multiple conflicts from the early nineteenth century down to the years following the end of the Pacific War. The end of the Chinese Civil War,[96] with its attendant outside involvement, was followed by further conflicts, both domestic and international with the cold war. All this gets fed into the contemporary collective memory and finds expression in the national past, where some events are remembered, others carefully forgotten, and over time these self-understandings accumulate material.[97] The material is selective as some events are read in, whilst others are read out.[98] One aspect, noted by Callahan,[99] is the official embrace of the notion of national humiliation, a reading of the history of the country, one widely disseminated through schooling and the media, that urges citizens to help build the country in the face of ever dangerous and unscrupulous foreign powers.

International Relations within the Region

Beijing is the core of the Chinese system, but it would be foolish to treat the polity as a single homogenous entity:[100] there are multiple factions within the elite levels located in Beijing, there are multiple peripheral agents located in provincial capitals, there is a nascent civil society (much of it web based) and, as the country is very large, there are many local communities with their own local concerns. The country revolves around the party-state apparatus; there is also an officially sponsored nationalism, and it revolves around the construction of the Han race and a stylized national past cast in terms of the depredations of foreigners and national humiliation. The nationalism also revolves around claims to a long history of civilization. Together, these domestic factors feed into the international relations of the country, the policy elite's self-understandings and understandings of others – the party-state authorities speak of socialism with Chinese characteristics, they speak of a socialist market economy, and they speak of peaceful rising or peaceful development.

Today China faces a number of crucial problems in the international relations arena: first, the long-running issue of relations with Taiwan; second, the equally long-running issue of the relationship with Japan; third, relatedly, their relationship with the USA; and fourth, the issue of the South China Sea.

CONCLUSION: AN AGENDA FOR THE DISCUSSION IN THIS TEXT

The discussion presented here will have roughly the following shape:

- the collapse of the Qing Empire and the creation of the nationalist Republic of China (ROC)
  o the failure of the Qing;

   o the rise of domestic resistance and mooted alternatives;
   o the Republic Revolution;
* the creation of the PRC
   o Mao's peasant revolution;
   o Deng's reform programme;
   o the emergence of today's China;
* the situation in contemporary China
   o domestic politics;
   o international politics;
   o future politics.

The discussion will offer an interpretive analysis of the logic of politics in China; it will be informed by the resources of historical institutionalism (and cognate ways of thinking) and will identify the crucial institutional structures, the party-state, along with the patterns of thought associated with these institutions, the ways in which inherited resources find expression in elite politics, public policy and the wider, still-developing public sphere, the arena of popular participation.

The text will set aside familiar characterizations of China's politics – authoritarian, communist, and so on – as such characterizations belong to a now defunct cold war era; it will also set aside their counterparts, those texts offering varieties of China-boosting; instead, it will offer an analysis grounded in a distinct intellectual approach and addressed to those concerned with a straightforward and realistic account.

NOTES

1. For a review of recent English-language work in political science and international relations, see Colin Hay 2002 *Political Analysis: A Critical Introduction*, London, Palgrave.
2. For a review of recent English-language work, see V. Lowndes and M. Roberts 2013 *Why Institutions Matter: The New Institutionalism in Political Science*, London, Palgrave.
3. A point nicely made by Zheng, Yongnian 2010 *The Chinese Communist Party as Organizational Emperor: Culture, Reproduction and Transformation*, London, Routledge, p.xv.
4. On the nineteenth century expansion of European (and later American) state-empires: on Britain, see Julia Lovell 2011 *The Opium War: Drugs, Dreams and the Making of China*, London, Picador, Robert Bickers 2011 *The Scramble for China: Foreign Devils in the Qing Empire 1832–1914*, London, Allen Lane, Carl Trocki 1999 *Opium, Empire and the Global Political Economy: A Study of the Asian Opium Trade 1750–1950*, London, Routledge, Brian Inglis 1979 *The Opium War*, London, Coronet; on France's role, see Bickers 2011; and on the post-1945 record, see R. Kedward 2005 *La Vie en Bleu: France and the French since 1900*, London, Allen Lane and see chapter 13, Robert Gildea 2002 'Myth, Memory and Policy in France since 1945' in J.W. Muller ed. *Memory and Power in Post-war Europe*, Cambridge University Press; on the late-comers America, Germany

and Japan, a classic exercise in comparative analysis was given by Barrington Moore Jr. 1966 *The Social Origins of Dictatorship and Democracy: Lord and Peasant in the Making of the Modern World*, Boston, Beacon Press – see in this context his chapter on China.

5. The mix of celebration of a long civilization plus remembered 'humiliation' by foreigners is pursued by W.A. Callahan 2010 *China: The Pessoptimist Nation*, Oxford University Press.

6. Available from the nineteenth century down through the cold war and on into the present day – see, for example, in the first, China as the 'sick man of Asia', in the second, China as a 'totalitarian communist dictatorship' and, more recently, China as a 'fragile superpower' (S. Shirk 2007 *China: Fragile Superpower*, Oxford University Press).

7. To be clear, China's route to the modern world has created a distinctive contingent result: territorially, it is a sub-continent; organizationally, it is ordered by a Beijing-oriented hierarchical double bureaucracy (the party-state), and then there are further provincial cores and peripheries; and thereafter the system as a whole is further inflected by personal networks, factions and so on – or in brief, 'China' is not the name of a neat and tidy nation state. The point is nicely made by Gail Hershatter 2007 'Forget Remembering: Rural Women's Narratives of China's Collective Past' in C.K. Lee and G. Yang eds. *Re-envisioning the Chinese Revolution*, Stanford University Press, pp. 70–1 – thus 'For scholars, "China" is a convenient shorthand, a way of organising our teaching, our production of knowledge, and our narrative of the nation ... Our persistent habit of talking about "China", however, obscures the extent to which all socialism is local. The working out of state policies is contingent upon geography, prior social arrangements, local personalities, and a host of endlessly variable factors.'

8. The notion of 'traditional' would be useful except for the prevalence within European and American thinking of ideas of 'modernization/globalization theory' where traditional societies are taken to be static, un-dynamic, superstitious and so on, none of which is true of pre-modern China (or, it could argued, anywhere else, see C. Bayly 2004 *The Birth of the Modern World 1780–1914*, Oxford, Blackwell), and where the end point of the posited process of modernization is exemplified by the contemporary West, or the USA in particular; see W.W. Rostow 1960 *The Stages of Economic Growth*, Cambridge University Press and F. Fukuyama 1992 *The End of History and the Last Man*, London, Hamish Hamilton, and on American nationalism, see A. Lieven 2004 *America Right or Wrong: An Anatomy of American Nationalism*, London, Harper Collins.

9. P.K. Crossley 2010 *The Wobbling Pivot: China since 1800*, Chichester, UK, Wiley-Blackwell, pp. 155–63.

10. A trio of classics: B. Anderson 1983 *Imagined Communities*, London, Verso; E. Gellner 1983 *Nations and Nationalism*, Cambridge University Press; E. Hobsbawm 1990 *Nations and Nationalism since 1780*, Cambridge University Press.

11. By traditional is meant China-before-the-modern-world – the detail of pre-modern China has to be specified – and historical institutionalism can do this – what is not meant by 'traditional' is anything like the simple oppositions of 1950/60s modernization theory.

12. The relationships of cores and peripheries is complex – the key issue for politics has been between concentrated power at a single centre (today, unitary state) versus dispersed power amongst a number of centres (today, a notion of federalism, or in China's recent past, warlord territories – on this see Crossley 2010).

13. X. Ren 2013 *Urban China*, Cambridge, Polity.

14. N. Stockman 2000 *Understanding Chinese Society*, Cambridge, Polity, p. 57.

15. K. Marx and F. Engels ([1847] 1986) 'The Manifesto of the Communist Party' in *Karl Marx and Fredrick Engels: Selected Works in One Volume*, London, Lawrence and Wishart, p. 39.

16. Bickers 2011– who is highly critical of these traders.

17. Bickers 2011.

18. Lovell 2011.

19. As the nineteenth century ran its course, the number of foreign 'concessions' grew – these are listed in R. Nield 2015 *China's Foreign Places: The Foreign Presence in China in the Treaty Port Era, 1840–1943*, Hong Kong University Press.

20. Callahan 2010 pp. 34–6 dates the discourse to the 1920s – May 4th/New Culture; it was picked up by Chiang Kai Shek, then from 1937 to 1990 disregarded, only reanimated after Tiananmen Square Incident 1989.

21. Regional (China was divided – north/south, rural/urban); social class (language, clan, economic position); popular (ethnic division, Manchu/Han); intellectual (conservative, reformer, insurrectionist, revolutionary). On the multiplicity of divisions within Chinese society, see Crossley 2010, chapters 1 and 3; see also Stockman 2000.

22. Moore 1966.

23. On the wars of the warlords, see S.C.M. Paine 2012 *The Wars for Asia*, Cambridge University Press; see also E.L. Dreyer 1995 *China at War 1901–1949*, London, Longman.

24. Thereafter, from 1949 there were extensive exercises in 'mopping up' pockets of resistance – as with the end of the war in Europe, so also in China, the violence continued before stability was re-established.

25. P. Short 2004 *Mao: A Life*, London, John Murray, pp. 476–504 puts the number of deaths at 25 million.

26. David Shambaugh 2008 *China's Communist Party: Atrophy and Adaptation*, University of California Press analyses the nature of the Communist Party in China and concludes that it has learned the lessons of the 1989–91 period – that is from 4 June 1989 through to the collapse of the Soviet Union; the party has analysed the collapse in systemic terms, that is, a moribund party presiding over an old fashioned isolated economy plus imperial overstretch and US hostility, and taken steps to upgrade the party's organization and performance in governance – successfully; amusingly, the text is grounded in cold war bloc-think and does not ask the question of how Soviet Union and China 'watchers' ever got themselves into the intellectual dead end they came to occupy.

27. Callahan 2010 p. 8 notes that holding the games in China were first mooted in 1908, as a way of combating national weakness. Callahan adds that the domestic meaning of the games was one of final recovery from a long list of humiliations.

28. Shambaugh 2008.

29. The civil war came to a nominal end when the KMT elite fled to Taiwan; however, civil wars do not come to neat and tidy ends, rather the reverse: they come to slowly drawn out unpleasant ends – for example, the years following the American Civil War or the British elite suppression of the Chartists or the Communist Party of the Soviet Union's suppression of opponents or Franco's suppression of the left-wing and so on. In China the CCP pursued its opponents for several years, with many casualties.

30. G. Davies 2009 *Worrying about China: The Language of Chinese Critical Enquiry*, Harvard University Press.

31. F. Christiansen and S. Rai 1996 *Chinese Politics and Society: An Introduction*, Hemel Hempstead, UK, Prentice Hall Europe, pp. 2–22.

32. A position spelled out by T. Saich 2004 2nd ed. *Governance and Politics of China*, London, Palgrave, see chapter 4, pp. 92–5.

33. Shambaugh 2008.

34. Shambaugh 2008 p. 13.

35. Shambaugh 2008 p. 175.

36. Saich 2004 p. 95.

37. Z. Bauman 1976 *Culture as Praxis*, London, Sage, characterizes the realm of ordinary life in terms of the idea of culture-as-praxis.

38. The CCP is not a party in the liberal-democratic sense; China does not have multiple parties, it does not have party competition, it does not have competitive elections as a mechanism for recruiting personnel for positions, but is better grasped as a bureaucracy – its focus is not administration, it is politics (mainstream European parties in recent years have been characterized by their 'professionalism' and remoteness from populations, so there are some similarities).

39. Zheng 2010.
40. Elizabeth Freund Larus 2012 *Politics and Society in Contemporary China*, Boulder, CO, Lynne Rienner Publishers, p. 108.
41. Cited in K. Brown 2014 *The New Emperors: Power and the Princelings in China*, London, I.B. Tauris, p. 20.
42. R. McGregor 2012 *The Party: The Secret World of China's Communist Rulers*, London, Penguin, p.xx.
43. McGregor 2012 p.xi – see diagram of The Party.
44. The machinery is detailed in Saich 2004, see chapters 5 and 6.
45. J.C.F. Wang 2002 7th ed. *Contemporary Chinese Politics: An Introduction*, Upper Saddle River, NJ, Prentice Hall, p. 70.
46. Larus 2012 p. 110.
47. L.R. Sullivan 2012 *Historical Dictionary of the Chinese Communist Party*, Lanham, MD, Scarecrow Press, p. 48.
48. Larus 2012 p. 112.
49. Such as Severe Acute Respiratory Syndrome (SARS); see Southern Weekly 2013 August 1 Understanding the Operation of the Politburo's Standing Committee (Chinese Version), Online. <http://www.infzm.com/content/93040> (accessed 21 January 2016).
50. C. Zhang 2016 *The Domestic Dynamics of China's Energy Diplomacy*, Singapore, World Scientific Publishing.
51. C.X. Zhou and T.T. Gui 2014 The Duties and Tasks of Small Groups for the Politburo's Standing Committee, Online. <http://news.qq.com/a/20140623/003192.htm> (accessed 21 Janaury 2016).
52. Sullivan 2012 p. 113.
53. Wang 2002 p. 78.
54. Wang 2002 p. 87.
55. Wang 2002 p. 87.
56. Wang 2002 p. 89.
57. Constitution of the People's Republic of China 2004, Online. <http://www.npc.gov.cn/englishnpc/Constitution/node_2825.htm> (accessed 21 January 2016).
58. The National People's Congress of the People's Republic of China 2016 State Structure of the People's Republic of China, Online. <http://www.npc.gov.cn/englishnpc/stateStructure/2007-12/06/content_1382098.htm> (accessed 21 January 2016).
59. Sullivan 2012 p. 47.
60. Constitution of the People's Republic of China 2004.
61. Constitution of the People's Republic of China 2004.
62. Larus 2012 p. 122.
63. Zheng 2010.
64. Zheng 2010.
65. Zheng 2010 – see pp. 7–15 (compare with Shambaugh 2008).
66. Zheng 2010 also considers lines of possible future development as revolution/civil war habits of thought and organization are revised over time (pp. 39–40).
67. As a model we get this: as revolution and civil war unfold, (i) received culture informs elite thinking (ii) who construct a party and (iii) engage in state making, and (iv) what they make is a party-state system, (v) thereafter wedded to the pursuit of development. Today the CCP is a large organization: in 2008 it had 73 million members and 'by 2006 the CCP had 3.6 million organizations, including both Party committees and Party branches at the grass roots level. More than 420,000 firms had established Party organizations. Out of 2.4 million firms in the non-state sector, 178,000 (7.4 per cent) had established Party organizations. In other words, Party organizations have penetrated all forms of firms, institutions and social organisations' (Zheng 2010 p. 4).
68. Zheng 2010 p. 61.
69. Zheng 2010 p. 64.
70. Zheng 2010 p. 73.
71. Zheng 2010 p. 84.

72. Zheng 2014 *Contemporary China: A History since 1978*, London, Wiley-Blackwell – see chapter two in particular.
73. Zheng 2010 p. 100.
74. Zheng 2010 p. 101.
75. Zheng 2010 p. 103.
76. Zheng 2010 pp. 104–6.
77. Zheng 2010 p. 108.
78. Zheng 2010 p. 111.
79. Zheng 2010 – Central Party School – part teaching operation for cadres, part research organization and part keeper of ideological line – used by the party to discretely float policy ideas, used by the party to run courses for low level officials, used to teach party leader's doctrines; there are other schools in provinces and cities and counties – some 2000 in all (p. 175).
80. Two issues are particularly important: control of judiciary and control of military – see Zheng 2010 pp. 112–17.
81. Zheng 2010 p. 139.
82. Shambaugh 2008 notes the way the party responded to the unanticipated collapse of the USSR: it upgraded its performance. Others would add that for its public it upgraded its nationalist rhetoric (C.R. Hughes 2006 *Chinese Nationalism in the Global Era*, London, Routledge; Zhao, Suisheng 2004 *A Nation-State by Construction: Dynamics of Modern Chinese Nationalism*, Stanford University Press).
83. Zheng 2010 pp. 176–7.
84. Zheng 2010 pp. 176–7.
85. Shambaugh 2008 – CCP looked at the collapse of the USSR and diagnosed a moribund inefficient system; CCP has looked to upgrade the party apparatus and engage with economic and social reform; plus there is a new stress on nationalism.
86. Notwithstanding numerous signs of local popular dissatisfaction – K. O'Brien and L. Li 2006 *Rightful Resistance in Rural China*, Cambridge University Press – plus netizens in cities voicing sharp criticisms of the regime (and many other things too).
87. Hughes 2006.
88. That is, Xi's reforms and nationalism are aimed at strengthening the party-state, not changing it (reports began to appear in the *Financial Times*, *Economist*, *South China Morning Post* and so on in mid-2015).
89. Hughes 2006.
90. On this see Gordon White ed. 1988 *Developmental States in East Asia*, London, Macmillan; Chalmers Johnson 1995 *Japan: Who Governs?*, New York, Norton; Robert Wade 1990 *Governing the Market*, Princeton University Press; L. Weiss 1998 *The Myth of the Powerless State*, Cambridge, Polity.
91. K. O'Brien and L. Li 2006.
92. Noted by X. Ren 2013 pp. 121 et seq.
93. M. Halbwachs (edited by Lewis Coser) 1992 *On Collective Memory*, Chicago University Press.
94. On this see Patrick Wright 1985 *On Living in an Old Country*, London, Verso.
95. On the wars, see Dreyer 1995.
96. On the protagonists, see J. Fenby 2005 *Generalissimo: Chiang Kai Shek and the China He Lost*, London, The Free Press; Short 2004.
97. Zhao 2004 – chapter 1 stresses the 'situational context' of Chinese nationalism, shaped by responses to events, especially wars – thus the Opium Wars feeds into the Self-Strengthening Movement, the (First) Sino-Japanese War feeds into the Boxer Rebellion and the overthrow of the Qing, the Versailles Treaty feeds into the May 4th New Culture Movement, the (Second) Sino-Japanese War feeds into national struggle, the Korean War feeds into consolidation of PRC, and the post-1989 criticisms feed into the CCP self-presentation as the defender of China, wedded to national development.
98. See W.A. Callahan 2006 'History, Identity and Society: Producing and Consuming Nationalism in China' in *Critical Asian Studies* 38.2 on national humiliation days.

99. Callahan 2010 pp. 8–14 – these claims produce, after Raymond Williams, a 'structure of feeling'.
100. Christiansen and Rai 1996.

2. China in the early twentieth century: collapse, recovery and war

In the late nineteenth and early twentieth centuries a mix of external pressures from foreign traders and empire builders coupled to domestic structural change – economic and social change along with an insurrectionary opposition – brought down the governing Chinese regime. The long-delayed collapse of the Qing regime ushered in a lengthy period of turmoil within China. The newly formed Republic of China (ROC) proved difficult to settle into place, and assorted elite-level conflicts plus extensive domestic social upheaval meant that those people with ideals, seeking progressive change, were disappointed. High ideals gave way to warlord violence, and it was not until the late 1920s that a semblance of order was secured, in the period of the Nanjing Decade. However, that period, too, was suffused with violence, as to the general confusions of the time (failed revolution, warlords and the continuing presence of foreigners) was added civil war and, a little later, outright inter-state war with Imperial Japan, an exchange later subsumed within the wider Pacific War, in turn a part of the global Second World War.[1] As matters unfolded, the end of the international wars ushered in a period of renewed civil war, finally resolved only in 1949 with the establishment of the PRC. This route to the modern world has shaped contemporary China, and in various ways these events have fed into collective memories, in turn shaping, in part, the ways in which the elite and mass conceive their futures.

CHINA AND THE SHIFT TO THE MODERN WORLD

The shift to the modern world began in Europe. The changes overturned long-established agrarian feudal forms of life, creating, in time, natural science informed industrial capitalism. All these changes were the serial consequences of a fortuitous set of initial circumstances. Beginning in the seventeenth century, and reaching a maximum disruptive expansionary dynamism in the nineteenth century, these processes entailed radical domestic innovative change and a related drive for external expansion.

The former drove metropolitan progress; the latter impacted and, in time, remade China. The earliest contacts were made by traders, quickly followed by others, and although the initial impact of these incomers was relatively slight, over the space of a relatively few decades they triggered the slow collapse of the long-established, distinctive Qing dynasty.

The dynamism of the modern form of life has not run its course. In particular, natural science continues its dazzling, disruptive and culturally central progress. There is no simple single shift from traditional to modern. There is no end of history.[2] The shift to the modern world is open-ended and ongoing. It is a process that can be unpacked, its multiple logics displayed. Here, first, we recall the impacts within Europe from the sixteenth through to the nineteenth centuries.

Europe – the Epicentre of the Shift to the Modern World

So, first, in Europe, as the functional logic of natural science based industrial production unfolded, hitherto settled relationships between social classes were disturbed. The established pattern of landed classes, with great houses, large domestic households with servants and retainers, related agricultural workers (peasants, tenants, share-croppers and so on) and relatively weak urban areas, with the whole ensemble understood and justified in terms of elite quasi-religious responsibility for family, land and attached retainers/workers, had to accommodate the rise of new classes: merchants, industrialists, middle classes and working classes. These disturbances proceeded at uneven rates, with different paces of change in different places, and they were all disruptive, requiring new sets of mutually agreed expectations, what one social class could expect of another, and sometimes they were violent, giving rise to assorted civil conflicts. Then, second, long-settled relationships between existing elites were disturbed as feudal arrangements with their trans-European networks of powerful families – royal, princely, local and so on – gave way to bounded sovereign states legitimated in terms of ideas of nation. The transition was slow, uneven and sometimes involved outright war (thus the Great War, which saw interlinked royal families involved in widespread inter-state warfare), with liberal democracy only becoming a general model after the Second World War.[3]

And third, cultural resources were disturbed, with inherited ideas questioned and new ideas interrogated, sometimes accepted and sometimes deployed. The long episode fed into the nineteenth century formation of the classical European tradition of social theorizing with its core concern with elucidating the dynamics of complex change.[4] So, finally, fourth, the politics of these sweeping changes were similarly disturbed. Landed elites had to accommodate the rise of new social groups, revolving around claims to wider participation in elite-level decision making, and claims and elite responses varied, and so the resultant patterns of political change varied: revolutions (successful, as in America,[5] France and Russia, or partial, as in Europe's 1848 Springtime of Nations, or blocked, as in the case of nineteenth century defeat of the English Chartists); accommodations (British elite gave ground via slow, partial political reforms); and resistance/reaction (radical nationalisms, as in Germany and Japan[6]).

As Europeans shifted into the modern world they exported their emergent form of life around the planet, for the system they had contrived was dynamic, and domestic intensification was coupled to external expansion. The drive for expansion was structural; it was built into the system, and individual agents read and reacted to these structural opportunities/imperatives. The keys to expansion were the drive for trade (buttressed by an elaborate ideology identifying its general beneficence) and a preparedness to use violence to secure desired ends (matters of technology, technique and opportunistic local alliances). And it was during this expansionary period that European elites created state-empires (various theories: structural economic, political competition and accident). Such state-empires were unified political structures, and internally they comprised a core (or cores) and a periphery (or peripheries), and both elements were remade as the shift to the modern world unfolded. In the case of the core, pre-modern forms of life were remade, and in the case of the periphery, pre-modern forms of life were remade. The metropolitan and peripheral elites interacted and cooperated, and the masses in the core and the periphery were obliged to adjust; thus, for peoples in both areas, there was some mix of exploitation and development.

The Impact on the Qing

The borders of 'China' have altered quite dramatically down the centuries, as with 'Europe', the geographical unit is not stable (as definitions vary), and nor are the borders of the polities within it (as they vary also).[7] The heartlands of the country lie between the two ends of the Great Wall, between the two great rivers, the Yangtze River and Yellow River, and thereafter peripheral areas have been sometimes incorporated, sometimes not, thus Tibet, Yunnan, Xinjiang, Mongolia, Manchuria and Taiwan. Within the heartland area polities have sometimes included all of it, sometimes not. The Qing Empire controlled a relatively large area, one with relatively settled borders.[8] The Qing Empire was precisely that, an empire with a core elite comprising a distinct ethnic group controlled a wide and varied periphery.

In the early nineteenth century the Qing regime was confronted by the disruptive pressures created by the burgeoning industrial capitalist form of life and these pressures presented themselves in the guise of European traders. When foreign traders arrived they disturbed the domestic balance (creating new problems for assertion of Qing control over local areas) and weakened directly the Qing centre (via their increasing presence and associated demands for privileges), and the regime's initial responses were uncomprehending. Later, following defeat in wars, there were attempts at reform, until finally the Qing regime collapsed as a result of a mix of accumulating foreign depredations to which the regime found no answer, coupled to domestic rebellions.

The Qing authorities had to read and react to these novel pressures, and they did so in terms of the ideas and institutions within which they dwelled. Amongst the Qing elite responses varied:[9] resistance (attempted opium trade suppression, 1842–60), pragmatic learning (Self-Strengthening Movement, 1861–95), attempts at rapid catch-up (the Hundred Days Reform, 1898), local rebellion (tacit support for Boxers, 1899–1901) and late attempts at catch-up (Late Qing Reforms, 1901–11). Chinese scholars and intellectuals participated in these debates, and an overall trajectory can be identified in a slow move from an initial inclination to learn so as to reform Qing China to a desire to replace the Qing and remake China in a modern form, thus opening the way to the revolutionary ideas associated with Sun Yat Sen. Cast in these sweeping terms, it all seems neat and tidy and amenable to reasoned debate, but the context was one of the slow dissolution of a politico-cultural system that in geographical extent embraced a sub-continent, and so matters were far from easy.

THE QING ERA: ELITE, MASS AND THE ROLE OF FOREIGNERS

The Ming Empire (1368–1644) came under external and internal pressures from around the turn of the seventeenth century: 'Political strife at the Ming court in Beijing over border policy was connected with competition between eunuch cliques and scholarly cliques, between networks of corruption and campaigns for reform, so that both border management and internal administration were paralyzed.'[10] A mixture of popular disaffection, rebellion and the pressures of the Manchu Qing in the north led in 1644 to the collapse of the Ming regime, and the last emperor committed suicide. Thereafter, the Qing faced the task of embedding their rule, and this was no simple matter, as the remnants of the Ming had to be brought under control and the machinery of the Qing state established. Crossley[11] comments that all this took most of the rest of the century, and whilst it was relatively straightforward in the areas north of the Yangtze, it was much more awkward in the southern areas.

The Condition of the Economy

The Qing dynasty ruled an essentially agrarian economy, and they did so in the context of a highly sophisticated culture, and so during the period of their rule, the economy prospered; this is borne out by population figures, so at the start of Qing rule the population was around 150 million, by mid-eighteenth century it was around 270 million, by 1800 it was 345 million, and in 1859 it was 430 million.[12] However, notwithstanding the successes necessary to sustain population growth, all this placed pressure on the agricultural sector. In pre-modern China it was not possible to radically increase agricultural output, and nor was it possible to shift population to modern industry. The country was predominant in porcelain and silk, so increasing numbers of people made ever more intensive demands on land, and although this could be a source of local-level conflict, the economy prospered. It was not until the nineteenth century that problems became apparent and the condition of the economy was in question. One economic argument suggests that the country was locked into a 'high level equilibrium trap', that is, it was efficient, successful and unable to generate the domestic impetus to make the structural changes necessary for a process of industrialization; however, Crossley[13] expresses doubts, noting the scale of the economy in the seventeenth century and the clear desire of European merchants to access this market in the eighteenth and early nineteenth centuries.

Commentators also argue that prior to the shift to the modern world, a world that had Europe at its centre, the world economy was Sino-centric, that is, it centred on China, and that the Chinese economy was highly sophisticated[14] and traded throughout East and Southeast Asia. A.G. Frank[15] argues that the growth of European economies was fuelled in part by participation in these Asian networks of trade. A key element of this participation was taking advantage of the high-level equilibrium trap of a sophisticated local agrarian economy unable to deal with industrialized economies; however, others might point to the more immediate role of violence-secured trade concessions, the business of system-carried intensification and expansion. All that said, it is the case that during the nineteenth century the macro global system reconfigured and Europe moved to the fore.

China was embedded within regional and global networks. The Qing maintained an extensive system of tribute/embassy[16] relations with local regional country powers. The economy had trade links with the region via coastal sea-trade, and the economy had links inland via the Silk Road through Central Asia to lands in the west. China exported manufactures (silk, ceramics) and agricultural products (tea), and it imported regional products, such as foodstuffs. Yet it resisted the importation of European manufactures. In the nineteenth century this was to be the occasion of a financial trade imbalance. Money flowed into China but, in the absence of Chinese imports, it was not recycled. One familiar strand of commentary on the occasion of the Opium War makes reference to this financial imbalance.[17] However, it is clear that prior to the arrival of the modern world, China was a major regional and thus global economic power.

It was in the nineteenth century that foreign traders entered the Chinese realm in significant numbers, and they superseded earlier traders for now they came with new products, new technologies, new knowledge, new social mores, new political ideas, new diplomatic ideas plus a disposition to the use of violence in order to secure their goals. They constructed numerous trading bases.[18] All these impacted extant Chinese ideas and practice, and whilst some prospered (sea-port merchants), others did not. The impact was uneven; the extent of local impact in question, but through this process China slowly entered the modern world.

The Condition of Society

The relationship between state and society was distant and particular: distant in that the power of the state did not reach down to local level and particular in that state and local society achieved a balance that worked. The system was hierarchical, with the elites remote, but, in principle, accessible via examination; the elite worked with ordinary people at the local level, where the official magistrate worked with local gentry landowners in the realm of day-to-day activity – a mix of elite-level demands and local-level practical cooperation.

Elite and mass – linkages
The Qing authorities' formal apparatus was a top-down affair, as with any empire. The core was the capital city, and thereafter provincial capitals, prefectural capitals and county towns. The last noted was base for the local magistrate, and this was the lowest level of formal machinery of

state; thereafter, the magistrate had to negotiate with local elites in small towns and villages, and so actual day-to-day practical politics was a matter of local-level discussion.[19] Crossley makes the point that the system had its own distinct logic: it worked:[20]

> Chinese history is not a history of despotism or unfettered authoritarianism, but one that has been sustained during long periods of peace and stability by the awareness of the limits on government power [set] by a volatile and organized public, and the limits on public expression presented by a government equipped to violently suppress what it regards as threats.

So, in general terms, it is possible to distinguish the elite (in principle, coherent) and the mass (in practice, very diverse). Thus, first, the elite was made up of those groups that animated the formal machinery of the state – the Qing elites plus the examination-recruited bureaucracy that enabled the state to reach down to local landowners, or gentry – plus Qing army groups, or Banner forces, who were encouraged to remain separate from the local population.[21]

Then, second, the masses were made up of the rest of the population – farmers, merchants, sea-farers and so on – dwelling within local communities and ordering their own affairs. The Qing asserted their authority over the population they controlled via a top-down state machinery; however, this machinery did not penetrate the underlying society – the linkage was formed by the relationship between state appointed magistrates (local officials) and local landowners (gentry). The magistrates represented and served the empire (law, taxation, infrastructure) whilst the gentry were embedded within the local society (family, kin networks, language group, locality). The local society thus continued in its own way; its pattern of life was local. The Qing state was a framework for local societies, and the relationship was contingent and could tip over into conflict. The claims of state were pitted against claims of local society. Characterizations of 'China' (and the 'Chinese') have (consequently) varied: a geographical place, a cultural form or civilization, a home to a race-based national people, or a modern nation that had 'stood up'.[22]

And then, third, cast in comparative terms, a contrast can be made with European society at roughly the same time.[23] In the long shift from pre-modern medieval Europe to the modern world in Europe the social world became more differentiated as social actors created distinctions. The intermingled nature of institutional forms within the medieval period (church, state, economy) became more clearly differentiated: the church's authority was reduced, legally and socially, and the state's authority was codified and unpacked into (variant forms of) executive, legislature and judiciary, and distinguished more clearly from private spheres of economic activity and domestic family realms. At the same time the economy became more clearly delineated in law and practice from state and society, as the pursuit of livelihood became understood and organized in terms of contractual relations between nominally free individuals. Other more restricted realms claimed similar discrete status: organizations intermediate between the local and state levels. Plus there was the crucial impact of long-distance trade, in particular, early on, money and foodstuffs from the Americas. However, these processes are lodged in history and are part of the unfolding historical trajectories of discrete societies; and the trajectory was different in China. The settled social world of the Qing saw little division between sacred and secular authority, both fused in the emperor. There was little division within the apparatus of the state; it functioned as a hierarchy of administrative roles (no separation of powers). The economy was predominantly rural and pursued peasant-based household production. In urban areas specialist trades continued in this guise, the institution of the private company with a distinct legal identity did not appear and cultural activities such as scholarship had little institutional autonomy. Stockman[24] suggests that cast in Habermasian terms the system was only partially uncoupled from the life-world, and one implication is that public sphere and civil society were only ever weakly developed in Qing China and, overall, the culture produced a stress on social integration which continued throughout subsequent periods and into today's China.

Fourth, the population of Qing China at the time of the arrival of significant numbers of foreign traders was around 350 million, and the bulk of these people lived in farming communities. These were locally oriented and ordered via kinship network, village, language group and so on. As with multiple languages in Europe prior to their print capitalism process of standardization, so there were multiple versions of Chinese.

All this, fifth, implies a mixture of great diversity, with local communities welded loosely together by overlapping cultural practices (all partook variously of a stock of common religions, festivals, literatures and so on) and managed in a distant fashion by the Qing state.

Sixth, local communities interacted with the Qing state via local gentry or landowners, and via magistrates appointed to an area by the state. The magistrates were the key local link to the administrative machinery of empire. The local magistrates were responsible to the Qing for local taxation and administration, were partially funded and were required to part self-fund, and this opened the way to links with local gentry landowners. Crossley[25] argues that the Qing authorities sought to set standards and regulations and then to devolve financial responsibility to the lower levels of the administration; so magistrates were funded for core functions and thereafter relied on links with local landowners, and this created a blurred dividing line between official and local (or private) activities. Crossley[26] adds two other related machineries – the local registration/tax unit and the local security unit – and both operated at a local level via magistrate/gentry – in the city, the neighbourhood block, and in rural areas, the village – and again were interlinked with local-level social networks; and so at the local level there was great diversity, with highly local mixes of magistrate/gentry powers.

Levels of living in urban and rural areas
The Qing presided over a sophisticated but essentially agrarian political economy. One important distinction was between rural and urban dwellers; thereafter, the levels of living of the population can be sketched – here, urban housing, health and education.

Urban and rural life: Zhao[27] reports that prosperity was evident in the urban areas of cities, there were busy marketplaces, a lively market atmosphere and stores of food and clothes, wine shops, shops for daily necessities (for example, comb, candle, wooden bucket), scissor shops, barbershops, pawnshops, drugstores, bath houses and shops for jewellery. Apart from fixed stores and shops, there were hawkers selling different kinds of food (for example, steamed buns and cakes, roasted sweet potatoes, steamed dumplings, fried shrimp and fish, tea, eggs), selling second-hand clothes and cloth, string, thread and hairclips, and providing services such as haircutting and pedicures. There were also knife sharpeners, street performers and fortune-tellers in markets. Many old and famous restaurants could be found in Beijing. They included 'Tranquil House with cold porridge, Taihe Building with delicious snacks made of flour, [and] Julan Building with snacks made of sugar and flour'.[28]

The economic activity of rural life was also ordered and integrated with the wider economy; the local agrarian form of life was integrated via regular fairs, which were primary markets in rural areas. There were rural fairs in county seats, towns and villages. The fair was approved and established by local magistrates to meet peasants' and grass-roots demands, jointly promote agriculture and business, guarantee commodity circulation and maintain social stability.[29] Rural fairs sold rice, tea, vegetables, fish and prawns, fruits, salt, daily necessities, cattle, silk, cloth, seeds and farm implements. Ren points out that the 'exchange in the rural fairs were primarily the distribution of resources (surplus rice especially) among small producers'.[30] But there were also professional markets in towns where travelling merchants would do business with individual farmers by using money. These towns, depending on their geographical position, specialized in the production of cotton and cotton cloth, silkworm and silk fabrics, pottery, fishery, mountain produce, bamboo and paper.[31]

Urban areas developed more quickly than related rural areas: a mix of indigenous developments plus the import of ideas from an increasingly visible foreign presence. All this was clear in housing, health and education.

Housing: class polarization was evident during the Qing Dynasty.[32] In Beijing the inner city areas were distinguished from outer areas. Under the Manchu-Han separate-living policy, all the lands and houses in the Inner City of Beijing were occupied by the Qing government and all the Han people, officials and merchants were ordered to move to the Outer City; the houses in the Inner City were then allocated to Manchu military and government officials according to rank.[33] Courtyard houses where Manchu military and government officials lived were a symbol of luxury, and in form they were 'a residential compound with a set of courtyards enclosed by the surrounding buildings and high walls on four sides'.[34] Raff notes that 'Han people were allowed to enter the Inner City in the daytime but were not allowed to stay overnight', adding that they could own properties in the Outer City,[35] but their living environment was poor because, as Hui remarks,[36] it 'was full of narrow and congested streets/ alleys and small houses'.

Health: the Qing government 'rarely intervened with medical issues'[37] and so health care was mainly provided by local charitable organizations on the basis of benevolence. These organizations, which were overseen by local elites, provided medication and coffins on credit, addressed the seasonal epidemics, such as malaria and cholera, and sponsored clinics and branch hospitals. Hospitals and clinics were established by wealthy philanthropists, local businessmen and the wider business community in order to provide the poor with free and year-round medication and treatment, free coffins and burial plots.[38] Popular books were printed by Chinese philanthropists to 'educate the public about health and medicine'.[39] As regards Western medical missionaries, they 'recognized medical philanthropy as a potent tool for granting acceptance and establishing a foothold in local community'.[40] Canton Hospital, which was the first Western-style hospital in China, was established in 1835, and the first church hospital in China was established in 1900.[41] Hospitals established by Western missionaries were originally funded by church organizations, and their associated fundraising activities, and later by domestic Chinese donations, and they provided free medical treatment to the poor and needy, prevented and treated eye diseases, promoted smallpox vaccinations and controlled epidemics such as plague and cholera.[42]

Education: until 1905 the civil service examination system, which focused on the study of Confucianism, was the main channel to recruit Chinese officials based on merit[43] and 'the only way to secure and maintain elite status … [however] … women were not allowed in the examination compounds'.[44] Wong notes that women's education 'was limited to the teaching of social ethics and family traditions with an emphasis on how to become a virtuous wife and good mother'.[45] However, during the Qing Dynasty, the advancement of women's education was promoted by Western missionaries in China to achieve gender and educational equality.[46] A girls' school was first established by British missionaries in Ningbo in 1844, and another girls' school was established in the Zhen-Jiang region along the Yangtze River in 1884.[47] In the late 1890s, Chinese writers such as Liang Qichao also supported women's education because they believed that education could 'liberate women from oppression … [and] … enable women to fulfil adequately their role as wives and mothers'.[48] In 1898, the Jing Zheng Girls' School was established in Shanghai, which became the forerunner of girls' schools organized by the local Chinese, and in 1907 the Qing government gave the official seal of approval to the development of a women's private educational sector.[49] Subsequently, the support for women's education turned into the support for the women's rights movement and, in the aftermath of the 1911 Revolution, there was the mushrooming of women's organizations, such as the Female Alliance and the Women's Organisation for Peace.[50]

The Role of Outside Powers

The collapse of the Qing can be unpacked in terms of internal matters and external contacts. The former revolve around the weakening of the state: pressures of population expansion; weakening of tax raising powers; local rebellions; and weakening of central control over peripheral figures in the bureaucratic hierarchy. And the latter revolve around the role of foreign traders; and, whilst their numbers were small, the culture, which enabled and underpinned their voyages and demands, was powerful. Individually, they may have been violent, acquisitive and cynical,[51] but this does not matter; what does matter is the culture standing behind them, that is, the expansionary drive of modern science based industrial capitalism.

The traders contributed to the collapse of the Qing in a number of ways: the goods they sold and the demands they made in respect of trading arrangements, along with their ready inclination to turn to violence to realize their goals. So, first, as British traders were restricted to Canton they were obliged to use local intermediaries or compradors, together the Canton System. Some goods were legal in China, such as woollens, cottons and some manufactures, but others were illegal, in particular opium. The Qing Empire interacted only in a limited way with local people, and local merchants could find the space in which to work with the traders, and so patterns of social hierarchy in China began to be modified. Second, British traders brought in large quantities of opium. The drug was known and produced and used in China; however, its production and sale was not done on a large scale, and the British traders made the drug readily available; its use was debilitating and Chinese public health was damaged. And third, foreign traders were joined by foreign missionaries, and their impact was significant; thus, incoming Christian missionaries offered religious ideas and charitable activities, but also the ideas that inspired the leader of the Taiping Rebellion.

Fourth, these traders opened up alternate lines of development for the country in the guise of practical trade links, plus new ideas cut against the authority of the Qing. Thus, fifth, settled forms of economic activity were disturbed with novel imported goods (requiring local agents and distribution networks), novel schedules of demands for locally produced goods (agents/networks) and novel sources of finance (new finance houses, payments systems and monies), and these in turn promoted new infrastructure in the form of ports, roads and, later, railways. And, finally, sixth, at the extreme, the foreign traders precipitated war: the Opium War,[52] the Arrow War and the creation of the Treaty Port System, which saw the implantation on Qing territory of communities with ties and loyalties to outside state-empires, a process of quasi-colonization.

The Politics of the Period

Crossley makes it clear that the system of government of the Qing was simultaneously stable and somewhat precarious. It had a distinctive logic: the empire's elite was socially remote from the lives of ordinary people, who, in turn, ordered their own local communities. It was a balance of core and peripheries, and both sides had distinctive anxieties. Crossley specifies three particular elite concerns:[53]

First was the development of partnerships, between local officials and local landowners or merchants, large enough and strong enough to threaten the state. Second was the emergence of locally based cliques whose tendrils might reach into the central government itself. Third was the development of resistance at the local level of a magnitude sufficient to overwhelm state credibility or power.

It was a balancing act. The arrival of foreigners disturbed this domestic system of order. Commentators record that the initial response of local officials to the arrival on their shores of foreign traders was negative: traders were restricted, trading was controlled, and then in the early nineteenth century, as relationships broke down and the foreigners deployed violence to press their case, local officials were unable to fashion an effective response. Their failures were compounded by a habit of relaying messages upwards along the networks of bureaucracy reaching up to the emperor, which claimed decisive successes against the foreigners. Julia Lovell[54] reports that it took several years after the violence began for Beijing to work out just what was happening.

The response of the central government
The apparatus of the state was limited, but it was the mechanism whereby the elite had to fashion a response to the demands of both local opponents and newly arrived foreign traders. The Qing state worked at a hierarchy of levels with relatively small numbers. Nineteenth century figures record their central offices had around 15–23,000 people; in Britain, 60,000; in the USA, 80,000. Today, China has around 11,000,000 state officials.[55] The reach of the central authorities was limited. It was likely that any response to unfamiliar foreigners making novel demands would be hesitant and slow, but the response was made more difficult by two factors: first, the unscrupulous violence of the foreign traders and, second, the grossly misleading reports made by local officials to their superiors.[56] When the British began demanding access the central Qing authorities had no real idea of who these traders were or what they wanted, and at first they were read as one more group of pirates. The depth of the problems posed by these traders only slowly became apparent, and the Qing did respond with treaties and indemnities for the foreigners, military upgrades to the army and navy, and administrative reforms to central state, all to no avail. After the First Opium War other Europeans and Americans joined in. The foreign pressure on the Qing increased, and their responses were rational, but to no avail; thus as domestic pressures increased, so too did the depredations of the foreigners.

The Qing authorities were faced with direct foreign demands, and after each Qing defeat there were new treaties: Treaty of Nanking (1842), Treaty of Tientsin (1858), Treaty of Aigun (1858), Convention of Peking

(1860), Treaty of Shimonoseki (1895) and the Boxer Protocol (1901). Each treaty further embedded foreign influence within the Chinese political economy (trade concessions, customs agreements and so on), and, in addition, the Qing authorities were obliged to pay onerous indemnities after each military defeat. Yet, on the other hand, these treaties did bring with them linkages to foreigners, illustrating again the ambiguous nature of the local-level processes that in total amounted to the Qing's deepening involvement in the unfolding shift to the modern world – the mixture of exploitation, development and learning.

The Qing authorities made domestic reform attempts, such as the Tongzhi Restoration.[57] Emperor Tongzhi's short reign (1861–75) gives the name to an episode of reform that was provoked by reaction to the failure of the Opium War and the disaster of the Taiping Rebellion, and the key to the reforms were newly empowered provincial officials.[58] The programme offered a mixture of moral uplift, ordered by a re-emphasis on Confucian learning, plus learning from the foreigners, with reforms to institutions (so as to deal better with foreigners) and the use of imported machine technologies (in particular for the military). The drive for reforms continued, overall characterized as the Self-Strengthening Movement, 1861–95.

The administrative reforms,[59] which were originally intended to be temporary, saw an office to deal with foreigners added to the Qing administrative system, the Zongli Yamen. Here Qing officials could interact with foreign representatives. Other work included translations of texts on international law, and thus the beginnings of a domestic shift away from the Sino-centric system. There were significant military upgrades.[60] The Opium War had shown that the foreign forces were vastly superior to local ones, and technology was one key; so reformers arranged for arsenals to be built, and these were sites for importing technology, training engineers and building weapons, whilst related reforms involved schooling in natural science based subjects, thus chemistry, physics and so on, and foreign missionaries playing a role in these changes.[61] These reforms were not welcomed by conservative minded officials. Given the nature of the foreign problems faced – traders backed by navies – the Qing reformers paid particular attention to building naval forces. The Qing reformers built arsenals, in particular at Shanghai, Tianjin and Nanking,[62] but there were many more.[63] However, in the latter part of the nineteenth century, central authority waned as regional authorities gained power, in particular, the Beiyang Intendency and the Nanyang Intendency;[64] both built arsenals and both built naval forces. However, there was competition between the two sets of leaders, and the organizational duplication had disastrous consequences: in the

Sino-French War 1884–85 the Southern Fleet based in Fuzhou was destroyed and the Northern Fleet did not come to its aid; later, in the Sino-Japanese War 1894–95, the Northern Fleet based in Weihaiwei and Port Arthur was destroyed and the Southern Fleet, such as it was after rebuilding, did not come to its aid;[65] the two fleets did not support each other.[66] These events fed the perception at the end of the century that the domestic Self-Strengthening Movement had failed, but in fact it achieved much, and the military defeats can be credited to local failures (ships, supplies, training and officering).

More generally, as a result of these reforms the country acquired new centres of power, particularly coastal trading cities, and the idea of self-strengthening took hold. The process of reform continued after Emperor Tongzhi's death, but ambiguously with Dowager Empress Cixi as ruler, and attempts to accelerate reforms in the late nineteenth century with the 1898 Hundred Days Reform programme of Emperor Guangxu[67] were rebuffed by Cixi. Key reformers fled, and Cixi's later support for the Boxer Rebellion 1899–1901 provoked reformers to look to insurrectionary change, and in time regional dissatisfactions with the core eventually provided an opportunity.

The responses of other important agents to these challenges

The Qing authorities in mid-nineteenth century faced many difficulties. There were numerous large-scale rebellions, and these were not local rebellions that could be suppressed by the central authorities; rather, they took the form of regional wars. The central authorities found them very difficult. In the process of their suppression, effective power (political/military) drifted away from the Chinese centre in Beijing to various subordinate groups (thus Beijing-appointed generals) or regional powers; in other words, these rebellions significantly weakened the empire's political structure.

The Taiping Rebellion[68] (1850–66) centred around the charismatic figure of Hong Xiuquan, who began teaching a species of millenarian Christianity around 1847, formed a society, gathered recruits from an impoverished and desperate population,[69] defeated the Qing's attempt at military suppression and was in open revolt from 1851. The rebels seized Nanking in 1853, and it served as their capital from 1853 to 1864. Crossley[70] reports that some landowners and foreigners did wonder if the Taiping might be an effective replacement for the Qing, yet they failed: they failed to press military advantage, they failed to secure urban support and they did not carry out the land reforms in rural areas that had been promised.[71] Eventually, regional armed forces plus mercenaries defeated the rebels, but the combined loss of life was very high, and estimates cite around twenty million. As a consequence of the disaster, power began to flow away from the Qing.[72]

The Nian Revolt[73] of 1851–68 comprised a scattered guerrilla-type rebellion centred on southern Shandong and parts of adjoining Henan, Anhui and Jiangsu, which again had been provoked by rural distress aggravated by flooding when the Yellow River changed course in 1855. These disturbances were slowly suppressed by the Qing.

The Boxer Rebellion[74] was initiated by the Boxers, who began in 1898 in Shandong as an anti-foreigner secret society and had by 1900 entered Beijing. In June the Dowager Empress Cixi embraced their cause, and so the rebellion was now official, but in August the rebellion was crushed by a foreign expeditionary force, and this Qing failure further undermined their position.

Add to all this that there were further opportunistic demands from foreigners – treaties, indemnities and punishments – all oriented towards extending the reach of foreign power in China with the practical intention to reorder Chinese economic affairs, ostensibly to 'mutual benefit' in the light of the ideology of the efficacy of free trade.

The response of ordinary people
These unfolding events had little immediate impact on peasant-based farming as it continued unless otherwise disrupted or challenged. There were two broad sources of change: economic (new demands and opportunities) and social disruption (warfare and other breakdowns of customary order).

The pressures of social and economic change were significant. Incoming foreigners brought new opportunities (merchants in coastal cities prospered and new employment opportunities opened up in trade and manufacturing). Incoming foreigners brought new ideas and practices (schools and hospitals, and along with them ideas of technical education, health and hygiene). Incoming foreigners brought new challenges and opportunities in respect of conceptions of humankind (thus, religion with Christianity). And, added to all this, the pressures occasioned by violence were also significant. The wars and other social breakdowns of the period caused massive social disruption, with millions killed or injured or displaced.

These twin pressures created pressures for movement, migration. There was internal migration, with flows from impoverished rural areas towards either coastal provinces, now increasingly linked to foreign trade networks, or to better off or underexploited rural areas. And there was external migration, flows in particular to the Nanyang, to Latin America and to North America. Conditions were poor in the last pair, with exploitation and racism, but in the Nanyang Chinese migrants were better able to find niches within extant societies and settled in large numbers.

The collapse of the Qing in collective memory
The popular view amongst foreigners takes shape in the nineteenth century and is thereafter subject to modification, as with any other memory; it takes two main forms or discourses. First, the Qing Empire was a formerly great but now moribund civilization (the deep history, cultural resources and contemporary practices are both acknowledged and dismissed as the ensemble of ideas and practices are judged not to measure up to the demands or standards of the modern world). And second, extensive reforms were necessary to the economy, society and polity, and the key to inaugurating these reforms was trade. Trade was the key to 'opening up China', and these ideas were bound up in an elaborate ideology of free trade for commerce would bring new products and ideas; 'opening up' meant opening up to the full schedule of ideas and practices that characterized then European modernity, and, in principle, all would benefit. All that said, more recently, there have been revisions to this tale as the history has been revisited (necessarily as the European-centred wars of the twentieth century dampened the enthusiasm of Europe-boosters[75]), and it can now be granted that the Chinese were to some extent victims of rapacious foreigners.

The popular view amongst Chinese takes shape in the nineteenth century and is thereafter subject to modification, as with any other memory. First, the Qing elite saw rapacious violent foreigners, initially seen as one more group of coastal pirates and only later as representatives of a distant powerful civilization. Second, Qing conservative scholars/administrators saw materialistic foreigners plus missionaries as a threat to long-established cultural ideas and practices. Third, local merchants in the coastal cities saw opportunities, for the European traders could not operate in China without Chinese partners. Fourth, reformers amongst the elite saw a sketch of what a modern China might look like, and what the difficulties might be, and how the foreigners might work to facilitate their interests; hence the Self-Strengthening Movement, through Tongmenghui to the New Culture Movement and the May 4th 1919 demonstrations; and, more recently, an elite promulgated yet popular view is one of a century of humiliation during which rapacious foreigners coupled to a weak, ineffectual Qing regime brought disaster upon the country.[76]

THE FATE OF THE REPUBLIC

The domestic and external problems of the Qing regime came to a head in the early years of the twenty-first century when the immediate issue was one of control of railway financing.[77] The deeper occasion was provided by the changes running through both the elite machinery and the wider social environment within which they worked. Or, in brief, the authorities ran out of both capacity and legitimacy whilst the wider society was not in a position to provide any replacement, and the result was disintegration, both state and society. Barrington Moore offers the following diagnosis:[78]

> The flurry of reforms under the Dowager Empress in the opening years of the twentieth century … strongly suggest that her real goal was the establishment of a strong centralized bureaucratic government over which she would be able to exercise direct personal control … [T]he main point for our purposes is that the social basis for such a regime was lacking in China … The central feature of such a regime … is a coalition between sections of the old agrarian ruling classes … with an emergent commercial and industrial elite with some economic power but political and social disadvantages.

Moore argues that neither class was available for such an alliance; the former were both conservative and relatively privileged and the rural gentry were gaining local power as the authority of the centre faded, whilst the latter were influential in the coastal trading cities, otherwise too weak. Yet there were many intellectual critics of the Qing. Sun Yat Sen and the Tongmenghui represented one strand of opinion, favouring insurrection. Yet, as noted, it was the narrower issue of railway financing that finally provoked an effective response, and as provincial-level resistance to demands from Beijing gathered strength, the rebellion snowballed. However, when the breakdown finally occurred, the optimism of those who initiated the revolution did not long survive the post-revolution politics.

The Condition of the Economy

The late nineteenth century saw rapid, albeit uneven, development in China and these developments showed all the now routinely noted problems of rapid change: exploitation, inequality, environmental degradation and varieties of conflict.

In the economy, foreign traders had served as the vehicle for the introduction of modern commerce and industry, whilst the state paid

attention to armaments factories, shipyards and the like. Foreign investment built up new mines, ports and railways, and foreign money was
invested in new forms of silk production. Local officials and reformers
followed their lead, and iron and steel complexes were built, the bulk of
these activities being concentrated in coastal concessions. Otherwise,
most industrial-type activities remained small scale and traditional in
character, that is, craft-based, low-tech and ordered via guilds.[79] Rural
China was largely untouched, with peasant based production, hence
landlords, poverty and periodic local famines. However, in some rural
areas farmers were able to respond to new market demands and produced
new cash crops such as cotton and tobacco,[80] and there was also
rural–urban migration to the industrializing coastal cities, where conditions for new migrants were poor.

These structural changes found domestic support in the Hundred Days
Reform of 1898; however, the reformers also found conservative opponents and the movement was blunted, even as the processes of structural
change ran on, as did the activities of the foreigners now carving up
China into a series of interlinked quasi-colonies.

The demands of structural change plus the activities of foreigners plus
the apparent inability of the Qing authorities to deal with either structural
change or the foreigners, or even comprehend the scale of their problems,[81] led to growing domestic opposition (elite reformist as noted;
insurrectionary as with the Boxers or the early efforts of Sun Yat Sen's
Revolutionary Alliance), and there was a broader process of learning as
foreign ideas and examples were studied, including materials from
America, Europe and Meiji Japan; or more directly, the poorer sections
of society (workers, hawkers, migrants and the like), confronted with
poor conditions and pay, staged strikes and demonstrations.[82]

The final debate that precipitated revolt against the Qing had centred
on the ownership and finance of railways, but the intermingling of
economic change and local politics were complex.[83] In 1912 a republic
was proclaimed; however, as regards the economy, by the early twentieth
century the impact of the modern world had begun to remake the
economic base of the country.

The Condition of Society

The impact of the modern world's system-carried preference for industry
and democracy, in the initial guise of foreign traders, later supplemented
by domestic efforts at self-strengthening, further supplemented by late-
Qing reform efforts (administrative and economic), all pointed towards
greater social differentiation within the society; however, there was

relatively little change, and the economic base of the country remained peasant agriculture; changes were slow.

The Politics of the Period

The final years of the Qing regime saw accumulating domestic problems and continuing foreign pressures, and, as noted, the final trigger for collapse turned out to be a dispute about the financing of railways; once the rebellion had begun in central China it spread rapidly.

Late Qing reforms, 1901–11

The first moves were made during the 1898 Hundred Days Reform as the young Emperor Guangxu and his supporters issued a series of decrees: reforms to education (introducing modern ideas/skills); reforms to economy (upgrading manufactures and commerce); and reforms to governance (new agencies for new activities). However, elite-level manoeuvring and confusion saw the reform programme stopped, and the Dowager Empress Cixi imprisoned the emperor. Nonetheless, domestic and foreign pressures remained. In 1905 the Qing court abolished the traditional scholarly examinations, new ideas flowed into Chinese debates and local chambers of commerce were encouraged; and in 1906 Cixi ordered the preparation of a new constitution and administrative structure for the country. In 1908, the year Cixi died, the court announced plans for the reform of governance, and provincial assemblies, elected on a restricted franchise, were formed in 1909, with wider debate thereby encouraged. The court promised further reforms, but their efforts at reform-from-above were undone by the rebellions occasioned by the business of railways. Provincial assemblies, plus provincial leaders, plus units of the New Army, plus popular proto-nationalist pressures all pointed to the end of the regime, nonetheless, the regime remained powerful.

Domestic opposition

There were various groups, various understandings and various actions. The groups included: factions within the elite, thus new merchant groups, provincial assemblies, provincial leaders, units of the New Army, intellectuals and other reformers, insurrectionary plotters; along with local-level discontents amongst ordinary people. In this environment novel political ideas were invoked to shape these diverse resentments; thus socialism, nationalism, Marxism, liberalism and so on.

Rebellion and formation of the republic

The final rebellion against the Qing was begun in the autumn of 1911 by accident by revolutionists in Wuhan, as in the context of wider debates about railway financing a mistaken insurrectionist bomb explosion precipitated a rising.[84] It succeeded, and other cities rose against the Qing, and through the autumn of 1911 various factions manoeuvred to secure change. The Qing authorities retreated, and Yuan Shikai was invited by the Qing to rule as premier. Sun Yat Sen returned to China in early 1912 and was invited by the rebels to become provincial president. In February 1912 Pu Yi abdicated and passed authority to Yuan Shikai, so the empire was gone but the country now had two leaders.

The fading Qing regime had established a National Assembly in Peking in late 1910, and this institution became crucial in the subsequent power struggles. In early 1912 the revolutionaries inaugurated a national council in Nanjing. Sun Yat Sen appreciated that the revolutionaries could not match Yuan's armed forces and sought to draw him into the nascent democratic structures by recognizing him as provisional president; elections were organized and held on a restricted franchise in 1912, and the results were announced in January 1913. The parliament convened in Peking; however, there were disputes, and Yuan effectively seized power in early 1913; the parliament was dissolved in early 1914.

Yuan's base of support was in northern China. His regime had difficulty in raising taxes, and loans were secured from foreign banks; the regime thereafter began a reform programme and various aspects of governance and economy were reformed. However, Yuan flirted with the idea of restoring the monarchy, but his power waned and he died young in mid-1916. Thereafter, factional intrigue grew and the era of warlords began, with hundreds of local groups. Some warlords pursued regular governance and reforms whilst others were merely locally successful bandits. The era saw multiple wars.

Collapse into warlord era

Yuan's death in 1916 left the new republic without any clear leadership; political power devolved to those controlling the means of violence, and legitimacy tended to be self-proclaimed as an era of warlord rule began. These warlord groups varied in the base of power they controlled and the manner in which it was deployed; some had spun out of earlier Qing era armies, others were rooted in former local administrations, whilst others, as Spence notes, were simply gangsters.[85]

These warlords controlled numerous territories and engaged in equally numerous wars. There were numerous, very local, polities. The nominal republican government continued a muted existence in Beijing, and warlords in the north competed to control this institution as it provided a kind of continuity and a kind of international status, as China had contributed to the Allied war effort in France and had attended the Versailles Conference. However, the Chinese delegation had found itself outmanoeuvred in respect of former German concessions in Shandong, which were transferred to the Japanese, circumstances that provoked the May 4th 1919 demonstrations, and, more broadly, the period produced the New Culture Movement, 1915–21.

The warlord era was thus in retrospect a period of deepened confusion within an already confused Chinese polity. The twists and turns of the various alliances are many and the costs to ordinary Chinese were high, as instability and warfare were familiar.

The republic in today's collective memory
Sun Yat Sen is remembered as one of the founding figures of today's China. And the warlord era is remembered as one more nadir in the colonial-power inspired degradation of China. But it is also the period when intellectual resistance to the situation began, with the New Culture and May 4th Movements, the foundation of the Kuomintang Party and, at roughly the same time, the establishment of the Communist Party (notwithstanding their later and continuing conflicts).

Zheng Yongnian notes that the episode had consequences that run on into the present day, both organizationally and ideologically (with Sun Yat Sen as everybody's founding father). As regards the first noted, Zheng[86] argues that the 1911 Revolution aimed at a party-based parliamentary-style system and, as it failed and the country collapsed into warlordism, both the KMT and the CCP opted for a strong state, thus the party-state system. After 1949 Mao created a highly centralized system, and although it is not clear what the ultimate goal was as the system dissolved into an ideological struggle, nonetheless the basic structure was in place when Deng moved to the fore and began dramatic reforms. Zheng[87] argues that the elite control the party, the party controls the state and the party-state controls society. Political exchanges amongst elite factions find key expression in reworking the state bureaucracy and inventing (rational) intellectual-political programmes. The CCP has control; it adjusts and changes.

THE NANJING DECADE

The period following the death of Yuan Shikai in 1916 witnessed great confusion as the warlord era saw China dissolve into multiple local military areas; prospectively, there were two broad strands of response. In the southern part of China there was a period of political endeavour in trying to sustain the republic, and then the emphasis shifted towards military endeavours. And here the Northern Expedition was a key operation. The Northern Warlords were then dealt with either via military suppression or via co-option. The CCP were routed in Shanghai and the remnants retreated to a number of impermanent, insecure 'liberated zones' in the countryside. All this culminated in the establishment of a Nationalist China government in Nanjing, and from 1928 Chiang's regime ruled a nominally united country.

So, first, sustaining the republic proved to be very difficult. The initial efforts had collapsed into warlord rule. The proponents of a republican, nationalist China were merely one group amongst others, and in addition to warlords two political parties vied for power: Sun Yat Sen's KMT formed in 1912 and the CCP formed in 1921. Now both parties manoeuvred for advantage amongst sections of the local population, both parties came to create distinctive positions in respect of the future of China, both parties were supported by the newly formed USSR and both parties had to face the presence of foreign powers, powerful business enterprises backed by forces assembled within their concession areas, and, in turn, backed by foreign state military forces. Sun Yat Sen, who established a military government based in Canton in 1923 and became a figurehead until his death in 1925, allowed the already powerful military to come to the fore, with Chiang Kai Shek at their head.

Then, second, the turn to the military gathered pace during this period. The Comintern had offered assistance to Sun Yat Sen's political movement with assorted organizational advice for the party and the establishment of a military academy at Whampoa in 1924. Chiang Kai Shek made this his power base. Chiang deployed his new armies against three local warlords,[88] and victories helped build the army. Chiang then launched the Northern Expedition in 1926. The nationalist armies moved northwards towards Shanghai, Nanjing and Wuhan, all on the Yangtze River. The expedition involved pitched battles, and it also involved local warlords or their commanders switching sides. In this advance the role of the CCP was to organize peasants and workers ahead of the main armies, and in Shanghai they were particularly strong; however, Chiang negotiated with local business and gangster leaders, and the CCP forces and organizations were violently suppressed; some resistance by other CCP groups in the area of Wuhan was similarly suppressed.

Chiang now turned his forces towards Beijing, the key base of the Northern Warlords, but the situation was complicated by the presence of the Japanese in Shandong. A military clash took place at Jinan in May

1928 and Chiang's armies were checked in their advance, but the assassination by Japanese army officers of a key Northern Warlord, Zhang Zuolin, at Mukden in June 1928, saw resistance to Chiang come to an end as the remaining warlords settled. By the end of 1928 Nationalist China enjoyed a kind of unity, with many local tensions plus the continued presence of foreign powers, and thereafter the task was to build the state and govern. In all, Chiang Kai Shek's government secured a measure of control over China: it required accommodation with multiple warlords (some were militarily defeated, some were bought off, others variously accommodated); it also involved a low-level civil war against the Communist Party plus all the whilst the government had to deal with the presence and demands of foreigners – European, American and Japanese. Eventually it was to become involved in an inter-state war with Japan along with a related but, in practice, minor role in the wider Second World War.

The Economy during the Nanjing Decade

The bulk of the population lived in rural areas, and land was the key productive base; there was little change from the Qing era: local officials linked up with landlords; human labour power was central in planting, harvesting and transporting crops; there was low life expectancy and low literacy; and the general level of living was close to subsistence levels. In these circumstances any disturbance could tip large groups of people into destitution. In the early 1930s rural people were confronted with a series of disasters, including the Yangtze River floods in 1931, the Japanese seizure of Manchuria from 1931 onwards, which blocked seasonal migration and removed a productive area from Nanjing's control, plus the impact of the Great Depression, which cut demand, domestic and foreign, for agricultural cash crops.[89]

Urban areas fared much better. Shanghai was a key metropolis and the city was rich, corrupt and unequal. It was home to foreign traders, financiers, manufacturers, gangsters and many thousands of poor locals. And in the 1930s it was also the recipient of refugees from Europe.[90]

One great success for Chiang's government was recovering control of tariffs, and this raised the state's tax income significantly.[91]

The Condition of Society: Urban and Rural; Elite and Mass; Presence of Foreigners

Society was buffeted by a series of disruptive episodes: the collapse of the Qing, the initial failure of the republic, the depredations of warlords, and then political unification secured by military force; all impacted or overlaid an initially diverse social world of regions, towns, villages, clan and kin networks, languages and economic activity. All this produced a fragmented pattern of social life. But there were some overlying commonalities such as ethnicity, rituals and residues of the emperor system in common political culture, hence the practices of deference and hierarchy.

The Nanjing government sought to overlay these diverse local patterns of life with top-down programmes of national development, but such efforts achieved relatively little as a result of the un-clarity of the regime's goals, inefficient execution and the running sore of continuing foreign military involvement.

The Nanjing government had to contend with the presence and demands of foreigners in the guise of traders, financiers and industrialists plus the apparatus of concessions (quasi-colonial areas), with these foreigners being directly supported by their respective governments, not merely diplomatic exchanges but also soldiers and naval forces.[92] At the extreme such demands shaded into direct military intervention – later, with Japan, invasion.

Society evidenced multiple lines of fracture, hence little national-level unity.

The Politics of the Period

Often dismissed as chaotic and corrupt, with Chiang Kai Shek character-ized as just another warlord,[93] the warlord era plus civil war plus Sino-Japanese War provide the backdrop, and so there was extensive violence, with one estimate of the number of casualties put at around 35 million dead.[94] Cast in these terms, another line of commentary argues that the KMT faced a very difficult task in trying to construct a modern state and a modern nation; the key was nationalism and mobilization for war against Japan. So it was in this situation that they tried to construct an independent China.[95]

The key actors: their understandings and actions
The task facing the KMT after their military victory was establishing the apparatus of a state. The capital was moved from Beijing to Nanjing, and the government apparatus was designed to assert the agenda of the elite. It was top-down. The core of the state machinery was the State Council with its sixteen members. Chiang was chairman; thereafter, the system of five main Yuan (Executive, Legislative, Control, Judicial and Examin-ation). The inspiration for the model was provided by the ideas of Sun

Yat Sen, and Chiang sought to legitimize the regime by installing the body of Sun Yat Sen in a grandiose mausoleum in June 1929.

Chiang sought to mobilize the population via a top-down, promulgated ideology, in the main, moral exhortation, the idea of the New Life Movement. All this involved an amalgam of Social Darwinism, quasi-military mobilization and borrowings from the southern European variant of fascism (Mussolini was admired). It had limited utility. An off-shoot of this aspiration to top-down mobilization was the military sourced Blue Shirt Movement, nationalist, anti-communist and activist, and in time a secret police apparatus serving the core of the KMT regime.

All this was pursued in what turned out to be a brief period of comparative calm, some five years between 1928 and 1931. The Nanjing government was inaugurated in 1928, but tensions with Japan turned violent very quickly: the 1931 Mukden Incident and 1932 Shanghai Incident. The 1933 Tanggu Truce demilitarized the border between Nationalist China and Manchukuo. But in 1937 outright warfare began, the Second Sino-Japanese War.

The impacts of events on ordinary people and their responses

Spence reports 'immense change to Chinese life';[96] urban change involved improved roads, medical care, schools, power stations, steamer transport, new trains, cinemas, radio, photographs, Western-type fashions, entertainment complexes and shopping, and cigarette smoking became fashionable; however, in contrast, rural life continued much as before, despite some efforts on the part of the government.

The role of foreign powers

The Treaty Port System had been inaugurated by the state-empire system of the Europeans, America and Japan. In the nineteenth century they were powerful, but by the 1930s they were also coming to the end of their period of unchallenged hegemony. The system of state-empires existed in a period of slow crisis as deep-seated tensions found expression in conflicts in the heartland territories of Europe along with conflicts in the peripheral holdings of these state-empires. The system was in the process of change, and elites in metropolitan countries recognized this; there was some talk of handing over power to local nationalists, there was talk of development, but there was relatively little practical action prior to the final breakdown occasioned by the Second World War.[97]

In China, foreign state-empires found expression in two forms: concessions (traders, financiers, sojourners and so on, all buttressed by contingents of the various empires' military forces) and international treaties (all those treaties secured by foreigners from the Qing regime and its successors) – in sum, the Treaty Port System.[98]

As the confusions in China rolled on, the inhabitants of the concessions sought to protect their interests; there were elite contacts with contending Chinese groupings and the provision of some armed security to afford protection to the resident populations of foreigners, protections also provided in times of crisis to local Chinese, and on occasion this extended to bearing witness to some of the atrocities of warfare.[99]

The period of civil war

The alliance of the two parties, the KMT and the CCP, that emerged from within the failed revolutionary era, roughly the second decade of the twentieth century, was fragile from the outset, and many have noted that the two parties, whilst oriented towards the future sketched by Sun Yat Sen, were nonetheless ideologically distinct and crucially drew their support from quite different and antagonistic social bases.[100] Foreign allies, in particular the USSR, urged an alliance, and this was duly formed in 1923. Sun Yat Sen needed assistance, which the USSR could provide, and the CCP was relatively weak and so also had an interest in the alliance.[101] However, the arrangement was one-sided, as the KMT was more powerful, and as KMT thinking shifted after Sun's death, from politics towards the military, the alliance became ever more implausible.

The first period of civil war was inaugurated in Shanghai in April 1927 by Chiang Kai Shek and local business and gangster allies; the local CCP was destroyed, and some early efforts at rural organization were suppressed around the same time. In late 1927 Mao Zedong launched the Autumn Harvest Uprising, an early effort at rural peasant based revolution, and it failed, just as other similar insurrections came to naught. The CCP remnants retreated deeper into the countryside, where they endeavoured to regroup, and they did so in the context of very poor peasant communities.

Mao and his close allies developed the idea of guerrilla warfare and established a base area as the Jiangxi Soviet. The KMT sought to suppress it, but a number of encirclement campaigns failed. Chiang Kai Shek then sought assistance from National Socialist Germany, receiving military advice and advanced production facilities in exchange for rare mineral supplies.[102] The fifth encirclement campaign involved road building and numerous blockhouses, and it was successful; the CCP and its army elected to retreat. The breakout took place in October 1934, and in January 1935, at the Zunyi Conference, Mao joined the leadership group, slowly taking over the military leadership. The retreat took months, and cost many lives until the remnants met local forces and were able to construct a new base at Yan'an, in October 1935; the episode was remembered as the Long March.[103]

Chiang's attacks continued, but they were blocked in late 1936 in Xi'an by the actions of the warlord and KMT general Zhang Xueliang, who seized Chiang and demanded a change of course. After some confusion the CCP sought a second alliance, this time aimed primarily at the incursions of the Japanese, and Chiang reluctantly acceded to these demands. This second united front was no more stable than the first, but it took the pressure away from the CCP. Now revolution, civil war and inter-state war became intermixed, in all leading to a further period of chaos for China.

Inter-state war: the 1937–45 Sino-Japanese War

The Japanese route to the modern world came to shape their elite's perceptions of China. The Meiji Restoration in 1868 set Japan on a path of rapid national development, which is to say, they 'caught up and joined in', and this record offered an example to anti-Qing reformers, such as Sun Yat Sen and Chiang Kai Shek; however, what the Japanese elite joined was a global system of state-empires. The system of state-empires was centred in Europe and America and comprised a number of large political units each with a metropolitan core coupled to wide multi-ethnic territories bound together by mercantile trading linkages, these state-empires competed for territory; and the whole business was legitimated in terms of the models offered by the advanced civilizations of the core countries. The Japanese elite came to read their local circumstances in these terms, so empire was both a necessity and an obligation.

The Japanese elite sought an empire in Northeast Asia. Around the turn of the twentieth century the rising power of Japan came into conflict with the expansionary intentions of the established powers of the Qing Empire and the Czarist Empire. A number of wars ensued around control of the Korean Peninsula, home to the Hermit Kingdom. The Sino-Japanese War 1894–95 saw the aspirations of the Qing Empire in Korea defeated, and Japan secured primacy in Korea; later, the territory was annexed, Taiwan was ceded to Japan and influence was secured in Manchuria. The Russo-Japanese War 1904–05 saw the aspirations of the Czarist Empire in Korea/Manchuria defeated, and Japan secured access to Manchuria. Japan allied with Britain/France during the Great War and secured control of former German concessions in Shandong. At this point Japan was recognized by the elites of the state-empires as a 'power'. However, in the 1920s to 1930s American anxieties along with those of the leaders of British dominions in the region, plus the impacts of depression upon domestic politics, had the effect of redirecting the thinking of the Japanese elite, and they now saw an empire in Northeast Asia as a defensive bloc; it was an increasingly military conception.

In 1931 the Mukden Incident saw Japan take effective control of Manchuria, and from this base they moved southwards; a series of exchanges with nationalist armies followed. In 1937 open warfare began, and over the next eight years most of China was occupied. The military campaigns were large scale, and whilst the Japanese were able to advance against their generally weaker and less well organized foes, they were not able to effectively garrison and hold the territory that they captured. The result was a kind of stalemate. Nationalist armies did most of the fighting, the CCP's forces accomplished less, but from late 1941, as the fighting in the region grew to include European and American forces, in particular, the latter, both party elites, the KMT and CCP, took for granted the eventual defeat of Japan; thereafter, each moved with an eye on eventually resuming the civil war.

The Pacific War
A number of factors can be cited in respect of the choice for war made by the military elite in Japan: ideas of Pan-Asianism, which posited Japan as the replacement for a collapsed China as leader of Asia; acute diplomatic and industrial–military tension with the USA; a desire to secure raw materials in Southeast Asia to buttress both the state-empire in Northeast Asia; and war production and the fact that European state-empire holdings in the east were vulnerable given core warfare.[104] The final trigger, however, was American pressure, where newly imposed controls on scrap iron and oil exports meant that the Japanese war machine, in particular the navy, would within a measurable period become un-useable. After some debate the military determined upon a war to the south, designed to secure resources; however, the first requirement was to neutralize the American naval forces.

In late 1941 and early 1942 a series of ambitious attacks on American and European military forces and territorial holdings in the wide Pacific Asia region secured a vast territory for the Japanese, as in addition to their territories in Northeast Asia and China they now controlled the bulk of Indo-China and Southeast Asia plus a swathe of island territories in the Central and Western Pacific Ocean. However, American reaction was rapid, and their forces began a two-pronged advance: from the South Pacific towards the Philippines archipelago; and through the Central Pacific directly towards the Japanese homeland via an island hopping campaign, which secured a series of air and naval bases, eventually enabling, thereby, the virtual elimination of the Japanese navy and air force, plus opening the way to a strategic bombing campaign targeted at the cities of the home islands. These two campaigns were slated to be supported in Southeast Asia by the British and in Northeast Asia by the USSR. But in the event, the island hopping campaign led to the decisive defeat of the Japanese.[105] American forces occupied the home islands. The British along with other European powers returned, albeit briefly, to former colonial territories in Southeast Asia, whilst the Soviet Union, late in the day,[106] acquired some territories in the northern areas of hitherto Japanese territories.

The human and material costs of the war were high: the military and civilian casualties were measured in tens of millions, and throughout the region infrastructure was damaged and societies were disrupted.[107] The geo-strategic consequences were profound. Japan was occupied and reorganized by the SCAP[108] authorities, and the pre-war European state-empire presence in the region was removed; cast in terms of decolonization, their withdrawal was unavoidable, the influence of the Soviet Union was enhanced and its influence in China grew, and America emerged as the dominant power within the Pacific Asia region.

And in all this the two key parties in China manoeuvred for advantage against each other. The KMT was supported by the USA in the cause of the military defeat of Japan and the CCP was supported by the USSR in the same cause. The relationship of both foreign supporters to their erstwhile Chinese allies was difficult, and as the Pacific War ended the civil war amongst the Chinese resumed.

American involvement; European withdrawal; early cold war

The civil war resumed shortly after the end of the Pacific War. The Americans supported the nationalists with money, materiel and logistics, whilst the USSR offered support to the CCP. The resumption of fighting saw the rapid defeat of the KMT, and Mao declared the PRC in October 1949 as the remnants of the KMT retreated to the island of Formosa, now styled the ROC. American politicians reacted badly and spoke of 'losing China', and the Korean War 1950–53 fixed in place a cold war in East Asia. These changes were supplemented in a similar time period as the Europeans withdrew from their state-empire colonial holdings in the region. So, in the late 1940s, East Asia was divided into two blocs: one looks to Washington, the other to the (provisional) double centre of Beijing and Moscow.

The Nanjing Decade in Collective Memory

It is possible to identify two broad readings – external (the components of collective memory in the West) and internal (the components of collective memory in China) – and both readings carry shifting meanings down the post-war decades.

The West's Nanjing Decade: this reading notes that the ruling KMT was supported by the USA. The relationship is recalled in a number of phases: (i) from 1927 to 1937(41) when the KMT was supported first against the CCP and then against the Japanese and the regime was read as a progressive modernizing force; (ii) from 1941 to 1945 when the nationalist government was a wartime ally, a period in which the KMT received financial and military aid; (iii) from 1945 to 1949 when the KMT was directly supported in their civil war against the CCP. Plus, (iv) de facto independent Taiwan remains an ally to be supported against the declarations of the CCP. A number of themes run through the literature on this period: (i) regime incompetence and corruption; (ii) regime quasi-fascism (Leadership cult, New Life, Blue Shirts); (iii) Nanjing compared to Weimar; (iv) exoticism (Shanghai as rich, unequal, corrupt, energetic, louche); and (v) in summary retrospect, reading the history in hindsight, Nanjing as a doomed regime, perhaps unfairly damned.

The CCP's Nanjing Decade: this reading notes a period of violent suppression and conflict. Again there are a number of phases picked up in memory: (i) from 1927 to 1937, Nanjing was the capital city of a declared enemy of the CCP (recall, the KMT rule began with the massacre of communists in Shanghai, and during the early phase the KMT regime ran a series of military campaigns aimed at extirpating the influence of CCP, crucially, encirclement campaigns against the Jiangxi Soviet, an episode that provided one founding myth of the PRC, that is, the Long March); (ii) from 1937 to 1945, the KMT was an unreliable temporary wartime ally against the Japanese; (iii) from 1945 to 1949, the KMT was a declared enemy, supported by the USA; and (iv) from 1949 to the present day, the KMT remains an issue for Beijing (thus, the KMT fled to Taiwan and the status of that territory was contested as it is de facto independent but de jure claimed by Beijing). A number of themes can be identified in contemporary thinking, and they revolve around the unfinished business – so far as Beijing is officially concerned – of the civil war; thus Taiwan is a 'renegade province'. The Nanjing Decade and the rule of the KMT are read in terms of regime reaction, corruption and enmity, and these ideas flow into contemporary relations with Taiwan, although, recently, the role of nationalist armies during the war against Japan has been acknowledged, so history can be revisited in the light of changing circumstances.

CONCLUSION: COLLAPSE, RECOVERY AND WAR

The collapse of the Qing Empire as a consequence of external and domestic pressures ushered in a period of chaotic violence in China as revolution was followed by warlords in turn followed by civil war, in turn succeeded by inter-state war itself subsumed within the regional arena of the Second World War. The Chinese people had, perforce, to endure all this confusion and violence. It was only in 1949 that a measure of stability returned to China and to its people.

Yet there were further challenges. Externally, the American sponsored cold war in East Asia, in particular the Korean War, which drew in Chinese forces, placed further demands on the country as the elite shaped their actions in the light of possible external military intervention. Thereafter, the tasks of domestic reform placed further burdens on the people. The record of the first half of the twentieth century was one of almost continual strife and there was more to come: the costs of the revolution were high as the CCP built its state machine throughout China in the wake of the defeat of the organized armies of the KMT and the costs of Mao's experiments were high (the GLF and the Cultural Revolution).

It was only after 1978 that the leadership was able to set the country on a relatively peaceful and prosperous trajectory. Ideologically informed experimentation was set aside in favour of a pragmatic concern for improving the livelihoods of the ordinary people – in brief, the pursuit of economic growth (with its attendant functional demands for social and political reform). In order to give shape to this new policy, the leadership looked to the record of their near neighbours – the countries of the East Asian region – and found not merely a better record (that is, put simply, much better rates of economic growth) but also the keys to a model, a recipe – expert-led national development. In sum, the elite borrowed from the model of the East Asian developmental state.

NOTES

1. Names count: wars involve different participants and give rise to different memories.
2. The claim of one proponent of modernization/globalization; see F. Fukuyama 1992 *The End of History and the Last Man*, New York, The Free Press; and the earlier classic text

was W.W. Rostow 1960 *The Stages of Economic Growth: A Non-Communist Manifesto*, Cambridge University Press.

3. On the UK, see T. Nairn 1988 *The Enchanted Glass*, London, Radius; and more generally see A. Mayer 1981 *The Persistence of the Old Regime*, New York, Croom Helm.
4. There are many texts that tell this tale; see, for example, Z. Bauman 1987 *Legislators and Interpreters*, Cambridge, Polity; J. Habermas 1989 *The Structural Transformation of the Public Sphere*, Cambridge, Polity; A. MacIntyre 1985 2nd ed. *After Virtue*, London, Duckworth; F. Jameson 1991 *Postmodernism: Or, the Cultural Logic of Late Capitalism*, London, Verso; or in contemporary political science terms, C. Hay 2002 *Political Analysis: A Critical Introduction*, London, Palgrave.
5. On this, B. Anderson 1983 *Imagined Communities*, London, Verso – the idea of nation takes shape first in North America, then parts of Europe and Latin America, and later in sometime colonial territories.
6. On these cases, Barrington Moore Jr. 1966 *The Social Origins of Dictatorship and Democracy*, Boston, Beacon.
7. On the distinction between geographical territory and polity in respect of Europe, see Norman Davies 1997 *Europe: A History*, London, Pimlico. In regard to the Qing Empire, the PRC has inherited this very large territory.
8. Pamela Kyle Crossley 2010 *The Wobbling Pivot: China since 1800*, Chichester, UK, John Wiley, pp. 66 et seq.
9. Lin Zexu (1785–1850), Li Hongzhang (1823–1901), Kang Youwei (1858–1927), Liang Qichao (1873–1929) and Sun Yat Sen (1866–1925).
10. Crossley 2010 pp. 23–4.
11. Crossley 2010 pp. 24–5.
12. Data is from A.G. Frank 1998 *Re-Orient: Global Economy in the Asian Age*, University of California Press (Crossley mentions population issues and pressures leading to migration, pp. 44–50).
13. Crossley 2010 pp. 36–7.
14. Thus Chris Bayly on 'industriousness', see C. Bayly 2004 *The Birth of the Modern World 1780–1914*, Oxford, Blackwell.
15. Frank 1998.
16. Crossley 2010 p. 37 offers this characterization.
17. The tale is more complicated and involves money systems, commercialization and tax raising, plus international trading created problems for authorities in Beijing; that is, it was not just the issue of funding opium consumption (Crossley 2010 pp. 37, 62–3).
18. Eventually around 80 or so, see R. Nield 2015 *China's Foreign Places: The Foreign Presence in China in the Treaty Ports Era, 1840–1943*, Hong Kong University Press.
19. Norman Stockman 2000 *Understanding Chinese Society*, Cambridge, Polity, p. 47.
20. Crossley 2010 p. 15.
21. On this, see Crossley 2010 p. 53.
22. On 'Chinese-ness' various lines are noted by Stockman 2000.
23. Stockman 2000 pp. 203 et seq.
24. Stockman 2000 p. 208.
25. Crossley 2010 pp. 26–30.
26. Crossley 2010 p. 31.
27. Zhao, Shiyu 2014 *The Urban Life of the Qing Dynasty*, Reading, UK, Paths International, pp. 223, 229–31.
28. Zhao 2014 p. 216.
29. Ren, Fang 2010 'The Rural Market in Late Imperial China' in *Asian Social Science* 6.6, p. 43.
30. Ren 2010 p. 43.
31. Ren 2010 pp. 45–6.
32. Hui, Xiaoxi 2013 Housing, Urban Renewal and Socio-Spatial Integration: A Study on Rehabilitating the Former Socialistic Public Housing Areas in Beijing, Online. <http://

abe.tudelft.nl/index.php/faculty-architecture/article/view/hui/pdf> (accessed 20 January 2016), p. 104.

33. D. Raff, S. Wachter and S. Yan 2013 'Real Estate Prices in Beijing 1644–1840' in *Explorations in Economic History* 50, p. 371.

34. Liu, Ying and Awotona, Adenrele 1996 The Traditional Courtyard House in China, Online. <http://iaps.architexturez.net/system/files/pdf/1202bm1029.content.pdf> (accessed 20 January 2016), p. 1.

35. Raff et al. 2013 p. 371.

36. Hui 2013 p. 104.

37. Yu, Xinzhong, and Yang, Luwei 2013 'Modernity: A Rose with Thorns: Reflection on the Modernity of Sanitation Construction in the Late Qing Dynasty' in *Journal of Cambridge Studies* 8.3/4, p. 48.

38. Zhang, Xiulan and Zhang, Lu 2014 'Medicine with a Mission: Chinese Roots and Foreign Engagement in Health Philanthropy' in Jennifer Ryan, Lincoln C. Chen and Tony Saich eds. *Philanthropy for Health in China*, Bloomington, Indiana University Press, pp. 84–6.

39. Zhang and Zhang 2014 p. 87.

40. Zhang and Zhang 2014 p. 87.

41. Zhang and Zhang 2014 pp. 87–8.

42. Zhang and Zhang 2014 pp. 88–9, p. 95.

43. Zhou, Jinghao 2003 *Remaking China's Public Philosophy for the Twenty-first Century*, Westport, CT, Praeger.

44. Bonnie Smith 2008 'Civil Service' in Bonnie G. Smith ed. *The Oxford Encyclopedia of Women in World History (Volume 1)*, Oxford University Press, p. 398.

45. Wong, Yin Lee 1995 'Women's Education in Traditional and Modern China' in *Women's History Review* 4.3, p. 345.

46. Wong 1995 p. 356.

47. Wong 1995 p. 356.

48. Wong 1995 p. 357.

49. Wong 1995 p. 356.

50. Wong 1995 p. 356.

51. R. Bickers 2011 *The Scramble for China: Foreign Devils in the Qing Empire 1832–1914*, London, Allen Lane.

52. J.D. Spence 2013 *The Search for Modern China*, New York, Norton, pp. 152–8; Brian Inglis 1976 *The Opium War*, London, Coronet; C.A. Trocki 1999 *Opium, Empire and the Global Political Economy: A Study of the Asian Opium Trade 1750–1950*, London, Routledge; Julia Lovell 2011 *The Opium War: Drugs, Dreams and the Making of China*, London, Picador.

53. Crossley 2010 p. 18 – Crossley adds that although the PRC state is much larger, 'it is too small and too uncoordinated to truly permeate the wide and very complex space of the PRC' (p. 18), so the balancing act – the wobbling pivot – continues in the absence of any reforms.

54. Lovell 2011.

55. Crossley 2010 p. 26.

56. Lovell 2011 pp. 115–8.

57. Spence 2013 pp. 186–96.

58. Crossley 2010 pp. 118–25 mentions the consequences of regional power in the wake of Taiping War 1850–66; thus regional power centres grew and the Qing declined. In particular, the period sees the start of the rise of Northern Beiyang Intendancy (at Tianjin) and Nanyang Intendancy (at Fuzhou). Crossley adds that the familiar discussion of Dowager Empress Cixi is not that relevant.

59. Spence 2013 pp. 191–6.

60. Spence 2013 pp. 189–90; B.A. Elman 2004 'Naval Warfare and the Refraction of China's Self Strengthening Reforms into Scientific and Technical Failure 1869–1895' in *Modern Asian Studies* 38.2.

61. Spence 2013 pp. 198–200.
62. Crossley 2010 p. 92.
63. Elman 2004 p. 309.
64. Crossley 2010 p. 123.
65. Spence 2013 pp. 213–5, Crossley 2010 pp. 93–5.
66. Elman 2004 p. 319.
67. Spence 2013 pp. 220–1; relatedly, claims to 'Chinese essence, foreign practicality', p. 217.
68. Crossley 2010 pp. 101–17.
69. Crossley 2010 p. 102, notes that this took place in context of social dislocation occasioned by core failures and foreign adventuring.
70. Crossley 2010 p. 110.
71. Spence 2013 p. 173.
72. Crossley 2010 pp. 116–8.
73. Spence 2013 pp. 178–81.
74. Spence 2013 p. 222.
75. On the scale of the catastrophes of the twentieth century in Europe and in East Asia, see P.W. Preston 2010 *National Pasts in Europe and East Asia*, London, Routledge.
76. Lovell 2011 pp. 337–60; the issue of 'humiliation' is pursued by William Callahan 2010 *China: The Pessoptimist Nation*, Oxford University Press.
77. A tangled story as in the last few years of the nineteenth century foreign investors began to plan and build railways, and after a few years a nationalist 'rights recovery movement' took shape, arguing that local Chinese investors should put their capital to use; but in 1910 the Qing authorities decided that all railways should be nationalized, and it provoked a reaction; when a group of conspirators in Hankou accidentally set off a bomb, a local uprising was triggered and it spread; see Spence 2013 pp. 238–42, 250–4.
78. Moore 1966 pp. 184–5.
79. Spence 2013 p. 303.
80. Spence 2013 pp. 215–6.
81. Moore 1966.
82. Spence 2013 pp. 228–33.
83. Spence 2013 pp. 238–54.
84. Spence 2013 p. 250.
85. Spence 2013 pp. 273–4.
86. Zheng, Yongnian 2014 *Contemporary China: A History since 1978*, Chichester, UK, Wiley-Blackwell – see chapter 1 in particular.
87. Zheng 2014, see chapters 10 and 11.
88. Spence 2013 p. 308.
89. Spence 2013 pp. 356–65 notes that around this time social scientific rural community studies were carried out in China and Manchukuo, providing much valuable data.
90. B. Waserstein 1998 *Secret War in Shanghai: Treachery, Subversion and Collaboration in the Second World War*, London, Profile, pp. 140–50.
91. Spence 2013 p. 333.
92. Available to deploy force; a number of episodes of violent repression of local Chinese demonstrators or strikers took place in the 1920s, and these fed local political hostility to the foreign presence, yet, paradoxically, at times of acute crisis these same concessions served as refuges for local people.
93. J. Fenby 2005 *Generalissimo: Chiang Kai Shek and the China He Lost*, London, The Free Press.
94. R.J. Rummel 1991 *China's Bloody Century*, London, Transaction, p. 12.
95. H.J. van de Ven 2003 *War and Nationalism in China 1925–45*, London, Routledge.
96. Spence 2013 p. 336.
97. Matters pursued in P.W. Preston 2010.
98. Nield 2015.

99. Reportage in regard to the Nanjing Massacre was made available by a German business man, John Rabe – the massacre has now passed into the official Chinese national past; on this aspect, as it is expressed in museum displays, see K.A. Denton 2007 'Horror and Atrocity: Memory of Japanese Imperialism in Chinese Museums' in C.K. Lee and G. Yang eds. *Re-envisioning the Chinese Revolution: The Politics and Poetics of Collective Memories in Reform China*, Stanford University Press.
100. Moore 1966, Spence 2013.
101. Spence 2013 pp. 302–3.
102. Spence 2013 p. 374.
103. The track of the retreat and creation of the myth are revisited in Sun, Shuyun 2007 *The Long March*, London, Harper.
104. On this see A. Iriye 1987 *The Origins of the Second World War in Asia and the Pacific*, London, Longman; A. Iriye 1997 *Japan and the Wider World*, London, Longman.
105. For an overview of the late stages of the war in the Pacific, see Max Hastings 2008 *Retribution: The Battle for Japan*, New York, Alfred Knopf.
106. On the end game of the war against Japan, see Tsuyoshi, Hasegawa 2005 *Racing the Enemy: Stalin, Truman, and the Surrender of Japan*, Belknap Press of Harvard University Press.
107. C. Thorne 1986 *The Far Eastern War: States and Societies 1941–45*, London, Coronet.
108. SCAP = Supreme Commander Allied Powers – the acronym is often used as a shorthand for the occupation authorities, mostly American.

3. New China I: the revolutionary era of Mao

The period 1937–49 wreaked havoc on the economy, society, culture and politics of China. For some eight years the country was swept by continuous warfare. There were numerous combatants: the Japanese, the KMT, the Communist Party, assorted warlords, local regional wartime states, Americans and a multiplicity of more local groups including self-defence militias, party forces and simple bandits. The formal declaration of the PRC marked the CCP elite's embrace of this inherited chaos; it was the starting point for their work in rebuilding China, and this project entailed radically remaking the country.

The events of the civil war, the military victory of the armies of the CCP in 1949 and the subsequent difficult and often violent pacification of the country along with the expulsion of the forces of the nationalists established the overall shape of contemporary China, that is, New China. There were distinctive domestic and international aspects to this episode. The domestic establishment of a state-socialist system evidenced both successes and familiarly noted failures: the creation of an effective state machine, the expulsion of foreigners and the achievement of a measure of social order and economic recovery, plus the costs of inaugurating these programmes, the latter exemplified by the events of the GLF. Thereafter, in a wider international context, the domestic reactions of the elite of the USA[1] to the so-called loss of China were severe, as it was read as a major geo-strategic defeat, and it helped usher in the business of cold war in East Asia. This general political environment plus the Korean War, along with subsequent tensions around Taiwan and wars in neighbouring Southeast Asian countries, reinforced the perceptions amongst the elite in Beijing that they had, perforce, to fight for their revolution against domestic opponents and foreign enemies.

INTER-STATE WAR, CIVIL WAR AND REVOLUTION – THE LATE 1940s AND EARLY 1950s

The domestic history of China during the early twentieth century following the final decay of the Qing regime involved numerous conflicts. At the outset the Republican Revolution of 1911 had not been followed by the successes imagined by the proponents of change; instead, the country was repeatedly swept with violence. The country saw the emergence of many warlord rulers. And from the late 1920s there was fighting between the KMT and the CCP. Moving into these domestic conflicts, the Imperial Japanese began to deepen their involvement in China during the early 1930s, in particular in Manchuria, thereafter in adjacent areas of northern China. In 1937 there were significant Japanese forces present in northern areas of China, and both Chinese and Japanese troops were based on the railway linking Beijing and Tianjin. In July 1937, at the Marco Polo Bridge, there was a minor local clash which escalated. Japanese forces deepened their grip on northern China, and Chiang Kai Shek responded by opening another area of conflict in Shanghai. In the early phases of fighting a failed nationalist bombing attack killed hundreds of local citizens and thereafter from August both the nationalists and the Japanese reinforced their armies until in November the battle was in effect over and the nationalists retreated. The Japanese forces advanced, and in December 1937 Nanjing was seized, whereupon a local massacre ensued. Following these events in the early months of 1938, the Japanese advanced again and took Wuhan in late 1938. Now Chiang's forces retreated again, and in the course of this retreat, in order to delay the Japanese, Chiang's forces destroyed the dykes on the Yellow River. There was extensive flooding, which destroyed some 4,000 villages, killing untold numbers of civilians.[2] The Japanese advance continued, as did the retreat of the nationalists, which finally ended in Chongqing in the far southeast of the country. The city was remote, cut-off and heavily bombed; it became the wartime base of the nationalists.

In the campaigns of the late 1930s the Japanese armed forces drove the KMT forces out of northern and central China.[3] The KMT steadily retreated to the southwest, and during these war years it was based in Chongqing. Meanwhile, the CCP, which was based in Yan'an, controlled areas in central northern China. Much of northern and coastal China was in the grip of the Japanese. And in 1942, following the start of the wider Pacific War, the Japanese renewed their campaigns; however, attempted moves into central southern China were unsuccessful, and a kind of stalemate developed where the Japanese could make military advances but could not adequately garrison their holdings, and nor could Chinese forces remove them. For a period southwest China provided the Americans with a base region for bombing campaigns against the Japanese further north, but in the summer of 1944 the Ichigo campaign saw Japanese forces extend their control of wide areas of southern China, seeking to disable these American attacks.

In this chaos a number of local regional governments were formed.[4] Spence remarks that the once unified territory was now divided into 'ten separate major units'.[5] At this time five nominally independent states emerged: Manchukuo, Federated Autonomous Government of Mongolia, the Provisional Government of the Republic of China (based in Peking), Reformed Government (based in Nanjing) and Taiwan. All were dependent upon the Japanese. Plus there were the nationalists in Chongqing and the CCP in Yan'an. Thus, the chaos of war produced a chaotic political/administrative pattern, and whilst many Chinese rallied to the last two noted groups, most did not – they stayed where they were and made the best of their local circumstances, dealing pragmatically with whichever group(s) held local power.[6]

At the local level, during these various military campaigns ordinary people had to adjust as best they could. In all, it was a chaotic situation comprising multiple players, with some large army formations plus guerrilla activity, plus puppet regimes and collaboration. The latter could involve a variety of local-level engagements with the occupying power. Brook[7] notes compulsion, cooperation, agreement and support, and so the activities were diverse, and all are difficult for historians to access as records are scanty and Chinese collective memory tends to speak schematically of heroic resistance, violent occupation and traitorous collaboration with all detail and nuance thus lost.

Yet during this period, as the Sino-Japanese War overlapped with the Pacific War two non-Japanese sponsored governments continued to operate: the nationalists in Chongqing and the CCP in Yan'an. Both were isolated, both lacked resources,[8] both sought to evade the attacks of the Japanese, both sought to develop their areas and both had great difficulty asserting the power and authority of their nascent state machineries over the populations they nominally controlled. And both sought to manoeuvre against the other. Historians record that the nationalists were the weaker party and were haphazard and corrupt, whilst the CCP better understood the need to gather support from the majority, that is, the peasants. However, for both elites the overwhelming issue was warfare; first against the Japanese and then against each other. And with the opening of the wider Pacific War, the latter moved to the forefront of elite thinking as both nationalists and the CCP anticipated the eventual defeat of the Japanese.[9] At the same time, the contending parties also noted the growing might of the USA and the virtual elimination of the presence of the state-empires of the Europeans. The KMT in particular were assiduous in their courtship of the Americans. It was clear that the post-war period was going to be quite different from what had gone before, and the key political issue was which group was going to be central in determining its new shape.

****

The Pacific War was brought to a formal end in August 1945. The cost to the Chinese of the war against the Japanese was around 12 million dead.[10] And as the fighting ceased the practical business of ordering matters on the ground began: the Japanese had some 2.25 million troops in China (these were intact military formations) plus around 1.75 million civilians.[11] Add to this the numerous displaced persons, the depredations of continuing fighting between the KMT and CCP, and the matter of interned foreigners[12] along with some foreign military personnel, and it is clear that the situation was one ripe with tensions.

The KMT and CCP forces secured the surrender of these troops and the people in the areas that they controlled, and they competed to place troops in those areas outside their immediate control (unlike mainland Europe where there were agreements amongst the allies about respective post-war control areas). After the defeat of the Japanese there were attempts at agreement between the two parties, but these failed. With the help of the USA, Chiang Kai Shek moved troops into Manchuria, and in late 1945 attacked the forces of the CCP; and whilst the USA endeavoured to mediate, its evident partiality for the KMT undermined its efforts. There were clashes between the KMT and CCP in many areas of China, and local CCP forces increasingly treated American troops as enemies; there were clashes, and eventually the USA gave up attempts to mediate. In late 1946 the CCP armies in Manchuria, which were no longer guerrilla formations but instead conventional armies, began to advance southwards. The number of troops involved was large, and in total both armies numbered around four million. In a relatively short time, the PLA defeated the armies of the nationalists; by late 1948 the CCP had reached the Yangtze River, and by late 1949 they had reached Canton and Chongqing, and the KMT remnants retreated to Taiwan.

The scale of the fighting throughout East Asia during the 1930s and 1940s entailed many casualties, huge numbers of displaced people along with social breakdown and great political confusion. The USA emerged as the key power, whilst China dissolved into civil war and revolution. European and American colonial powers sought briefly to recapture former territories, whilst local nationalist movements sought independence, and once in power, these replacement elites faced the daunting tasks of order, security and development.

CONDITIONS IN CHINA – FROM THE LATE 1930s TO THE EARLY 1950s

By the middle of the 1930s the population of China was some 479 million,[13] and the systematic information available from local social scientists[14] showed that the growth of industry in the cities had lifted levels of living for many; however, many remained poor, and the situation in rural areas remained parlous. In the cities, in new industries hours were long, conditions and pay were poor, and unions were weak; nonetheless, the better-off workers could live on their incomes. Others were not so lucky, and where the cities hosted extensive slum areas, the rural areas fared worse. Social scientific field studies[15] were made, revealing population pressures and exploitative patterns of land ownership, and these studies also revealed great regional diversity in patterns of life; however, the overall pattern was one of rural distress, and many led lives that hovered around bare subsistence.

Social conditions for people in cities and rural areas were uneven, generally poor. The KMT in the 1930s had sought to pursue development: it had secured tariff autonomy in 1928 and this had increased the state's tax take[16] but revenues did not match expenditures. Urban areas grew, and Shanghai grew rapidly, whilst rural areas remained poor,[17] with conditions resembling those of the Qing era, that is, the routine use of hand-power in production along with village localism and landlordism.[18] Spence argues that the KMT never managed to construct an effective state machine[19] – it remained weak and liable to corruption. And from the late 1930s onwards the depredations of warfare weakened the economy and society further. With fighting and multiple administrations, existing levels of living in urban areas declined sharply, so too rural areas. However, the changes in rural areas around the weakening of familiar patterns of organization opened the way to CCP organization,[20] and by the late 1940s the KMT was failing, American support faltering and the sometime influential foreigners with their extra-territoriality and concessions rapidly fading from the scene. Change swept through an already chaotic country and the clue to Mao's revolution was the embrace of the peasantry as the crucial class grouping.

The politics of the period of the late 1940s saw the end of the Pacific War, the end of the civil war and the beginnings of the cold war in East Asia. However, whereas the ending of warfare ought to have simplified matters, political life for the elites was anything but straightforward; indeed, it would better be characterized in terms of a series of urgent crises.

In 1949 the CCP faced the task of establishing domestic control: removing class enemies (rural/urban), taking control of the machineries of the state (all the routine operations) and securing border areas with the October 1949 failed attack on Quemoy, the October 1950 invasion of Tibet and the October 1950 intervention in the Korean War. In brief, the violence of civil war and inter-state war that had begun in the 1920s warlord era carried over into the 1950s, and the legacies of the 1940s and 1950s included the deep animosity of the political elite of the USA, hence cold war in East Asia.

THE POLITICS OF THE PERIOD OF REVOLUTION – 1950s ONWARDS

The end of the civil war meant that the new CCP government could move ahead with reconstructing the Chinese state and thereafter pursuing development; however, these matters were far from straightforward.

CCP Ideals, Dissent and Disputes, and Lines of Commentary

In the late Qing era and around the time of the republican experiment, activists in China, both intellectuals and political agents, looked to various examples from Japan, America and Europe. Many ideas were imported, and they offered a wide spread of ideas for reforms that could or should be adopted in China. Famously, Sun Yat Sen identified the three principles of nationalism, democracy and livelihood. However, the importation of ideas from Japan, America and Europe was anything but straightforward, for all these political ideas were deeply embedded within wider cultural milieu and once moved to their new location had to be read in terms of available ideas; that is to say, new ideas were made intelligible within the context of older received traditions. In all, this was an instance of the widely familiar intellectual process of engaging with the modern world and identifying new forms of local practice.

Then, in this period, the 1917 Russian Revolution offered these activists both encouragement, as the Czarist absolutist state was overthrown, and a model of how to build a progressive polity, and some strands of activism in China embraced the new model. It led to the formation of the CCP.

The early period of the republic saw many flows of new ideas, and these debates tended to belong to urban elites; and then a further impetus to debate was given in 1919 by the May 4th Movement. Such flows of ideas mingled with early investigations into Marxism,[21] investigations reinforced by the 1917 Revolution and, in particular, declarations from Soviet leadership about nations and decolonization. In 1919–20 several communist groups were established in China and in France, and from these strands grew the CCP; its first meeting was held in Shanghai in July 1912,[22] and it was a very small group, which made an early decision to ally with the KMT.

Thereafter, down the years, the party was involved in various debates: thus tactics (how to respond politically to shifting events), policy (what should be done – the 'party line') and, more reflectively, ideology (just what was the appropriate application of the theories of Marx to the situation of China). In respect of political analysis it was noted that China was embroiled in warlord violence, had a weak republican state and was deeply penetrated by foreign powers. And in an economic perspective, China had a weak economy that was rural centred and host to a peasant-dominated form of life. The conclusions reached by party theorists were always provisional, and debates amongst elite were fluid, plus more local groups also had their own ideas, so there was never a monolithic party line. Moreover, given the size and complexity of the country, any such top-down lines of argument could never have been translated neatly into practice, so debate and practice were intertwined and substantive claims about the correct path for the party were always provisional.[23]

In all these debates, one answer came from Mao Zedong, as his experience as a young man organizing peasants in poor, rural areas of central China had convinced him that much could be done by encouraging the activity of the peasantry, and this was to remain a characteristic of his thinking. Another answer came from those aided by Comintern agents, who looked to the example of the USSR, and their politics looked to urban areas, to the role of industry and to the strengthening of the urban working class. This stance opened up a role for elite-level planners and technocrats, which was a distinction that would come to be more important after the party had won power. These debates ran on down the years. Mao's GLF programme celebrated peasant agency, and one reading of the Cultural Revolution posits a tension between revolutionary action as championed by Mao and the bureaucratic order of an industrializing state, that is, the tendency for political power to drift towards elite central bodies staffed by professionals, political, administrative and technical, and relatively detached from the mass of the people. The debate amongst the party elite was difficult. In broad terms, the debate was settled in the period following the death of Mao as radical leftists disposed to follow Mao's line and celebrate the power of the peasantry were purged and technocrats came to the fore, with these latter groups associated with the rise to paramount power of Deng Xiaoping; thereafter, the lines of reform continue to unfold.

Looking at China and the CCP, there are many lines of American and European political analysis. Fleming Christiansen and Shirin Rai[24] list some ten approaches to the study of politics in China, and these include notions of totalitarianism, factionalism, clientelism, class struggle, Confucianism and others. One recent influential study[25] looks at China in a comparative fashion and argues that the CCP has adapted successfully to recent changes – externally, the 1989–91 collapse of the Soviet bloc, and internally, to the shock of the 1989 Tiananmen Square episode. The adaptation has seen the party upgrade its own structures and those of the state, and thus the CCP's recent successes are not just down to materialism plus nationalism. A newer text argues that the local political structure is best read in terms of institutions and ideas, where the last noted embrace the legacy of earlier phases of development in China, that is, the inheritance of the emperor system. The upshot is that the party-state is best seen as an 'organizational emperor';[26] it is the machinery which orders political exchanges and around which groups manoeuvre for position.

The historical institutionalist approach favoured in this text invites analysts to look at shifting sets of structural circumstances and at the response of variously located agent groups as they build institutions, formulate plans and promulgate them (disseminate/legitimate) amongst their target audiences; that being so, in 1949 the CCP faced the tasks of recovery from warfare and thereafter the pursuit, like other developing countries, of order, stability and development.

The Task of Securing Political and Social Order

The constitutional structure was set in place in the first instance by the 1949 Common Programme established by a group of delegates at a consultative conference, and it functioned as an interim constitution. In it, political and administrative power was distributed around three pillars, the party, state machine and army, and the CCP sat at the heart of this organization. The country was divided into six regions; these had taken shape during the period of warfare and were partly military boundaries and partly the natural regions into which the country fell. Thereafter, within each region, the tripartite system was followed.[27] And given the track record of the key members of elite level bodies and the generation to which they belonged, by the early 1950s the party-state was powerful and effective in securing desired changes, although, nonetheless, the structure allowed the expression of familiar tensions between regional authorities.

A formal constitution was adopted in 1954 by the first meeting of the National People's Congress.[28] The political structure was reordered,[29] the six regions abolished and the system was remade in a centralized fashion with Beijing at the centre. There were twenty-one provinces, five autonomous regions and two municipalities along with two thousand or so county governments. This apparatus was supplemented by the party, as below this level there were many local branches of the Communist Party. The model has endured.

The 1949 Common Programme affirmed the key role of the Communist Party and identified two areas of development, rural and urban; however, as Spence[30] points out, the crucial early tasks were to reconstruct a war-damaged economy and society; thereafter, reforms oriented towards the future could be pursued in rural areas and also the cities.

In rural areas, through the late 1940s and early 1950s there were extensive reforms, and the key was land reform carried out as a staged class struggle.[31] It was begun slowly. It transferred ownership from the long-established landlord classes to the poor peasantry so that peasants could be liberated from economic oppression and an equal distribution of land could be achieved,[32] and in the event, poor peasants 'more than doubled their average farm size'.[33] It was not merely an economic reform, as the process was also intended to break the hitherto existing class structure, and so on a broader scale it was in fact an act of state building 'designed to break landlord power, generate peasant support, and create the foundation for a new socialist state'.[34] By overthrowing the feudal landlord class, political activists and party members emerged as new village leaders loyal to the CCP;[35] local-level reform groups were established and tasked with carrying out the changes, and so, perhaps inevitably, the process was attended by violence, with later estimates putting the numbers of dead at around one million.[36] Critical commentators argue that Mao believed that violence was necessary to demolish the existing foundations of political and economic power in rural areas,[37] but in the context of the times it is difficult to see how significant change could have been achieved quietly or consensually.

In the cities reforms were more difficult as CCP cadres were unused to city life, but the party slowly remade urban administrations, propagandized against class enemies and built new administrative structures that reached down to the level of local neighbourhoods. In all, not an easy relationship or simple reform process.

One key strategy used by the party was the 'mass campaign'.[38] The CCP had become adept at organizing mass campaigns during its time in Yan'an and later Manchuria during the latter phases of the civil war. These techniques involved a mixture of top-down direction, small local active groups and the accumulation of extensive knowledge of local conditions. The campaigns worked, and in the early 1950s four key mass campaigns were undertaken, each directed to some particular political and economic goals; the first sought to mobilize the population against an external enemy, the USA, whilst the succeeding trio of campaigns were turned towards domestic opponents and associated problems.

The first mass campaign was the 1950–51 Resist America and Aid Korea Campaign, a part of the war effort of the Chinese state in respect of the political disintegration into civil war that took place in Korea. The Korean conflict in both its development and prosecution involved significant outside involvement, in particular from the USA, and the actions of the armies of General MacArthur in advancing towards the Yalu River border drew in the Chinese army, nominally volunteers, which forced an American retreat, with the fighting ending along the 38th parallel, reinstating the pattern that had held from the 1945 division of the country.[39] At home the mass campaign embraced a wide purge of foreigners in the country, and with 'beating American arrogance' as its central slogan, the Chinese government aggressively mobilized support for their intervention.[40]

Thereafter, the second related campaign was directed at domestic opponents, and the 1950–51 Campaign to Suppress Counterrevolutionaries was in effect both a purge of society in the wake of the civil war and a process of dis-arming the population, where decades of warfare had led to the widespread dissemination around the country of military knowledge along with the parallel distribution of a profusion of modern weaponry. Millions of people who had been in the KMT party or had served in nationalist armies were put under the category of class enemies, spies and bandits.[41] Then, the third mass campaign was focused on the apparatus of the new communist state; thus the 1951 Three Antis Campaign was directed against corruption, waste and bureaucracy,[42] and the target of the campaign were party cadres who took bribes, used public money for personal use and indulged themselves in a luxury lifestyle.[43] Then, somewhat later, the 1952 Five Antis Campaign was directed against the wider national bourgeoisie for a variety of economic crimes, which included tax evasion, bribery, cheating on government contracts and stealing state property and state economic secrets.[44]

In the early years of the PRC the mass campaigns served the purposes of strengthening the power of the party and legitimizing its programme of the 'people's dictatorship'. The campaigns also served to defeat 'the resistance of anyone who was in a position to challenge the new regime'.[45] These constitutional, political and popular measures ensured the success of the revolution; thus the new party-state secured its power (security and order). Next came development.

Development – Ideas and Achievements

The model adopted by the CCP drew directly on the experience of the USSR with its rapid industrialization pursued by means of state planning; and there was significant technical help from the USSR. The initial impetus to the pursuit of industrialization was given by the simple fact of the absence of warfare and the need to rebuild, and thereafter a number of further questions drove the work. Thus, further encouragement was given by rural land-reform programmes and by urban reforms, including infrastructure. The implementation of basic, local-level government services (hygiene, health and the like) helped drive development and further impetus was given by the introduction of a stable currency, the renminbi, with government spending controlled and funded via bonds. The basic model of development via rapid industrialization saw private consumption suppressed in order to build up industrial and agricultural infrastructure for future production.[46]

The First Five Year Plan (1953–57) 'concentrated on the development of heavy industry financed with Soviet assistance'[47] and was a great success. In this period the Soviets built more than 200 industrial plants in China, and there were about 10,000 Soviet and East European advisers in China working on more than 300 industrial projects.[48] The programme constituted a major drive to upgrade the economy, and in this process important 'industries, including iron and steel manufacturing, coal mining, cement production, electricity generation, and machine building were greatly expanded'.[49]

During this period Liou notes that 'the Chinese government successfully attained its political objective of public ownership of the means of production',[50] as privately owned firms no longer existed because they were either sold to the state or converted into joint public–private enterprises under state control.[51] Under the state-planning model, the government 'made all production and investment decisions ... [and] set the prices for virtually all products'.[52] The urban work unit system of a factory 'functioned as a self-sufficient "welfare society"'.[53] It provided employees with life-long employment and basic income protection, health care and housing benefits, and services in areas such as food, education and recreational activities free of charge or at a nominal charge, and this led to an increased dependence of urban employees and their family members on the work units and their loyalty to the party.

All these factors were cast in voluntaristic terms in line with Mao's intellectual and moral commitment to the vitality of the masses, and as the bulk of the population were peasant farmers they carried a considerable burden; nonetheless, their circumstances were much improved over the wartime period. From 1952 onwards private peasant farming was reorganized towards the model of cooperatives and then communes, with small-scale reforms at first, then more ambitious reforms, and production increased whilst private plots were particularly successful, one illustration of the tensions that could arise between formal socialist goals and the accidents of the pursuit of rapid development. The reform process in rural areas went through a number of phases, first, low-level cooperative schemes, later formal cooperatives, and then schemes of much larger scale involving many households, and these, in turn, were to become the keys to more ambitious commune schemes.

The first stage began in 1952 with the formation of mutual aid teams that comprised up to 20 households cooperating during the cultivation and harvest months.[54] Labour was pooled but agricultural land, animals and tools remained in private hands.[55] The second stage was the formation of lower-stage Agricultural Producers' Cooperatives (APCs) in 1954 that combined mutual-aid teams and pooled agricultural land, animals and tools for cultivation. Peasants retained private ownership of land and 'received income in relation to the proportion of the size of the shares of property originally invested'.[56] The third stage was the formation of higher-stage APCs in 1956 that comprised between 100 and 300 households, with agricultural land and other means of production becoming collectively owned.[57] Peasants received income 'according to man-hours of work after necessary deduction on account of depreciation of means of production, state reserve and public welfare fund'.[58]

In 1958, people's communes were formed to 'direct and manage the multiplicity of rural activities that sprang up under the aegis of the [Great] Leap Forward',[59] and they 'combined governmental functions of township government and economic functions of Agricultural Production Cooperatives into one entity'.[60] These organizations were informed by Mao's notion of peasant self-reliance, and so 'each commune was to be capable of producing its own basic necessities'.[61] And so apart from carrying out agricultural work, people's communes were also in charge of 'industrial work, trade, education, military affairs, health, village administration and social welfare'.[62] Mao regarded each commune as 'a self-sustaining economy, cultural centre, and a military unit held together and led forward by the CCP'.[63] People's communes were organized into three levels, which consisted of a central commune administration, the production brigade and the production team, and each 'commune contained an average of fifteen production brigades of around 220 households and 980 people'.[64] Thereafter, each 'brigade, in turn, was divided into an average of seven production teams'.[65] Those peasants who lost their private land to the communes were placed on production teams to cultivate the land according to targets that were passed down from the communes to the brigades.[66]

The farmers working these lands received income according to a 'half supply, half wage formula in which 50 per cent of peasant wages were paid in goods and services and 50 per cent in cash'.[67] However, their crops could only be sold to state procurement stations at prices set by the state, and these were kept low.[68] All this meant that for farmers their incomes were low and their consumption level was also low. Confronted with top-down demands for hard work coupled to low rewards for the work that they did, they lost incentives to work hard.

The results of the First Five Year Plan were in some respects a disappointment to the CCP elite as rural growth was slow, and there was debate amongst the elite, the upshot was an attempt to accelerate growth. The drive began in late 1957; peasant vitality would provide the power, and larger units of organization would provide the vehicle, and so the system of large communes was embraced. A good harvest was reported in 1958 and this encouraged optimism, but this was short lived as problems emerged and it became clear that success had been overstated. In the late 1950s, during the experiment of the GLF, the lack of incentives to cultivate land, together with bad weather and poor pricing and procurement policies resulted in a dramatic decrease in grain production and severe famine.[69] By mid-1959 large communes were being dismantled, whilst elite-level disputes continued; yet by late 1960 the idea was discredited. But in the countryside, in practical terms, the failure of the GLF led to severe problems, and between 1959 and 1962 there were several areas of famine, and on some estimates around twenty million are thought to have died.[70]

The tensions surrounding the policy of building socialism via peasant-oriented communes included the role of intellectuals and other professionals in New China. Technicians of all kinds were needed to build an industrial society; however, such groups had perforce to be educated. In the early years of the PRC such groups had responded variously – supporting or acquiescing; then, as problems emerged in wake of the first plan period, domestic and international, the core leadership of the party invited criticism. The period May–June 1957 saw the Hundred Flowers Campaign[71] open critical debate; however, leadership cadres within the party did not care for such criticism and obliged the leadership to backtrack. In June the Anti-Rightist Campaign began, and all public criticism was suppressed. One consequence was the falling away of technical expertise available to the state, and another was the opening of the way to ideologically informed experiments in development.

CCP elites continued to debate the issue of the development trajectory of the country, and as elite leaders made study tours, they discovered problems of corruption in the CCP organization, and a mass education campaign followed: the Socialist Education Campaign. The tension between agent-centred mobilization on the one hand and technocratic planning on the other continued, and the period 1962–65 saw the latter group recover the ground lost in the GLF; the voluntaristic policies favoured by Mao fell out of favour. But the debate was not finished and one element of the contending elite groups began a debate around the socialist spirit, or lack thereof, of a theatre play running in Beijing. All these debates were recycled once again in the guise of the Great Proletarian Cultural Revolution.

The Cultural Revolution was launched early in 1966.[72] Ostensibly a debate about the nature and direction of the CCP and China, the episode also embraced other strands: Mao's anxieties about his age and future, questions about lines of development for the country, along with senior-level faction fights.[73] Put directly, the Cultural Revolution was an attempt made by Mao to reassert his authority over the CCP and undo Liu Shaoqi's and Deng Xiaoping's post-GLF economic policies, which emphasized a market-oriented economy, material rewards and technocratic expertise rather than mass mobilization and ideological purity.[74] Mao thought that Liu and Deng were following the 'capitalist road' and worried that corruption and the economic privileges enjoyed by party cadres would lead to social inequality in a society. Such tensions were evident. Thus, within the wider society there were groups of frustrated students, alienated urban youth and lower-level industrial workers, in other words, a large pool of discontented citizens. In July 1966 Mao swam in the Yangtze River in an episode celebrated by his supporters. Mao in turn celebrated the model of the Paris Commune 1971 and called on the nation's youth to unleash their revolutionary spirits in order to purge revisionist elements and overthrow his enemies. Thereafter, the students and other radical supporters, now tagged Red Guards, were encouraged to widen their protests, and they were invited by Mao to smash the Four Olds, which referred to old ideas, old customs, old habits and old culture. They were also invited by Mao to oust Liu Shaoqi and Deng Xiaoping, who were criticized by Mao for moving towards revisionism and lacking revolutionary zeal. The protests had numerous targets and quickly became violent as the movement began to run out of control.

Red Guards ransacked houses and confiscated the property of targeted families belonging to 'the so-called Five Black Categories of landlords, rich peasants, counterrevolutionaries, "bad elements," and rightists'.[75] They physically attacked and humiliated party cadres, along with their teachers, school administrators, parents, relatives, friends and neighbours. They destroyed public property, temples and churches, historical and cultural relics, and burned books and paintings. Many people were imprisoned, beaten, tortured, or became mentally ill or committed suicide. Millions of intellectuals were struggled against and sent to the countryside to engage in hard rural labour.[76]

Eventually, the violence involved the hitherto carefully separate PLA, the core machinery of the state, at which point elite factions agreed the business had run out of control.[77] The PLA reasserted elite control, and the chaos was slowly brought under control; something like order was restored by mid-1968. But the episode had a final note when in September 1971 a key supporter of Mao, Minister of Defence Lin Biao, was reported killed whilst fleeing to the USSR in the wake of a failed coup. Spence comments that this episode did little to reassure grass-roots citizens that the CCP knew what it was doing.[78] The death of Mao and the subsequent 1976 fall of the Gang of Four brought the Cultural Revolution to an end; thereafter, pragmatists and technocrats came to the fore as the pursuit of development was placed at the centre of the concerns of the party-state.

But the Cultural Revolution had catastrophic and far-reaching impacts on Chinese society, education and economy. Numerous commentators have listed the negative impacts. The Cultural Revolution seriously damaged social harmony.[79] All schools and universities were closed down and students deprived of a decade of education.[80] The work of the 'institution of science was destroyed, scientists purged, and talent wasted'.[81] The talent of intellectuals was wasted on manual work in the countryside. And an outbreak of xenophobia during that period 'gave rise to an almost complete self-imposed national isolation … [and] foreign trade stagnated'.[82] 'The transportation network was seriously disrupted … [as] trains and railway stations were reserved for Red Guards.'[83] It led to the blockage of a million tons of intermediate goods, including coal, steel, cements and minerals.[84] Industrial production was paralyzed. It has been estimated that the death toll of these sequential upheavals was about three million people.[85] Macfarquhar and Schoenhals[86] comment that the deprivations of the Cultural Revolution were so evident and so far reaching that they provoked a strong reaction and it took the form of a decisive elite-turn towards the pragmatic policy stance of Deng Xiaoping.

International Stance and the Diplomatic Aspect

The newly established PRC had to build relationships with the wider international system. The key relationships included the USSR as an ally, supporter, supplier and latent opponent, the USA as an implacable enemy, and the countries of what now is tagged the Global South. The new Chinese state adopted a distinctive stance: China was active in the Non-Aligned Movement; the country was drawn into the US-sponsored cold war in East Asia; and yet the Chinese elite sought to keep a low profile. The foreign policy stance adopted by the elite was shaped by a complex interplay of political, economic and ideological forces, and during Mao's era there were various shifts and changes in Chinese foreign policy.

The broad framework of policy was given by the cold war conflict between the USA and its allies on the one hand and the group of state-socialist states on the other. The cold war can be read in a number of ways. The standard American or Western reading is that the cold war was occasioned by the behaviour of an expansionist Soviet Union in Europe after 1945 along with related events in East Asia which saw the violence-assisted establishment of a communist regime in China in 1949. The characterization of the policy of the USSR in terms of Soviet expansionism had deep roots in domestic American electoral red-baiting, and American anti-communism found expression in characterizations of the post-war settlement in Europe which were cast in terms of a betrayal at Yalta of Eastern bloc countries. In respect of China, sections of the American elite reacted very badly to the military victory of the PLA and the establishment of the PRC, and it was read in Washington in terms of an idea of 'the loss of China'. Thus there was available cold war hostility deployed in both Europe and East Asia. And such hostility was reciprocated as the Soviet Union under Stalin was never going to relinquish control of its newly acquired buffer zone in Eastern Europe and was quickly drawn into a diplomatic and military confrontation with erstwhile wartime allies. And in East Asia the newly victorious PLA saw the Americans more directly as an enemy, both militarily, as the USA had supplied the KMT with money and war materials and had placed an aggressive nationalist in power in South Korea and allowed him to run out of control, and historico-strategically, that is, as the core of a global imperialism hostile to people's communism. By 1950 the cold war was up and running; two blocs confronted each other: state-socialist regimes confronted liberal-democratic regimes. There was military/diplomatic competition, economic competition, cultural and ideological competition and various aid-donor competitions and proxy wars amongst countries in the Global South.

On 1 October 1949, the PRC was established under the leadership of Mao Zedong. Mao's immediate goal was to consolidate power, re-establish order and reconstruct the ruined and backward economy after years of war and poverty. Mao put forward the concept of the 'two camps, which divided the world into two irreconcilable camps: the communist East led by the Soviet Union and the capitalist West led by the United States'.[87] Since Mao was committed to moving China along the path of communism, he adopted a 'lean-to-one-side' foreign policy that aligned with the Soviet Union in order to combat the forces of imperialism and colonialism.[88] In February 1950, China signed a Treaty of Peace, Friendship, and Mutual Assistance with the Soviet Union. This treaty led to China obtaining substantial financial and technical assistance and military support from the Soviet Union. However, the close relationship between China and the Soviet Union did not last long. Their disputes over ideology, economic development, security and the border caused their relationship to deteriorate and finally drove these two states apart in the early 1960s.

However, Beijing's relations with Moscow were never smooth and unproblematic, and an ideological conflict between China and the Soviet Union occurred in 1956 when Stalin's successor, Nikita Khrushchev, launched a political campaign of de-Stalinization and pursued a foreign policy that favoured peaceful coexistence with the West. Khrushchev condemned Stalin for his brutalities, mass repression and irrational deportations. Mao was discontent with Khrushchev's de-Stalinization because it seriously undermined his legitimacy and the legitimacy of other communist regimes elsewhere. Besides, he argued that Khrushchev's embrace of peaceful coexistence with the West undermined the Sino-Soviet alliance[89] and 'active struggle was necessary for undeveloped countries'.[90] He thought 'Khrushchev had betrayed not only the Stalinist Road but also Marxism and Leninism.'[91]

The adoption of the Soviet model of economic development that put emphasis on industrialization and urban growth led to a structural imbalance between agriculture and industry. There was inadequate agricultural production to support further industrial expansion and feed the rapidly growing population.[92] This led to Mao launching a radical campaign of GLF that aimed to rapidly increase industrial output by mass mobilization.[93] Mao wanted to 'catch up with and surpass the Soviet Union and to demonstrate that China's economic development model was superior to that of the Soviet Union'.[94] But Mao was criticized by Khrushchev for deviating from the Soviet economic model.[95] Mao, in turn, criticized the Soviets, who branded the GLF as 'economically unsound and dangerously fanatical'.[96] However, the GLF ended in failure. In June 1960, 'Khrushchev withdrew all 1,390 Soviet advisers working in China, leaving a number of major industrial and infrastructural projects in limbo.'[97]

On the aspect of security, the dispute between China and the Soviet Union 'over how best to handle India, Taiwan and the United States, with Mao favouring a more uncompromising hard-line policy',[98] meant that these allies drifted apart. China publicly criticized Khrushchev as 'revisionist' when Khrushchev was inclined to have a peaceful coexistence with the USA. But the tensions in the Sino-Soviet relationship became more and more apparent after the Second Taiwan Strait Crisis (1958–59) and the Sino-Indian border issue of 1959. Mao unilaterally provoked the Taiwan Strait crisis, which threatened nuclear war with the USA,[99] and it resulted in the Soviet Union abrogating 'its nuclear aid agreement and recall[ing] its experts from China'.[100] In the armed conflicts on the Sino-Indian border of 1959, China was unhappy with the Soviet Union's position of neutrality and the Soviet call for resolving the conflicts by peaceful means.[101] China thought that the Soviet Union should have supported its action when this was a conflict between a socialist state and a bourgeois state. In 1960 the Sino-Soviet split became official.

In the early 1960s, China adopted a more confrontational approach to foreign policy. Mao became anti-American and anti-Soviet at the same time, and in 1962 he put forward the 'Three Worlds Theory', which 'aimed at opposing both U.S. imperialism and Soviet revisionism'.[102] According to Mao, the countries of the world were divided into three groups: the first world included the two superpowers of the USA and the Soviet Union; the second world included the developed countries of Canada, Europe and Japan; and the third world included all the developing countries of Asia, Africa and Latin America. The first world exploited the third world, whilst 'the second world, controlled by the first, [also] oppresses the third world'.[103] In order to end this exploitation and oppression, Mao advocated violent revolutions in the remaining foreign colonies in Africa and in the Middle East, whilst at the same time declaring China as a leader of the third world in its struggle for self-determination. His support for violent and continuous revolution led to six countries in the third world ending or suspending their diplomatic relations with China in the 1960s.[104]

In March 1969, China and the Soviet Union had military clashes on Zhenbao (Damanskii) Island, which was located near the Chinese bank of the Ussuri River. Both sides suffered casualties. Following armed conflicts on Zhenbao Island, the Soviet Union used nuclear threats to compel China to have border negotiations.[105] The Soviet threat to China's security drove China to readjust its security strategy. China labelled the Soviet Union as a social-imperialist country, which was the most dangerous enemy of the world proletarian revolution. The conflict drove China to seek rapprochement with the USA.[106]

Meanwhile, the USA, which wanted to 'improve relations with China to contain the spread of Soviet power',[107] signalled her readiness to communicate with China by relaxing trade and travel restrictions in China and halting reconnaissance fights over Chinese territory.[108] In 1971, the Sino-US relation was normalized when the American table tennis team received an invitation from the Chinese government to visit China. Known as ping pong diplomacy, the American table tennis team's visit to China broke years of isolation between China and the USA and paved the way for President Nixon's historic visit to China in February 1972. The first Shanghai Communiqué of 1972 laid a foundation for developing direct cooperative ties between China and the USA.

MAO IN NATIONAL PAST AND COLLECTIVE MEMORY

Mao died in 1976 and whilst his immediate successor, Hua Guofeng, celebrated his work, this did not last for long. Hua had the core quartet of the Cultural Revolution, the 'Gang of Four', arrested. This move signalled the latest phase of an elite faction fight, and this, in turn, was resolved in 1980–81, as Hua stood down from the leadership, in favour of Deng Xiaoping, at which point the leftists associated with Mao were displaced, and in the early 1980s a turn began towards an adoption of the available model of the East Asian developmental state.

The CCP has been the key organization involved in founding and thereafter establishing New China: the party eventually won its long drawn out war with the KMT; the party successfully established an effective state system (the first modern state in the history of China[109]); and the party successfully pursued development, including security within the global system of states, order within the domestic sphere built around an effective state and development, and the provision of better lives for the population in question, those whom the elite sought to organize. In the early period of the rule of the CCP – 1949–57 – the record was good; so after decades of destructive warfare the country was relatively stable and was able to pursue development after the style of the early Soviet Union. The GLF of the late 1950s was a setback, but the overall advance continued.[110]

All that said, there is a less happy counterpart to the story: (i) the inevitable[111] violence in securing domestic control; (ii) the violence used in resisting outside pressures along the country's periphery and relatedly in asserting earlier patterns of control over far-flung regions (Tibet, Xinjiang); (iii) the multiple errors in regard to the opinions of available experts, thus, again, paradigmatically, the elite's response to the Hundred Flowers Movement and the subsequent Anti-Rightist purge; (iv) the errors in over confident top-down development projects, paradigmatically, the GLF; and (v) the pursuit of destructive experiments cum faction fighting, hence the Cultural Revolution, where extensive disruption was caused for seemingly little gain. Thus, in all, with the death of Mao in 1976 and the subsequent removal of his key supporters, the stage was set for a review of the record of the revolution, both in the official national past and more slowly and diffusely in collective memory.

Mao has a settled place in the official national past. In June 1981 the CCP formally adopted a text[112] detailing the party's history and a number of points can be noted. First, that the positive record of the party was noted: the creation of a unified state, the removal of extant ruling groups and the expulsion of foreign influences, or in brief, the creation of New China and the subsequent near on 20 years of development, and in all this the central role of Mao. And second, the GLF was a failure. Then, third, the episode of the Cultural Revolution was a disaster and the responsibility was identified as that of Mao, a figure now characterized as having made more than a few errors, with the Cultural Revolution being the most grievous. Fourth, that his overall contribution to China was positive. And, finally, that the party's accumulated knowledge of Marxism–Leninism plus Mao Zedong Thought can guide the way for the country.

In regard to the record of the revolution:

The victorious Chinese revolution put an end to the rule of a handful of exploiters over the masses of the working people and to the enslavement of the multinational Chinese people by imperialists and colonialists ... Among the many outstanding leaders of the Party, Comrade Mao Zedong was the most prominent.[113]

In regard to the GLF, there was 'lack of experience' and 'inadequate understanding' plus:

> More important, it was due to the fact that Comrade Mao Zedong and many leading comrades, both at the centre and in the localities, had become smug about their successes, were impatient for quick results and overestimated the role of man's subjective will and efforts.[114]

In regard to the Cultural Revolution:

> The Cultural Revolution, which lasted from May 1966 to October 1976, was responsible for the most severe setback and the heaviest losses suffered by the Party, the state and the people since the founding of the People's Republic. It was initiated and led by Comrade Mao Zedong.[115]

In regard to the overall record:

> Comrade Mao Zedong was a great Marxist and a great proletarian revolutionary, strategist and theorist. It is true that he made gross mistakes during the Cultural Revolution, but if we judge his activities as a whole, his contribution to the Chinese revolution far outweigh his mistakes.[116]

In this way Mao is firmly located within the record of the party and his record evaluated. His place in the national past is clear: he is a key figure in the foundation myth of contemporary China, the victory of the CCP and the establishment of the PRC.

Against the clarity of the claims of the national past, Mao does not have a settled place in collective memory, where there are various strands of recollection. Mao died in 1976, now around 40 years ago, and as an active political and national figure he has faded into memory; the official national past records his key role in the founding of New China, and it adds that in later years his contributions were increasingly negative, with finally the chaos of the Cultural Revolution. As with all official discourses it offers a simplified but not inaccurate general summary, and it is available to be invoked in various ways and is open to a number of lines of critique; in both cases the past is being read into the present in order to guide action oriented towards the future.

The official past can be invoked as a model. There is a popular level appreciation of the work of Mao Zedong as the Deng Xiaoping reforms opened up both the chance for rapid economic growth and the equal chance for corruption. Commentators remark that the period of government led by Jiang Zemin fuelled the drive for growth and made corruption commonplace in the party, the state, the army and business. The drive for growth has created great inequality and those on the bottom of the heap are able to invoke Mao as representing an earlier, more honest period in Chinese life. At a popular level distress has found expression in 'rightful resistance' as the poor invoke the rules against the high-handed or corrupt officials of the party-state.[117] These sorts of sentiments were given voice politically by Bo Xilai, whose Chongqing model harked back to 'red culture', and more broadly by commentators tagged 'the New Left',[118] those looking to deal with inequalities via explicit state action (the comparator being the Guangdong model built around its free-market SEZs and the pursuit of outward-oriented trade).

The official past can be invoked and critiqued. China has a large number of official memorial sites; some refer to the Sino-Japanese War – they detail the depredations of the Japanese and the suffering of the local people; popular television documentaries have been made. There are also unofficial memorial sites, and whilst their focus may be quite similar, the attention to local history adds detail to official lines of remembering. In a similar way, oral histories can be taken, and these materials show a much more detailed picture of the war years and the role of the CCP and Mao. And similar strategies of critical reflection can be found in the work of contemporary artists: film directors returning to themes from the past and examining the past in the present, journals of commentary and books.

The official national past seems to be firmly fixed in place. Mao's portrait hangs on the wall of the Forbidden City in Beijing and is printed on banknotes, but the collective memory of Mao is perhaps more fluid. The memory can be invoked, and it can be subject to criticism. In this context, scholarly memory work has a dual function as it reads the past in order to better grasp the details of events and the manner of subsequent strategies of recollection; and in reading the past in this way it enriches contemporary social and political debate.[119]

CONCLUSION: THE SHIFT TO THE MODERN WORLD, COLLAPSE AND RECOVERY

Commentators, writing today, in the early part of the twenty-first century, can be inclined to overlook or misconstrue the violence of the first half of the twentieth century. Those who simply overlook the manifold conflicts permit themselves thereby to criticize the regime of Mao Zedong as an irrational, unfortunate and ideologically driven deviation from the obvious rational path of modernization; and those, on the other hand, who acknowledge the conflicts but prefer to turn their gaze to the subsequent years, permit themselves thereby to cast the history in terms of the heroism of the cadres of the CCP (and thereafter the Chinese people).

But both lines of commentary overlook the substance, that is, the years of sustained conflict, violence and loss suffered by the people of China.

With all its chaos, the first half of the twentieth century was the historical epoch within which the CCP was formed; it was the historical epoch within which Mao and his leadership colleagues were formed and perforce operated; it was the historical epoch within which grass-roots cadres were formed and operated; it was the nature of the period that shaped both the revolution and the drive for reconstruction and advance that followed. The episode can be recalled schematically in three phases: an initial exchange with the modern world, a dramatic collapse and thereafter a slow process of recovery and advance.

Over the long period of the nineteenth century, foreign-centred state-empires asserted their interests at the expense of the Qing, whose collapse slowly became inevitable. The traders who sought access to China in the early nineteenth century sought access to the domestic market; their key good was opium, sold to the population against the wishes of the government, and backed, wherever and whenever necessary, by the use of force – paradigmatically, the two Opium Wars. Recent commentary has identified both the economic role played by the opium trade[120] and the unscrupulous, sometimes racist, nature of the traders and their political backers.[121] Confronted with the demands of the modern world in this perverse guise, the Qing regime slowly gave ground and finally collapsed.

The collapse of the Qing Empire and its administrative apparatus was followed by an extended period of conflict. A simple list makes this clear: thus, first the 1911 Revolution, which did not long survive before being overtaken by political strife; then the 1916–28 period of warlords, during which the country dissolved into a multiplicity of local area units built around those with access to the means of violence; a first period of civil war, 1928–37, precipitated by the KMT and relentlessly pursued by them; the 1937–45 Sino-Japanese War, which saw large areas of the country fall under the nominal control of the Japanese; the 1941–45 Pacific War and the Second World War, during which period further damage was inflicted upon the people of China; and the second phase of civil war, 1945–49, when the question of which group was to lead an independent China was settled by means of arms.

In 1949 Mao declared the establishment of the People's Republic of China. It was the first modern state in China, and its creation was the first step in rebuilding the country; however, the country was in a parlous state, and so the task of the CCP was by any account daunting; it was also beset by further conflicts – both domestic, as former supporters of the KMT were tackled, and international, as the new regime moved to secure the borders of the state.

NOTES

1. On the domestic party politics of American anti-communism and red-baiting, see G. Kolko 1968 *The Politics of War*, New York, Vintage.
2. J.D. Spence 2013 *The Search for Modern China*, New York, Norton, p. 402.
3. For a military history of 1937–45 Japanese wars in China, see Mark Peattie, Edward Drea and Hans van de Ven eds. 2011 *The Battle for China: Essays on the Military History of the Sino-Japanese War of 1937–1945*, Stanford University Press.
4. Spence 2013 p. 403.
5. Spence 2013 p. 403.
6. On local collaboration, see T. Brook 2005 *Collaboration: Japanese Agents and Local Elites in Wartime China*, Harvard University Press; D.P. Barrett and L.N. Shyu eds. 2001 *Chinese Collaboration with Japan, 1932–1945: The Limits of Accommodation*, Stanford University Press.
7. Brook 2005 pp. 3–12.
8. The KMT repeatedly sought military and financial assistance from the USA, and it was an awkward relationship; the relationship of the CCP and the USSR was analogously awkward, so in neither case did the nominal ideological commitments of the participants translate neatly into coordinated agreed practice.
9. Clear from two biographies: P. Short 2004 *Mao: A Life*, London, John Murray; J. Fenby 2005 *Generalissimo: Chiang Kai Shek and the China He Lost*, London, The Free Press.
10. It is difficult to make estimates of the dead during the wars of the early part of the twentieth century; see P.W. Preston 2010 *National Pasts in Europe and East Asia*, London, Routledge; see chapter 2 for various estimates of the numbers of dead.
11. Spence 2013 p. 434.
12. For an English audience, recalled by J.G. Ballard 1988 *Empire of the Sun*, London, Grafton, plus his later final memoir J.G. Ballard 2008 *Miracles of Life: From Shanghai to Shepperton: An Autobiography*, London, Fourth Estate.
13. Spence 2013 p. 356 et seq.
14. Spence 2013 pp. 356–65.
15. Spence 2013 pp. 360–4; on the poverty, see also J. Spence and A. Chin 1996 *The Chinese Century: A Photographic History*, London, Harper.
16. Spence 2013 p. 333.
17. A history is available which reveals the poverty; see Spence and Chin 1996.
18. Spence 2013 p. 335.
19. Spence 2013 pp. 333–4.
20. Spence 2013 p. 440.
21. Spence 2013 pp. 295–300.
22. Spence 2013 p. 298.
23. Insight into the complex tale is given in Tony Saich 2004 *Governance and Politics of China*, London, Palgrave.
24. F. Christiansen and S. Rai 1996 *Chinese Politics and Society*, London, Routledge.
25. D. Shambaugh 2008 *China's Communist Party: Atrophy and Adaptation*, University of California Press.
26. Zheng, Yongnian 2010 *The Chinese Communist Party as Organizational Emperor: Culture, Reproduction and Transformation*, London, Routledge.
27. Spence 2013 pp. 465–8.
28. First of a sequence as politics developed: 1975 Constitution, 1978 Constitution and the 1982 Constitution, which reverts, mostly, to 1954 Constitution.
29. Spence 2013 p. 485.

30. Spence 2013 pp. 461 et seq.
31. A.G. Walder 2015 *China under Mao: A Revolution Derailed*, Harvard University Press, p. 40.
32. Walder 2015 pp. 40–1.
33. Walder 2015 p. 50.
34. Walder 2015 p. 53.
35. Walder 2015 p. 45.
36. Spence 2013 p. 463.
37. Walder 2015 p. 45.
38. Spence 2013 pp. 478–83.
39. On the history of Korea and the 1950–53 war, see Bruce Cummings 1997 *Korea's Place in the Sun*, New York, Norton; in brief, the USA insisted on dividing the country, with the USSR acquiescing, subsequently importing a US-based emigre right-wing nationalist to rule the south.
40. Chen, Jian 2001 *Mao's China and the Cold War*, University of North Carolina Press, p. 88.
41. E.F. Larus 2012 *Politics and Society in Contemporary China*, Boulder, CO, Lynne Rienner, p. 62.
42. James Gao 2004 *The Communist Takeover of Hangzhou: The Transformation of City and Cadre, 1949–1954*, University of Hawaii Press, p. 159.
43. Yang, Keming 2013 *Capitalists in Communist China*, New York, Palgrave, p. 36.
44. Tsai, Kellee S. 2007 *Capitalism without Democracy: The Private Sector in Contemporary China*, Cornell University Press, p. 47.
45. Larus 2012 p. 63.
46. Spence 2013 pp. 484–93.
47. Lin, Zhen and Zobisch, Michael A. eds. 2006 *Resource Use and Agricultural Sustainability: Risk and Consequences of Intensive Cropping in China*, Kassel University Press, p. 48.
48. Walder 2015 p. 83.
49. X. Zhang 2014 *Enterprise Management Control Systems in China*, Berlin, Springer, p. 4.
50. T.K. Liou 1998 *Managing Economic Reforms in Post-Mao China*, Westport, CT, Greenwood Publishing, p. 11.
51. Zhang 2014 p. 4.
52. Walder 2015 p. 86.
53. J.C.B. Leung 1998 'The Transformation of Social Welfare Policy: The Restructuring of the "Iron Rice Bowl"' in Joseph Y.S. Cheng ed. *China in the Post-Deng Era*, The Chinese University of Hong Kong Press, p. 618.
54. W. Kraus 1982 *Economic Development and Social Change in the People's Republic of China*, New York, Springer-Verlag, p. 76; T. Saich 2004 *Governance and Politics of China*, New York, Palgrave, p. 34.
55. Saich 2004 p. 34.
56. Saich 2004 p. 34.
57. K.L. Datta 2004 *Central Planning: A Case Study of China*, New Delhi, Concept Publishing, p. 34.
58. Datta 2004 pp. 34–5.
59. P.P. Jones and T.T. Poleman 1962 'Communes and the Agricultural Crisis in Communist China' in *Food Research Institute Studies* 1, pp. 6–7.
60. Yang, Zhong 2015 *Local Government and Politics in China: Challenges from Below*, New York, Routledge, p. 43.
61. Li, Xiaobing 2007 *A History of the Modern Chinese Army*, University Press of Kentucky, p. 195.
62. Saich 2004 p. 34.
63. Larus 2012 p. 84.
64. Walder 2015 p. 56.
65. Walder 2015 p. 56.

66. Larus 2012 p. 73.
67. Larus 2012 p. 73.
68. Walder 2015 p. 57.
69. Larus 2012 pp. 79–81.
70. Spence 2013 p. 523.
71. Spence 2013 pp. 505–12.
72. Spence 2013 pp. 541–51.
73. A detailed history of the Cultural Revolution is given by R. Macfarquhar and M. Schoenhals 2006 *Mao's Last Revolution*, Harvard University Press.
74. Larus 2012 pp. 84–5.
75. Larus 2012 pp. 91.
76. Jonathan Spence 2001 Introduction to the Cultural Revolution, Online. <http://spice.standford.edu> (accessed 9 November 2015).
77. Spence 2013 p. 551.
78. Spence 2013 p. 555.
79. Minority human rights were suppressed due to political, religious and cultural differences; see, for example, Arzo Beyazit 2014 'Human Rights Violations against Uyghur Turks in China' in *Human Rights Review* 4.8, p. 140.
80. More generally, Lu argues that through 'immersion in the rhetoric of the Cultural Revolution the Chinese masses were deprived of their critical-thinking abilities'. Lu, Xing 2004 *Rhetoric of the Chinese Cultural Revolution: The Impact on Chinese Thought, Culture, and Communication*, University of South Carolina Press, p. 199.
81. Cao, Cong 2013 'Science Imperilled: Intellectuals and the Cultural Revolution' in Chunjuan Nancy Wei and Darryl E. Brock eds. *Mr. Science and Chairman Mao's Cultural Revolution: Science and Technology in Modern China*, Lanham, MD, Lexington Books, p. 135.
82. Gregory Veeck, Clifton W. Pannell, Christopher J. Smith and Youqin Huang 2011 *China's Geography: Globalization and the Dynamic of Political, Economic, and Social Change*, Lanham, Rowman & Littlefield, p. 242.
83. R. Ash 2002 'The Cultural Revolution as an Economic Phenomenon' in Werner Draguhn and David S.G. Goodman eds. *China's Communist Revolutions: Fifty Years of the People's Republic of China*, London, Routledge Curzon, p. 131.
84. Ash 2002 p. 131.
85. H. Grice 2009 *Asian American Fiction, History and Life Writing: International Encounters*, London, Routledge, p. 12.
86. Macfarquhar and Schoenhals 2006, p. 3.
87. Larus 2012 p. 376.
88. Larus 2012 p. 376.
89. Lu, Zhouxiang and Hong, Fan 2014 *Sport and Nationalism in China*, New York, Routledge, p. 90.
90. Larus 2012 p. 377.
91. Lu and Hong 2014 p. 90.
92. Saich 2004 pp. 36–7.
93. Saich 2004.
94. Shen, Zhihua and Xia, Yafeng 2015 *Mao and the Sino-Soviet Partnership, 1945–1959: A New History*, Lanham, MD, Lexington Books, p. 285.
95. Mark, Chi-kwan 2012 *China and the World since 1945: An International History*, New York, Routledge, p. 47.
96. Larus 2012 p. 85.
97. Lo, Bobo 2008 *Axis of Convenience: Moscow, Beijing, and the New Geopolitics*, Washington, DC, Brookings Institution Press, p. 25.
98. M.B. Share 2007 *Where Empires Collided: Russian and Soviet Relations with Hong Kong, Taiwan, and Macau*, The Chinese University of Hong Kong Press, p. 11.
99. Li, Xiaobing ed. 2012 *China at War: An Encyclopedia*, Santa Barbara, CA, ABC-CLO, LLC, p. 261; Share 2007 p. 11.

100. Hu, Shaohua 2012 'Russia and cross-Taiwan Strait Relations' in George Wei ed. *China-Taiwan Relations in a Global Context: Taiwan's Foreign Policy and Relations*, New York, Routledge, p. 142.
101. M.Y. Prozumenschikov 1997 'The Sino-Indian Conflict, the Cuban Missile Crisis, and the Sino-Soviet Split, October 1962: New Evidence from the Russian Archives' in *Cold War International History Project Bulletin*, Issue 8–9, p. 251.
102. Zhu, Liqun 2014 'China's Cold War Experience and Its New Security Concept' in Vojtech Mastny and Zhu Liqun eds. *The Legacy of the Cold War: Perspectives on Security, Cooperation, and Conflict*, Lanham, Lexington Books, p. 337.
103. Larus 2012 p. 378.
104. Larus 2012 p. 378.
105. M.S. Gerson 2010 The Sino-Soviet Border Conflict: Deterrence, Escalation, and the Threat of Nuclear War in 1969, Online. <www.cna.org> (accessed 3 November 2015), p.iv.
106. Larus 2012 p. 378; T.W. Robinson 1994 'Chinese Foreign Policy from the 1940s to the 1990s' in Thomas W. Robinson and David Shambaugh eds. *Chinese Foreign Policy: Theory and Practice*, Oxford, Clarendon Press, p. 560; Chen, Jian 2003 'The Path toward Sino-American Rapprochement 1969–1972' in *GHI Bulletin Supplement* 1, p. 29 noted, 'a rapprochement with the imperialist United States, an enemy now less dangerous in comparison, became feasible and justifiable for Beijing's leaders'.
107. Khoo, Nicholas 2005 'Realism Redux: Investigating the Causes and Effects of Sino-US Rapprochement' in *Cold War History* 5.4, p. 529.
108. Larus 2012 p. 380.
109. Walder 2015 p. 2.
110. C.K. Lee and G. Yang eds. 2007 *Re-envisioning the Chinese Revolution*, Stanford University Press, revisit the period. Two pieces are of great interest; both pick up gender and record that women in the period experienced positive changes in their social status – see the pieces by Gail Hershatter and K.E. Manning.
111. The end of the Pacific War and the later end of the civil war did not mean any neat and tidy endings to conflicts; conflicts continued – both within the region (as local nationalists lodged claims to independence against reluctant colonial powers and as America began its anti-communist wars in the region) and within China (as their domestic wars ran down); the political generation that came to power through the region at this time had careers suffused with violence – the experience of war and rebellion and revolution; reading the violence as somehow voluntary on the part of leaderships or leaders is misleading.
112. Report to Central Committee June 1981 Resolution on Certain Questions in the History of Our Party since the Founding of the People's Republic of China, Online. <www.marxists.org/subject/china/documents/cpc/history/01.htm> (accessed December 2015).
113. Central Committee June 1981 pp. 5–6.
114. Central Committee June 1981 p. 17.
115. Central Committee June 1981 p. 19.
116. Central Committee June 1981 p. 35.
117. On this see K. O'Brien and L. Li 2006 *Rightful Resistance in Rural China*, Cambridge University Press.
118. W.A. Callahan 2013 *China Dreams: 20 Visions of the Future*, Oxford University Press, pp. 24–5.
119. One such arena has been investigated by Callahan 2013 – he identifies a number of dreams for the future of China amongst a growing civil society – a spread of intellectuals, commentators, artists and the like; ideas are drawn from many quarters, but in his exposition Mao is not a central resource.
120. C. Trocki 1999 *Opium, Empire and the Global Political Economy: A Study of the Asian Opium Trade 1750–1950*, London, Routledge.

121. See R. Bickers 2011 *The Scramble for China: Foreign Devils in the Qing Empire 1832–1914*, London, Allen Lane; J. Lovell 2011 *The Opium War: Drugs, Dreams and the Making of China*, London, Picador.

4.   New China II: the reforms of Deng Xiaoping

The final phase of Maoist-style state-socialism saw the fall of the 'Gang of Four' and the rapid ascent to power of Deng Xiaoping, who was a long-time elite player in the CCP[1] and was styled a pragmatist. Deng, along with allies, inaugurated, cautiously at first, a reform programme. It had a number of elements including agricultural reforms, urban reforms and diplomatic reforms that opened China to the wider global system. Crucially, economic policy was revised, the state-directed planned economy was reformed and aspects of a competitive market-oriented system were progressively introduced. SEZs were established in coastal sites, one was adjacent to Hong Kong, and these reforms enjoyed rapid success and gathered pace down the years. There were also expectations of political reforms. Deng's reforms opened the way for rapid development, producing a mix of sought for rapid economic and social change along with an associated spread of familiar problems. Most commentators report that these reforms set aspirations to socialism aside, lifted millions from poverty, made China an emergent great power and cost the country in terms of environmental pollution, widespread corruption and the persistence, after a number of domestic protests, of a restricted political sphere.

   In total these reforms can be read as the Beijing elite embracing a variant of the East Asian developmental state model of development: state-directed growth for national development,[2] and it is a model that became entrenched and has been followed by subsequent leaders.

DENG'S ERA AND THE OPENING OF CHINA: POLITICS AND ECONOMICS

Break with Maoism

The Cultural Revolution caused considerable confusion within China.[3] The most active period was between 1966 and 1968; however, the downstream consequences ran on for many years, and amongst them two might be noted: first, political confusions in respect of patterns of elite-level power and related matters of the direction of policy; and second, economic confusions, again in respect of policy, matters made more pressing by the evident comparative poor performance of the Chinese economy. Taiwan, in particular, was advancing more rapidly in this regard than the mainland and, more broadly, around this time capitalist East Asia was beginning its subsequent dramatic rise.[4]

Spence[5] argues that matters rather came to a head during the year 1976. In January of that year Zhou Enlai died and Deng Xiaoping read the eulogy; a little later, in April, crowds gathered in Tiananmen Square to celebrate his memory. There were also criticisms of Mao and leftist radicals; arrests were made and Deng Xiaoping was dismissed from his official posts.[6] A campaign against Deng followed; Hua Guofeng became Premier, and in July Zhu De, a long-time revolutionary, died and Hua read the eulogy. In July a devastating earthquake struck in Hebei Province, killing around 250,000, and then in September Mao Zedong died. A period of official mourning followed, along with a state funeral; Hua made the eulogy. Spence then remarks that the final dramatic event was the arrest, ordered by Hua, of the Gang of Four.[7]

During this period Deng relocated to Guangdong, where he was protected by local allies, and he was reappointed to his posts in July 1977; thereafter, the differing stances of Hua and Deng in respect of political and economic matters were played out. The key question was in respect of economic development. The general idea of the Four Modern-izations was accepted; thereafter, it was a matter of strategy: self-reliance and local-level initiatives versus a measured opening to the wider world coupled to importing technologies and ideas. Deng's ideas slowly came to the fore. A key meeting was the Third Plenum of the Eleventh Central Committee Meeting of the CCP,[8] and the key innovation was granting local level players the freedom to pursue their own initiatives as central direction was wound back. It was successful in agriculture,[9] where changes were introduced very rapidly, and there were related initiatives in regard to village-level industry and more difficult changes for state-owned enterprises (SOEs). A crucial innovation was borrowed from the experience of capitalist East Asia: export processing zones. These were organized in restricted geographical areas, where regulations and taxes were favourably configured – thus SEZs. In 1979 four were established adjacent to prosperous capitalist areas – Zhuhai, Shenzhen, Shantou and Xiamen – and whilst success was not immediate, Shenzhen did take-off, producing economic growth, along with many unanticipated social prob-lems, thus corruption, prostitution, black markets and street crime.[10] The pace of change worried some members of the elite, but the exchanges between Hua Guofeng and Deng Xiaoping were resolved in favour of Deng, and the reform programme strengthened. Deng was represented as a pragmatist, pursuing development in a practical fashion, embracing the old injunction to seek truth from facts, buttressed now by the judgement of practical results.[11]

Old Generations and New Generations of Leadership

As the power struggle between Hua and Deng was resolved, two new figures joined the elite, Hu Yaobang and Zhao Ziyang, and they drove the reforms forward. Matters of Maoism and the former regime were settled with two operations: the trial of the Gang of Four in 1980–81 and the 1981 Central Committee's decision that Mao had been 70 per cent correct and 30 per cent mistaken. After this, moving forwards, policy making became increasingly the province of technical experts of one sort or another, and radical-left ideologists were set aside as rapid material development, that is, economic growth, became the key goal.

Reforming and Redirecting Party and State

Spence[12] comments that around the early 1980s the elite levels of the party-state were superior to the law, and elite personnel changed as a result of political manoeuvring, not procedure. Spence reports that this elite comprised around 25 key players, and they were supported by a network of specialists and a quartet of institutions – State Planning Commission, State Economic Commission, State Science and Technology Commission and Ministry of Finance – and thereafter a spread of line ministries plus provincial governments, with their own systems of administration. The machinery of governance was cumbersome.[13] In the early 1980s such formal machineries of administration (whether efficient or not) began to slowly replace the earlier post-revolution system of communes, and systems of law were upgraded whilst day-to-day responsibilities were pushed downwards in agricultural reforms, later urban industrial reforms. The issue ran on through the 1980s, and further reforms were mooted in the last years of that decade.

Popular Responses: Rural Reforms, Urban Reforms and Political Reforms

The rural reforms were generally successful, so too urban reforms, but such changes produced winners and losers, and there were calls in the 1980s for political reform, led by students. These calls were somewhat disorganized but vigorous, taking place in major cities and opposed by party-state figures. Deng Xiaoping also joined the condemnations. In January 1987 Hu Yaobang was removed from office. Spence reports that commentators debate Deng's role: bending to the wind or, in fact, conservative with only a limited reform agenda. Spence remarks that the latter seems the more plausible; thus, economic reform was crucial, political reform was not and any challenge to the status of the CCP was resisted. In mid-1987 there were further elite personnel changes as formal leadership passed to Zhao Ziyang and Li Peng, yet as the reforms moved ahead social problems accumulated – 'inflation, low grain production, labour unrest, graft, unregulated population movements, rapid population growth and illiteracy'.[14] The tensions finally found expression in the Tiananmen Square occupation, triggered by the April 1989 death of Hu Yaobang and violently suppressed by the party-state on 4 June. Deng dismissed the episode as of little real account, and the drive for economic reform would continue[15] whilst political reform was on hold.

DENG XIAOPING AND THE PROGRAMMES OF REFORM

Once Deng had secured his position he moved to inaugurate a series of reforms, and these were undertaken quite cautiously at first, but early successes encouraged further reforms and slowly the process of remaking Maoist peasant-oriented centrally directed state-socialism gathered pace. The programme of reforms was not without its critics, and the practice was not without its problems.

Economic Policy

Deng Xiaoping's reforms were cautious and carefully targeted; whilst he thought that it was important to 'preserve the Party-State, a sound political power and the only possible agent of change',[16] he also thought that the function of the party-state should be modified to 'build the market economy, putting aside for the moment the construction of Communism'.[17] Deng wanted to transform China into a rich and strong nation by implementing the interlinked policies of opening-up and economic modernization, and, in all, the reforms made a great contribution to the economic development of China.

The establishment of SEZs in 1980 was an experiment to test the efficacy of a market economy. The SEZs were first established in Shenzhen, Zhuhai, Shantou and Xiamen and were designed to 'attract foreign investors who, in turn, would bring technology and modern management methods to China to produce exports for hard currency'.[18] They offered foreign investors more liberal regulations, more relaxed government measures and preferential treatment such as lower land costs, flexible wage and labour policies, lower tax rates, tax exemption and reduced tariffs.[19] In April 1984, the Open Door policy was extended to 14 coastal cities, where Economic and Technological Development Zones were established to attract foreign direct investment, import foreign technology, learn modern management skills and provide more job opportunities. Similar to the SEZs, these economic development zones also gave preferential treatment to foreign investors. In 1985, the Open Door policy was further extended to 'the Yangtze delta, the Pearl River estuary, a triangle south of Fujian next to Xiamen and the Jiaodong and Liaodong peninsula'.[20] In 1988, the status of SEZ was given to Hainan Province, which was the largest SEZ in China.

The reform programme was successful, and the first four SEZs 'multiplied their GDP by eight between 1985 and 1990, with annual growth of 50 per cent'.[21] The Pearl River Delta also experienced high-speed economic growth, with Gross Domestic Product (GDP) drastically increased from 30.4 billion renminbi in 1985 to 87.2 billion renminbi in 1990.[22] 'In 1992 total trade in the 14 open coastal cities was worth US$29.2 billion, up 24.3 percent from 1991.'[23]

As to the broad policy of economic modernization, Deng looked to reforms in agriculture, industry, science and technology, and national defence. He abandoned the iron rice bowl system and favoured the principle 'to each according to his work'. In rural areas, the household responsibility system was implemented successfully to increase food supply and crop diversification. Under the new system peasants were given the right to decision making about production, and after fulfilling the production quota set by the state, peasants could sell the surplus of farm products on the free market. In urban areas, reforms were implemented to increase the incentives and efficiency of SOEs through the contract management responsibility system. Under the system 'the relations between the state and enterprises [were] set out as a contract … in terms of duties and rights'.[24] Greater autonomy was given to managers to make decisions about 'production plans and marketing, sources of supply, distribution of profits within the enterprise and the hiring and firing of workers'.[25]

As SOEs became nominally financially independent, they were allowed to keep a portion of their profits, and these could be used for capital investment, technological innovation, the provision of collective welfare and bonuses to staff. And, in addition, non-state sectors were allowed to flourish. These included sole proprietorship, collective enterprises, joint ventures, wholly owned foreign enterprises and TVEs. Also, a two-tiered price system was implemented to 'distribute the scarce resource to designated users at an official, below-market price',[26] whilst at the same time 'a second market was allowed to trade the scarce resource at market prices'.[27] The economic reform initiated by Deng significantly increased foreign trade and GDP growth, but it also created problems of unemployment, inflation and corruption, with this last noted slowly becoming ever more severe such that commentators in later years came to see it as more or less endemic.

Social Policy

In the reform period social policy was developed to accommodate economic reform. However, the outcome of social policy was less successful because both the central and local governments prioritized economic development. Social policy reforms were further influenced by the incorporation of preferences for market-based solutions. The sweeping nature of social policy reforms plus the introduction of the market principle into provisions led to the trade-off between efficiency and equality as economic reform created new social problems, such as unemployment and rising medical costs. These problems could not be easily solved as the accelerated speed of economic reform only made them much worse. Without past experiences as reference, the central and local government could only explore and experiment with pilot schemes in order to gain experience and search for a possible solution.

Education

Three aspects of education provision are noted here: first, the role of education in economic development; second, the establishment of a bifurcated educational system; and third, the policy of decentralization.

So, first, during Deng's era, the role of education was closely linked with economic development.[28] In May 1977, Deng talked with leading comrades in the Central Committee of the Communist Party of China and pointed out that education was the basis for the development of science and technology and the key to modernization, and that both knowledge and talented people should be respected.[29] Deng and the central government believed that education should accommodate economic development and played an important role in reducing illiteracy, cultivating talents and realizing the Four Modernizations in China.[30] Education could provide a labour force for agricultural, industrial and commercial sectors and equip labourers with technical and practical skills; and

besides, it could cultivate the talents and professionals with the knowledge of management and modern science and technology that could
contribute to national prosperity.[31]

In May 1985, the Central Committee of the Communist Party of China
issued *Decision on the Reform of the Educational Structure* (hereafter the
1985 Decision), which called for the development of junior, senior and
tertiary vocational education. The 1985 Decision stated that the development of vocational education should be closely linked to economic and
social development. The aim of developing vocational education was to
train the junior-, secondary- and tertiary-level qualified technicians,
management staff and skilled workers needed in economic modernization. Junior vocational education was given to primary school graduates. Secondary vocational education was given to junior secondary
school graduates, whilst tertiary vocational education was given to high
school graduates. Emphasis was put on the development of secondary
vocational education and expanding its total enrolment;[32] and further,
graduates from vocational schools were to be appointed on merit.

The 1985 Decision also increased the autonomy of higher education
institutions in running schools, and so higher education institutions had
the incentives and abilities needed for adapting to economic and social
development. They had discretion to recruit students, allocate their
budget, formulate their own teaching plans and school curriculum,
choose their own textbooks and teaching materials and collaborate with
other institutions to do research or technological development.[33]

Then, second, during Deng's era, a bifurcated educational system was
established. This consisted of a small, hierarchically structured 'elite
sector to train the first-class scientists and engineers necessary to meet
the ambitious targets of the Four Modernizations program'[34] and an
open, diverse mass sector to provide basic knowledge to the majority.[35]
The bifurcated educational system reflected Deng's educational line of
trying to find 'the appropriate balance between popularization (*puji*) and
the raising of standards (*tigao*)'.[36]

In China, as elsewhere, education is regarded as a crucial aid in
fostering upward social mobility within a modern society. In China, the
so-called key-point system[37] provided entrance to the elite school sector.[38] The key-point system had been condemned for reproducing educational inequality during the Cultural Revolution and was abolished, but
it was restored during Deng's era to accommodate economic development: 'In the face of resource scarcity, the government gives priority to
the development of a small number of establishments.'[39] Key-point
primary and secondary schools and key-point universities 'are those that
receive the most funding, recruit the best students, and have the highest

quality teaching staffs'.[40] Key-point schools are 'chosen in each respective jurisdiction, based on their past educational accomplishment ... [and they] served as teaching and learning models for ordinary schools'.[41] Schools that achieved a higher promotion rate to university could possibly become key-point schools,[42] and students that gained entrance to universities guaranteed better career prospects in future. However, the key-point system divided the elite from the mass and created educational inequality as rich families or families with higher social status could either use money or personal connections to send their children to key schools.[43] Besides, non-key-point regular schools found it impossible to compete with key-point schools in producing qualified students for entrance to universities.[44] Meanwhile, the concentration of resources in key-point schools 'demoralized the majority of students attending ordinary schools, who [found] themselves generally ignored'.[45]

A system of mass education was also important to support economic modernization through raising the cultural level, knowledge and skills of the ordinary people. In December 1980, the Central Committee of the Communist Party of China and the State Council jointly issued *Decision on Several Issues in Universalizing Primary Education* (hereafter the 1980 Decision),[46] which called for local governments to gradually universalize primary education. It required the economically developed regions to universalize primary education before 1985 whilst the less-developed regions and regions with lower population density could universalize primary education before 1990.

The 1985 Decision called for the implementation of nine-year compulsory education. A child of compulsory school age should attend school regularly, and local governments were responsible for formulating compulsory education legislation that determined the steps, methods and years of implementing nine-year compulsory education.[47] Training and examination should be given to teachers to ensure their teaching quality and stability. In 1986, the government promulgated the Compulsory Education Law of the People's Republic of China. According to the Compulsory Education Law, all the children at the age of six should have the right to receive nine-year compulsory education free of charge, regardless of sex, ethnicity and race.[48] The operating expenses and capital construction of compulsory education was raised by the State Council and local governments. However, education was regarded as a consumption item during Deng's era, and the fee-charging principle was introduced into the educational system.[49] Students, after receiving nine-year compulsory education, had to pay tuition fees if they wanted to receive upper secondary education. Students from wealthier provinces, urban areas or well-off families had better opportunities to receive upper secondary education or tertiary education. Those who could not afford to pay tuition fees often dropped out of schools and got a job in society. Since Deng's era, the problem of unauthorized fee collection has become 'rampant in the whole education sector, especially in primary and secondary schools'.[50]

And, finally, third, the central government retreated from the finance of education and decentralized educational finance to local government.[51] This was because the central government wanted local governments to invest in non-industrial construction, such as education, housing and culture,[52] which could avoid competition with 'central government projects for scarce raw materials and support services, or strain energy and transport sectors'.[53] Hence, the central government asked local governments to play a greater role in providing, financing and regulating education, but the decentralization 'in turn caused diverse changes in the structure, curriculum and ideology in education'.[54]

Under the policy of financial decentralizations, non-governmental sources and the non-education sectors were mobilized to become the key funders of education.[55] For the provision of basic education, the government followed the principle of 'walking on two legs' in the financing of primary education.[56] Villages were asked to bear the major financial responsibility to build schools and buy school furniture whilst the state was only responsible for subsidizing part of these expenditures.[57] Donations from local industries and the community became villages' major source of finance to build schools.[58] When the schools came into operation, they had to generate incomes on their own through school-run factories, shops or other economic activities in order to pay non-recurrent expenditures such as teachers' bonuses, repairs and improvement of teaching facilities.[59] Whilst teachers from public schools received standard salaries and were paid by state appropriation, 'community' teachers received floating salaries that were linked with the local economy and were paid by the community with little government subsidies.[60] The policy of financial decentralization cultivated a sense of local control and, in turn, increased local incentives to develop education.[61] Education became localized and was developed according to community and market needs.[62] However, education disparity became prevalent amongst provinces and between urban and rural areas. There was the coexistence of a 6–3–3, 5–3–3 or 5–4–3 structure for primary, junior secondary and senior secondary education, and the diversification of curriculum design and textbooks.[63] Disparity between localities was also 'tremendous in terms of school buildings and facilities, teachers' qualification and remuneration, educational opportunities and teaching quality'.[64]

To compensate for the lack of government funding, collective enterprises, individuals and the community were encouraged to provide different kinds of vocational education on their own or collaborated with the Ministry of Education to provide vocational education.[65] Collective enterprises, individuals and the community were asked to recruit teachers and qualified technicians on their own in order to train needed manpower. Many vocational high schools were 'joint ventures between employers and local education or labour authorities'[66] that taught practical skills.

Housing

During Mao's era, urban housing in China was characterized by state ownership and the exclusive control of the state over the production, 'distribution, rental service, maintenance and management of housing units'.[67] Urban housing could be treated as public housing because it was allocated by work units of SOEs or local housing bureaus to urban employees who only needed to pay a nominal rent far below the production costs of the housing units.[68] Urban housing during that period was an occupational benefit and payment in kind to compensate for cheap labour costs.[69] During Deng's era, however, the market principle was introduced to the urban housing system following the economic reform. Urban housing in China was transformed from a non-productive public-welfare provision to a market commodity,[70] and since 1979 'housing ownership [in urban areas] has become increasingly denationalized, the sources of financing diversified and the pattern of allocation of housing benefits marketized'.[71] Meanwhile, housing in rural areas was a neglected area of reform.

In April 1980, Deng's *Talks on the Construction Industry and Housing Issues* contained three important instructions, which marked the beginning of urban housing reform.[72] First, Deng stated that the construction industry should be treated as an arena of production that could generate revenue and accumulate wealth for the nation. It should be developed and put in an important position in the government's long-term plan because it could provide lots of employment opportunities and facilitate the development of the building materials industry.[73] Second, there should be 'housing commodification' (*zhufang shangpinhua*) so that urban residents could buy houses and also sell their old or new houses, and the 'housing cost could be paid in one instalment or in several instalments over 10 or 15 years'.[74] Third, housing rents should be gradually increased to promote home purchase,[75] so the level of rent should be high enough to make home purchase desirable.[76] In June 1980, the Central Committee of the Chinese Communist Party and the State Council jointly issued *The Report Outline of National Construction Conference* (hereafter the 1980

Report Outline), which officially announced the implementation of the housing commodification policy. The 1980 Report Outline allowed individuals to build, purchase and own their housing.[77] In December 1983, the State Council issued *Ordinance on Managing Private Housing in Urban Areas*, which legally protected the rights of citizens over their private housing. The ordinance included the details of registration of home ownership, buying and selling private housing, and leasing private housing.[78]

In 1981, experiments were carried out in more than 60 cities and counties to promote the sale of public housing at construction costs.[79] However, citizens were not enthusiastic about this home purchase scheme due to their low wages and limited purchasing capacity, and so in 1982 based on this experience the government implemented a subsidized home purchase scheme for both existing and newly built housing units in four pilot cities, which included Zhengzhou, Changzhou, Siping and Shashi.[80] Under this scheme, individuals had to pay one third of the sale price whilst the other two thirds was respectively subsidized by the government and the buyer's work units. Later, in 1985, the scheme was extended to 160 cities and 300 towns and counties;[81] nevertheless, the subsidized home purchase scheme was halted in 1986 due to the heavy financial burden imposed on the government.[82]

In February 1986, 'the Housing System Reform Leading Group of the State Council was founded to lead and coordinate the reform of the national housing system'.[83] In July 1987, the Housing System Reform Leading Group of the State Council issued *The Bulletin of Forum on the Pilot Reform on Urban Housing System*, which stated that housing-system reform was an integral part of the economic reform and that it was important to achieve housing commodification through rent increases, wage increases and the use of housing vouchers.[84] In January 1988, the First National Working Conference on Housing System Reform was launched in Beijing, which identified the ideas for housing reform.[85] Jun-sheng Chen, who was the Secretary-General of the State Council, said in the Working Conference that starting from 1988, housing-system reform would officially become the reform plan of both the central and local governments and would be implemented nationwide in stages.[86] He said that the ideas of housing reform would be achieved with housing commodification through rent increases, wage increases and encouraging employees to buy houses.[87]

In February 1988, the State Council issued *The Implementation Plan for a Gradual Housing System Reform in Cities and Towns* (hereafter the 1988 Implementation Plan), which clearly stated the goals and missions of urban housing reform.[88] The 1988 Implementation Plan stated that

housing-system reform should be implemented nationwide within three
to five years. The focus of the 1988 Implementation Plan was on the
creation and development of a housing market through implementing five
measures.[89] First, housing rent should be increased and the standard rent
should be calculated by taking the depreciation rate, maintenance fee,
management fee, investment interests and property tax into account.
Second, housing vouchers, which provided 'an artificial income cushion
to the rent increase',[90] should be given to employees for the purposes of
paying rents, purchasing or building houses. Third, housing funds should
be established, with funding coming from the local government, enterprises and individuals. Housing funds should be used for building houses,
purchasing houses and maintenance only. Fourth, enterprises were asked
to sell their newly built housing units first to their employees whilst
renting should be the second option. Newly built housing units should be
sold at full prices. Enterprises were also asked to sell the current housing
units to the current tenants first. Fifth, the section of real estate credit
should be established in banks in order to handle capital raising,
financing and credit settlement for real estate development. Unfortunately, the housing reform in 1988 ended in failure due to rising inflation
caused by an overheating economy and the political crackdown associated with the Tiananmen incident in 1989.[91]

In June 1991, the State Council issued *Notification of the Continuation
of Urban Housing System Reform in an Active and Stable Manner*, which
stressed the importance of realizing housing commodification and developing the property market. To achieve these two goals, the rent of public
housing should be increased gradually, public housing should be sold at
market prices, housing units should be built through different sources of
finance and the mortgage system should be introduced to encourage
employees to build or purchase houses.[92] After launching the Second
National Conference on Housing Reform in October 1991, the Housing
System Reform Leading Group of the State Council issued *Opinions on
Implementing Urban Housing System Reform on Full Scale* (hereafter the
1991 Opinions) in November 1991, which reconfirmed rent increase,
selling old and new public housing units and the establishment of
housing funds as the direction of housing reform. The 1991 Opinions set
up a five-year goal and ten-year goal for rent increase and stated that the
institutional and legal framework should be strengthened in order to
provide a healthy environment for the development of the property
market.[93] However, urban housing reform was less successful during
Deng's era due to the limited development of the property market.[94] This
was because there were still many tenants living in public housing, urban

employees mainly bought housing from their work units and the selling prices of housing units were still too low.[95]

Health care

During Mao's era, 'health services followed socialist values by treating medical care as a public good as well as a basic human need'.[96] In order to make health care accessible to the general public, a three-tiered medical institution network was established. The first-tiered medical institutions were street-level health stations that provided primary and preventive care for patients. The second-tiered medical institutions were district hospitals that provided both inpatient and outpatient services for patients. The third-tiered medical institutions were municipal hospitals that provided complex treatments and specialist care for patients.[97] Hospitals were nationalized. Medical fees at public hospitals 'were set at a level far below the recurrent costs'.[98] At that time, the Chinese government provided urban employees with free medical service through the Labour Insurance Scheme (LIS) and Government Insurance Scheme (GIS). Both the LIS and GIS were not 'actually an insurance scheme in the real sense because [they] involved no premium contributions and no insurance institutions to manage the schemes'.[99] The LIS was implemented in 1951 to provide employees in SOEs with free outpatient and inpatient services whilst covering 50 per cent of the medical costs of their direct dependents. The GIS was implemented in 1952 to provide 'free health care for government employees and retirees, army veterans, university and college students, staff [and retirees] in the cultural, education, health and science sectors'.[100] The LIS was financed by the work units whilst the GIS were financed by the state budget.[101] In rural areas, a Cooperative Medical System (CMS) was implemented in the mid-1950s to provide free basic medical services for peasants. It was funded by three channels, including household contribution, contribution from production brigades and subsidies from higher levels of government.[102] Those who were not covered by the LIS, GIS or the CMS needed to pay low out-of-pocket fees when seeking medical treatment.

During Deng's era, health care was subordinated to economic development, and the economic reforms implemented since the late 1970s have adversely affected both health care delivery and the financing system. Under the economic reform, the financial decentralization policy was implemented. Health spending decisions were put in the hands of local government.[103] Local government 'decided to make cost recovery the foundation of its health care financing system and reduced subsidies to hospitals'.[104] Meanwhile, it implemented a financial responsibility system in hospitals. Hospitals were granted financial autonomy, but they were responsible for their own profits and losses.[105] For this reason, hospitals became 'revenue-maximising organizations'.[106] They were 'driven by profit rather than the health service needs of the local population'.[107] Doctors also became profit-driven in order to get more staff bonuses.[108] The problem of supplier-induced-demand (SID) became prevalent amongst hospitals.[109] In order to generate more revenues for hospitals, doctors usually prescribed unnecessary or expensive drugs, conducted unnecessary medical tests or performed unnecessary surgeries. These unnecessary practices not only jeopardized patients' health, but also imposed a heavy financial burden on the work units and the government in urban areas. For the work units, the rising health care expenditures led to a big drain on profits and reduced their competitiveness.[110] Employees became 'underinsured' or 'uninsured' due to the financial incapacity of their work units to pay for their medical expenses.[111] From 1985 to 1987, the state faced about a 25 per cent increase in the average annual growth rate of health care expenditure.[112] A continued drain on the state budget also made it very difficult for the government to sustain the GIS.[113] In rural areas, communes were disbanded due to the implementation of the household responsibility system, which granted individual households autonomy over land use and agricultural production. The 'foundation of the rural CMS, which was based on collective production units and collective resources, nearly disappeared'.[114] This led to the collapse of the CMS.

Since the mid-1980s, implementing health care financing reform has become an urgent task, with cost containment as the primary objective. But prior to 1992, health care financing reform in China only belonged to an exploration phase. In April 1984, the Ministry of Health and the Ministry of Finance jointly issued *Notification of Further Strengthening the Management of the Government Insurance Scheme*, which encouraged local governments to carry out experiments on the GIS that could give reasonable medical treatment to patients without wasting medical resources.[115] In November 1985, the local government of Shijiazhuang in Hebei Province carried out trials in the social pooling of medical fees for retirees.[116] In March 1988, the Research Group on Health System Reform was established with the permission of the State Council to provide guidance for reforming the LIS and GIS.[117] In 1989, the Research Group produced a draft titled 'A Plan to Reform the Medical Insurance System for Employees', which suggested the introduction of cost-sharing into the health insurance scheme to increase the cost consciousness of patients. It suggested that the medical fees of the LIS should be jointly shared by enterprises and employees whilst that of the GIS should be jointly shared by the government and individuals.[118] In the same year, Dandong, Siping, Huangshi and Zhuzhou were chosen as pilot cities to implement medical insurance reform.[119] In November 1991, the Hainan government issued *Temporary Regulations on Medical Insurance for Employees*, which stated that both employers and employees starting from January 1992 should respectively contribute 10 per cent and 1 per cent to a medical insurance scheme that would cover employees' inpatient and outpatient expenses in public hospitals.[120] In 1992, more than 80 per cent of enterprises in China implemented trial schemes on health insurance for employees, with an aim to increase employees' cost consciousness whilst having access to basic medical services.[121] However, health insurance reform at this stage failed to solve the problems of limited medical coverage, rising medical expenditures and 'other fundamental weaknesses that existed in financing, payment and management within the GIS and LIS'.[122] Health care insurance reform only focused on urban areas, whilst rural residents 'had to rely on personal savings and assistance from informal networks to pay for medical costs'.[123]

Social security
Two aspects are noted here: urban workers and rural workers.

So, first, in respect of urban workers, during Mao's era, unemployment was not expected to happen in a socialist system, but when it came to Deng's era, unemployment became a common phenomenon due to the opening of China and the implementation of economic reform. The transformation of a socialist economy into a market economy created a competitive atmosphere amongst enterprises. Enterprises that lost competitiveness and productivity were on the verge of bankruptcy or became bankrupt. Many workers were laid off and became unemployed due to enterprise downsizing or the closing down of enterprises. They usually came from the SOEs. For this reason, there was a need to implement an unemployment insurance scheme to provide the necessary financial assistance for the unemployed. The compulsory unemployment insurance scheme was first implemented in October 1986 when the State Council issued *The Interim Regulations on Unemployment Insurance for Employees of State-owned Enterprises* (hereafter the 1986 Interim Regulations).[124] The implementation of the unemployment insurance scheme could serve two purposes. First, it could provide financial aid to support the basic needs of the unemployed. Second, it could be used by the unemployed to receive training so that the unemployed could re-join the work force. According to the 1986 Interim Regulations, the unemployment insurance scheme was funded by enterprises that contributed 1 per cent of their total wage bill, interests from the bank where the unemployment insurance fund was deposited and subsidies from the local public finance. The unemployed were entitled to receive a maximum of 24-month unemployment insurance payments. The unemployment insurance scheme covered the medical expenses, funeral expenses and bereavement payments of their direct dependents. It could also be used for paying vocational training expenses, supporting the self-production of the unemployed and exploring other job opportunities. However, the role of the unemployment insurance scheme was limited because it only covered the unemployed from SOEs.

During Deng's era, the establishment of an old-age insurance system was regarded as an important measure to protect workers' social security needs after retirement, reduce the financial burden of the state and enterprises, facilitate economic reform and maintain social stability.[125] In June 1991, the State Council issued *Decision on Reforming the Old-Age Insurance System for Enterprise Workers*, which stated that a three-tiered old-age insurance system consisting of the basic old-age insurance fund, the enterprise supplementary old-age insurance fund and individual old-age insurance fund should be gradually established following the economic development. The funding responsibility should be jointly shared by the state, the enterprise and individual workers. The contribution made by the workers should not exceed 3 per cent of their wages, whilst enterprises were required to make tax-free contributions on the basis of their total wage bill. The old-age insurance system should be set up at the provincial level so that the old-age insurance funds of permanent and contract workers could be united to achieve better pooling. The enterprise could set up a supplementary old-age insurance fund by using funding from bonuses and welfare funds, whilst individual workers could voluntarily participate in an individual old-age insurance fund. The Ministry of Labour and its bureaus at the district level would be responsible for managing the overall operation of old-age insurance funds in urban areas. At the same time, Old-Age Insurance Fund Committees should be set up by local governments to guide and monitor the management of the insurance fund. Whilst SOEs had to compulsory join the old-age insurance scheme, collective-owned enterprises, foreign enterprises and private enterprises were encouraged to join the scheme.

And second, in respect of rural workers, in rural areas the necessity and feasibility of establishing a social security system was discussed amongst experts and government officials from municipalities, provinces and autonomous regions during the Forum on Basic Social Security Work in Rural China in October 1986.[126] The problem of population ageing and the implementation of one-child policy were two main reasons for establishing a rural social security system.[127] In March 1987, the Ministry of Civil Affairs (MCA) published *The Report on Exploring the*

Establishment of a Basic Social Security System in Rural China, which highlighted three important principles for establishing the rural social security system. First, the social security system should be community based and voluntary in nature before extending it to counties and provinces. Second, there was no single model of social security system. Variations should be allowed amongst economically developed and underdeveloped regions as long as they followed the direction of the national policy. Third, the contribution of social security should start at a low level without going beyond the financial capacity of individual participants, local communities and the state. The benefit levels should also start at a low level, with the purpose of securing the basic living standard. The MCA was given the mandate to explore and experiment with schemes for old-age social security in rural areas.[128] Under the guidance of the MCA, 'more than 8,000 villages, 800 townships, and 190 counties in 19 provinces had participated in some sort of pilot scheme by mid-1989'.[129] There were more than 900,000 participants, with an accumulated fund of 41 million renminbi.[130]

In January 1991, the MCA issued *Trial Implementation Plan on Rural Social Insurance Pension at the County Level*. It aimed at implementing a voluntary social insurance pension scheme that covered all rural residents aged between 20 and 60. Contribution was primarily made by individual participants, with subsidies from enterprises and local communities.[131] Tax exemption would be given to enterprises that made contributions to the social insurance pension scheme. Individual participants could receive a pension from their accumulated account at the age of 60. In February 1991, a temporary Office for Rural Social Insurance Pension was established by the MCA to carry out local experiments at the county level.[132] However, the role of this social insurance pension scheme was limited due to a low participation rate and the problem of fund embezzlement in some rural areas.[133]

Foreign Policy

Deng adopted a peaceful and pragmatic foreign policy that could be conducive to rapid economic growth and modernization.[134] The objective was to avoid war and the creation of enemies in favour of the pursuit of domestic development. Deng thought that 'the markets, capital, technology and management techniques of the advanced countries and their raw materials had to be targeted'.[135] Deng realized that normalizing Sino-US relations 'was necessary to access Western sources of finance, credit, and developmental assistance'[136] and useful to reduce the Soviet Union's military threat to China, and Sino-US relations were normalized after the Joint Communique of the United States of America and the People's Republic of China was released on 1 January 1979.

Sino-Soviet relations had been very tense and poor since 1960 due to continued disputes over ideology and the border. In the early 1980s, China's deteriorating relations with the USA led to China and the Soviet Union beginning a round of talks to resolve border issues. However, the results were not fruitful due to the so-called three obstacles, which referred to the Soviet Union's unwillingness to give up its military build-up in Afghanistan, Vietnam and the Soviet border regions.[137] Sino-Soviet relations started to improve politically and economically when the new political leader, Mikhail Gorbachev, in July 1986 expressed his willingness to resolve the border issues in his speech at Vladivostok.[138] In late 1986, a major economic agreement was signed between China and the Soviet Union, which 'called for increasing the then U.S.$2 billion trade between China and the Soviet Union to U.S.$10 billion by 1990'.[139] Sino-Soviet relations moved towards full normalization when Gorbachev paid his first visit to China in 1989 and agreed with Deng that Sino-Soviet relations should be developed based on the principle of peaceful coexistence.

After the Tiananmen incident in 1989, China was economically sanctioned by the USA. Shortly thereafter the collapse of communist regimes in Eastern Europe and the Soviet Union in the period 1989–91 changed the world's geopolitical balance. These events also changed the direction of Chinese foreign policy and Deng adopted a cautious and low-profile approach to foreign policy. He issued a 24-Character Strategy, which stated that China should 'observe calmly, secure its position, cope with affairs calmly, conceal its capabilities, maintain a low profile and never claim leadership'.[140]

Tiananmen; Elite Response; Reanimating the Discourse of Humiliation

This issue is pursued by W.A. Callahan,[141] who argues that the elite were shocked by the events of Tiananmen, the demonstrations plus costs of suppression, and one aspect of the response was a renewed stress on patriotic education. The discourse of humiliation was reanimated. It offered a particular take on the history of the country and involved a mix of active remembering and active forgetting, creating a top-down heavy[142] 'national past'. The story, to simplify, presents the history of the country during the modern period as one of routine humiliation by foreigners and weak citizens leading to the quasi-colonization of the country with the implication (lesson) being that rallying to the support of the current regime in order to protect and build the country is an appropriate and pragmatic expression of patriotism.

Patriotic education is promulgated by the Central Propaganda Department and feeds into schools (via textbooks, especially history) and into mass media (via films, television and other media). A national past is constructed that centres on the idea of 'national humiliation': the national past is presented as a linear history (essentially nationalist, past leads directly to present) and is a history of successive humiliations at the hands of foreigners and weak locals, and over time these ideas merge with common sense ideas of history and are thus more effective.[143] The national past is presented to the population via the usual official mix of flags, parades, anthems and memory sites, but these ideas are not new. The idea of national humiliation has its origins in popular reactions to Japan's 1915 '21 demands'. It was an unofficial celebration from 1915 to 1926, then official from 1927 to 1940, until it lapsed during the years of warfare. Patriotic education was re-emphasized by Deng Xiaoping after 1989 and national humiliation day reappeared as National Defence Education Day in 2001.[144] The rhetoric of national humiliation is distinctive, not merely a history of conflicts but an invitation to the audience to become emotionally committed to a particular characterization of China, the Chinese and their history. The national past offers a structure of feeling,[145] it shapes understandings and emotional responses, and in the sphere of international relations it colours state and popular readings of relations with Japan, Taiwan, the USA and others. It is also an ambiguous construction, and Callahan is not clear that it is entirely under the control of Beijing; thus, emotional nationalism is a blowback from patriotic education.[146]

China as a Developmental State

The record of the reform programme inaugurated by Deng Xiaoping can be placed within a number of comparative frameworks,[147] and here two seem to be of particular note. First, as spelled out implicitly in the above discussion, domestically – that is, to note the differences between Deng's political and policy stance and that of his immediate predecessors, the radical Maoist left, those who had come to prominence during the ill-fated Cultural Revolution; and cast in these terms, Deng's policy initiatives constituted radical departures from what had gone before, that is, the new policies implied (and in the event, embraced) dramatic new initiatives and consequently sweeping economic and social changes.

However, a second comparative framework presents itself, and once again it is implicit in the spread of initiatives embraced and the overall goal implied by the set of new policies, and this comparative frame is regional. The records of the countries of East Asia were available to Deng and his colleagues, and it was clear that whereas China had spent a decade embroiled in the activities of the Cultural Revolution, their East Asian neighbours had spent the time forging ahead economically, socially and (perhaps to a lesser extent) politically, with the sum total of their successes being recognized by scholars and, more publicly, by the World Bank[148] in terms of the notion of the developmental state.

The core nature of the developmental state can be put in terms of a contrast between the claims of liberal market theorists and those affirming the notion of the developmental state. As an abstract theoretical debate it can be rooted in the late nineteenth century when German economists, in particular, Friedrich List, pointed out that late developers faced particular problems in joining in and catching up with existing established industrial economies, in particular when, as was the case, the dominant power formally affirmed the central role of the liberal marketplace and, by virtue of its position, dominated global trade. It was clear that an open liberal trading system was fine if your economy was well placed; otherwise the system presented great difficulties for new aspirant members of the club of the highly developed. The political and policy response was to eschew the goal of participation within a liberal market system in favour of the goal of national development; the shift was significant – the state now assumed the central role of building the local economy in such a fashion as to serve directly the interests of the local population.

In the nineteenth and early twentieth century the strategy was successfully followed in two notable cases, Germany and Japan, and in both cases their rapid rise led to clashes with established powers. More recently, in the post-Second World War era, the strategies of the developmental state have been put to use in East Asia; once again, Japan, now an American ally, has been at the forefront and has been followed by South Korea, Taiwan, Hong Kong and Singapore. All have pursued variant forms of the state-sponsored pursuit of national development. There is now a wealth of literature on this intellectual debate and the records of the examples indicated,[149] and these issues can be developed further in later chapters. For the moment it can be noted that it is here that Deng found a model or a recipe, which China could adapt to its own circumstances in order to drive the reform programme. It was in these ideas and these practical records that the Beijing elite found a model, but their practice was a variant form; thus, simply, China has a population of 1.3 billion, Singapore, say, around 4 million.

In his 1992 Southern Tour, Deng reaffirmed the drive for economic advance. The 1990s saw rapid economic growth, along with all the usual problems of such growth. Hong Kong and Taiwan were noted as economic successes,[150] later, Singapore was cited; collectively, the East Asian little dragons, as noted, were picked up in scholarship as embracing the developmental state.

CONCLUSION: THE SWEEPING REFORMS INAUGURATED BY DENG

Deng Xiaoping died in February 1997, almost the last figure in the generation that had worked with Mao to make the revolution, and his period in power had produced dramatic changes. Reviewing Chinese politics in general, Callahan comments that foreign commentary often tends to two extremes, where critics speak of a communist dictatorship, seeing China as a threat, whilst sympathizers see a reforming socialist example; but, realistically, it is neither: it is a right-wing authoritarian party-state that is legitimated in the eyes of its population by the material results of a harsh form of capitalism and a patriarchal nationalism.[151] Or, less critically, thanks to Deng's initiatives, China has contrived a variant of the East Asian developmental state, and the question for the present day is the nature of the legacies of recent history – modernity, civil war, Maoism and so on – that carry forwards into contemporary China, as the model is likely to continue for the foreseeable future.[152]

NOTES

1. M. Dillon 2015 *Deng Xiaoping: The Man Who Made Modern China*, London, I.B. Tauris.
2. Crudely put, in contrast, liberal theorists look to development as joining in the self-regulating market system in the expectation that the market will provide, and so liberal critics speak of authoritarian capitalism; in contrast, social democratic theorists look to development as engaging with the actual US-dominated global system in the expectation of broad national development; so China looks like an interesting model – part success (economic growth), part problem (pollution, corruption plus restricted public sphere).
3. R. Macfarquhar and M. Scheonhals 2006 *Mao's Last Revolution*, Harvard University Press, present a detailed narrative political history of this episode, casting it as Mao's attempt to combat what he took to be revisionism at home and in the USSR; other commentators see multiple motives amongst the players, with Mao's ambitions and anxieties at the core; see J.D. Spence 2013 *The Search For Modern China*, New York, Norton pp. 542–3.
4. Later celebrated and subtly mis-described in The World Bank 1993 *The East Asian Miracle: Economic Growth and Public Policy*, Oxford University Press.
5. Spence 2013 pp. 580–6.

6. Spence 2013 p. 582.
7. Spence 2013 p. 585.
8. Spence 2013 p. 590.
9. Spence 2013 p. 591.
10. Spence 2013 p. 605.
11. Spence 2013 pp. 608–9.
12. Spence 2013 pp. 623–9.
13. Spence 2013 gives three examples – coal mining, dams and oil – pp. 627–9.
14. Spence 2013 p. 655.
15. Spence 2013 pp. 663–4.
16. E. Bregolat 2015 *The Second Chinese Revolution*, New York, Palgrave, p. 9.
17. Bregolat 2015 p. 10.
18. M.E. Marti 2002 *China and the Legacy of Deng Xiaoping: From Communist Revolution to Capitalist Evolution*, Washington, DC, Brassey's, p. 8.
19. K.B. Bucknall 1989 *China and the Open Door Policy*, Sydney, Allen & Unwin.
20. Bregolat 2015 p. 45.
21. Bregolat 2015 p. 45.
22. Chen, Guanghan and Li, Sa 2006 'Evolving Trends in the Development of Manufacturing Industry in the Pearl River Delta' in Anthony Gar-on Yeh, Victor Fung-shuen Sit, Guanghan Chen and Yunyuan Zhou eds. *Developing a Competitive Pearl River Delta in South China under One Country-Two Systems*, Hong Kong University Press, p. 29.
23. C. Genzberger 1995 *China Business: The Portable Encyclopedia for Doing Business with China*, San Rafael, CA, World Trade Press, p. 18.
24. B. Taylor, K. Chang and Q. Li 2003 *Industrial Relations in China*, Cheltenham, UK and Northampton, MA, Edward Elgar, p. 54.
25. T. Saich 2004 2nd ed. *Governance and Politics of China*, New York, Palgrave, p. 62.
26. G.C. Chow 2015 *China's Economic Transformation*, Chichester, UK, Wiley-Blackwell, p. 45.
27. Chow 2015 p. 45.
28. S. Rosen 1985 'Recentralization, Decentralization, and Rationalization: Deng Xiaoping's Bifurcated Educational Policy' in *Modern China* 11.3, p. 308.
29. Deng, Xiaoping 1977 'Respect Knowledge, Respect Trained Personnel', from *The Selected Works of Deng Xiaoping*, Volume II (1975–1982), Online. <www.dengxiaoping-works.wordpress.com> (accessed 12 September 2015).
30. The Central Committee of the Communist Party of China and the State Council 1980 Decision on Several Issues in Universalizing Primary Education (Chinese version), Online. <http://www.chinalawedu.com/falvfagui/fg22598/368.shtml> (accessed 6 September 2015).
31. The Central Committee of the Communist Party of China 1985 Decision on the Reform of the Educational Structure (Chinese version), Online. <http://learning.sohu.com/20150528/n414011980.shtml> (accessed 6 September 2015).
32. The Central Committee of the Communist Party of China 1985.
33. The Central Committee of the Communist Party of China 1985.
34. Rosen 1985 p. 301.
35. Rosen 1985 p. 301.
36. Rosen 1985 p. 309.
37. Ye, Hua 2015 'Key-point Schools and Entry into Tertiary Education in China' in *Chinese Sociological Review* 47.2.
38. Rosen 1985 p. 302.
39. Ye 2015 p. 131.
40. Rosen 1985 p. 302.
41. Ye 2015 p. 132.
42. Rosen 1985 p. 310.
43. Chan, Chak Kwan, Ngok, King Lun and Phillips, David 2008 *Social Policy in China: Development and Well-being*, Bristol, UK, Policy Press, p. 160.

44. Rosen 1985 p. 323.
45. Rosen 1985 p. 330.
46. The Central Committee of the Communist Party of China and the State Council 1980 Decision on Several Issues in Universalizing Primary Education (Chinese version), Online. <http://www.chinalawedu.com/falvfagui/fg22598/368.shtml> (accessed 6 September 2015).
47. The Central Committee of the Communist Party of China 1985.
48. People's Republic of China 1986 Compulsory Education Law of the People's Republic of China (Chinese version), Online. <http://www.edu.cn/jiao_yu_fa_lv_766/20060303/t20060303_165119.shtml> (accessed 10 September 2015).
49. Chan et al. 2008 p. 149.
50. Chan et al. 2008 p. 164.
51. Chan, Kai-ming 1995 'Education – Decentralization and the Market' in Linda Wong and Stewart Macpherson eds. *Social Change and Social Policy in Contemporary China*, Aldershot, Avebury, pp. 70–87.
52. Rosen 1985 p. 326.
53. Rosen 1985 p. 305.
54. Chan 1995 p. 70.
55. Chan 1995 p. 72.
56. The Central Committee of the Communist Party of China and the State Council 1980.
57. The Central Committee of the Communist Party of China and the State Council 1980.
58. Chan 1995 p. 71.
59. Chan 1995 p. 72.
60. Chan 1995 pp. 72–5.
61. Chan et al. 2008 pp. 150–1.
62. Chan 1995 p. 85.
63. Chan 1995 p. 74.
64. Chan et al. 2008 p. 151.
65. The Central Committee of the Communist Party of China 1985.
66. Chan 1995 p. 80.
67. Lee, Peter Nan-shong 1995 'Housing Privatization with Chinese Characteristics' in Linda Wong and Stewart Macpherson eds. *Social Change and Social Policy in Contemporary China*, Aldershot, UK, Avebury, p. 115.
68. Chan et al. 2008 p. 170.
69. Lee 1995; Chan et al. 2008.
70. Chan et al. 2008 p. 169.
71. Lee 1995 p. 115.
72. People's Daily 2010 April 30 Deng Xiaoping: Talks on the Construction Industry and Housing Issues (Chinese version), Online. <http://news.163.com/10/0430/12/65H3DRDC000146BD.html> (accessed 13 September 2015).
73. People's Daily 2010 April 30.
74. People's Daily 2010 April 30.
75. People's Daily 2010 April 30.
76. Lee 1995 p. 129.
77. Chen, Jie 2009 A 60-year Review of Housing Development in China (Chinese version), Working Paper of Centre for Housing Policy Studies, Fudan University, Online. <http://www.chps.fudan.edu.cn/cn/content.asp?id=50> (accessed 13 September 2015).
78. The State Council 1983 Ordinance on Managing Private Housing in Urban Areas (Chinese version), Online. <www.szhome.com/new/publicinfo/four/3-3-1.htm> (accessed 13 September 2015).
79. Xinhua News 2014 March 3 A Historical Review of Housing System Reform in China (Chinese version), Online. <http://www.ce.cn/cysc/fdc/fc/201403/03/t20140303_2403808.shtml> (accessed 13 September 2015).
80. Lee 1995 p. 127.
81. Xinhua News 2014 March 3.

82. Lee 1995 p. 127.
83. Yang, Zan and Chen, Jie 2014 *Housing Affordability and Housing Policy in Urban China*, Berlin, Springer, p. 21.
84. The Housing System Reform Leading Group of the State Council 1987 The Bulletin of Forum on the Pilot Reform on Urban Housing System (Chinese version), Online. <http://www.bjfang.com/news/policy-235.html> (accessed 13 September 2015).
85. People's Daily 2000 January 15 The First National Working Conference on Housing System Reform in 1988 Identified the Ideas of Housing Reform (Chinese version), Online. <http://www.people.com.cn/item/lsjt/200001/15/19880115.html> (accessed 13 September 2015).
86. People's Daily 2000 January 15.
87. People's Daily 2000 January 15.
88. The State Council 1988 The Implementation Plan for a Gradual Housing System Reform in Cities and Towns (Chinese version), Online. <http://www.gdczt.gov.cn/adminfo/polipub/fgbrowse/comprehensive/201004/t20100415_17329.htm> (accessed 13 September 2015).
89. The State Council 1988.
90. Lee 1995 p. 130.
91. Richard L. Carson 1998 *Comparative Economic Systems: Transition and Capitalist Alternatives*, New York, M.E. Sharpe, Inc., p. 24.
92. The State Council 1991a Notification of the Continuation of Urban Housing System Reform in an Active and Stable Manner (Chinese version), Online. <http://www.law110.com/law/guowuyuan/2080.htm> (accessed 13 September 2015).
93. The Housing System Reform Leading Group of the State Council 1991 Opinions on Implementing Urban Housing System Reform on Full Scale (Chinese version), Online. <http://www.110.com/fagui/law_4874.html> (accessed 13 September 2015).
94. Chan et al. 2008 p. 173.
95. Chan et al. 2008 p. 173.
96. Chan et al. 2008 p. 117.
97. S.C.Y. Luk 2014 *Health Insurance Reforms in Asia*, London, Routledge, p. 42.
98. Chan et al. 2008 p. 117.
99. Luk 2014 p. 5.
100. Luk 2014 p. 5.
101. Luk 2014 pp. 4–5.
102. Li, Qiong 2009 *Zhongguo quanmin yiliao baozhang shixian lujing yanjiu* (Pathway to Realizing Universal Health Insurance in China), Beijing, People's Publishing House, p. 56.
103. J. Duckett 2011 *The Chinese State's Retreat from Health: Policy and the Politics of Retrenchment*, New York, Routledge, p. 36.
104. V. Pearson 1995 'Health and Responsibility; But Whose?' in Linda Wong and Stewart Macpherson eds. *Social Change and Social Policy in Contemporary China*, Aldershot, Avebury, p. 96.
105. Luk 2014 p. 64.
106. Chan et al. 2008 p. 121.
107. Chan et al. 2008 p. 120.
108. Chan et al. 2008; Luk 2014.
109. Luk 2014 p. 64.
110. Luk 2014 p. 65.
111. Luk 2014 p. 65.
112. Luk 2014 p. 59.
113. Luk 2014 p. 67.
114. Chan et al. 2008 p. 126.

115. Ministry of Health and Ministry of Finance 1984 Notification of Further Strengthening the Management of the Government Insurance Scheme (Chinese version), Online. <http://www.chinalawedu.com/falvfagui/fg22598/23676.shtml> (accessed 14 September 2015).
116. Li, Q. 2009 p. 41.
117. Li, Q. 2009; Luk 2014.
118. Li, Q. 2009 p. 42.
119. Li, Q. 2009 p. 42.
120. The Hainan Government 1991 Temporary Regulations on Medical Insurance for Employees (Chinese version), Online. <http://laws.66law.cn/law-79637.aspx> (accessed 14 September 2015).
121. Ding, Chun 2009 *Shijie zhuyao yiliao baozhang zhidu moshi jixiao bijiao* (Comparative Studies on Major Health Insurance Systems around the World), Shanghai, Fudan University Press, p. 385.
122. Dong, Weizhen 2001 Health Care Reform in Urban China, Online. <www.munkschool.utoronto.ca> (accessed 14 September 2015), p. 8.
123. Chan et al. 2008 p. 126.
124. The State Council 1986 The Interim Regulations on Unemployment Insurance for Employees of State-owned Enterprises (Chinese version), Online. <http://www.lawlib.com/law/law_view.asp?id=47542> (accessed 15 September 2015).
125. The State Council 1991b Decision on Reforming the Old Age Insurance System for Enterprise Workers (Chinese version), Online. <http://3y.uu456.com/bp_8fub99mey92mdyx42w57_1.html> (accessed 15 September 2015).
126. The Ministry of Civil Affairs 1987 The Report on Exploring the Establishment of a Basic Social Security System in Rural China (Chinese version), Online. <http://www.lawlib.com/law/law_view.asp?id=4175> (accessed 15 September 2015).
127. Zu, Yuebin and Zhang, Xiulan 2012 'Pension and Social Assistance: The Development of Income Security Policies for Old People in China' in S. Chen and J.L. Powell eds. *Ageing in China: Implications to Social Policy of a Changing Economic State*, New York, Springer, p. 49.
128. Chen, Hsiao-hung Nancy and Fu, Tsung-his 2009 'Older People's Income Security in China: The Challenges of Population Ageing' in T.H. Fu and R. Hughes eds. *Ageing in East Asia: Challenges and Policies for the Twenty-First Century*, New York, Routledge, p. 44.
129. Chen and Fu 2009 p. 44.
130. Li, Jian-fei 2009 Social Insurance in Rural China Should Be Legalized (Chinese version), Online. <http://paper.people.com.cn/rmlt/html/2009-12/11/content_425093.htm> (accessed 15 September 2015).
131. The Ministry of Civil Affairs 1991 Trial Implementation Plan on Rural Social Insurance Pension at the County Level (Chinese version), Online. <http://www.chinaacc.com/new/63/69/113/1992/1/ad3630295011131299115989.htm> (accessed 15 September 2015).
132. Chen and Fu 2009 p. 44.
133. Chen and Fu 2009 p. 45.
134. Bregolat 2015; T.W. Robinson 1994 'Chinese Foreign Policy from the 1940s to the 1990s' in T.W. Robinson and D. Shambaugh eds. *Chinese Foreign Policy: Theory and Practice*, Oxford, Clarendon Press.
135. Bregolat 2015 p. 19.
136. Marti 2002 p. 10.
137. T.W. Robinson 1994 p. 573.
138. Marti 2002 pp. 18–9.
139. Marti 2002 p. 19.
140. See A.S. Whiting 1995 'Chinese Nationalism and Foreign Policy after Deng' in *The China Quarterly* 142.
141. W.A. Callahan 2010 *China: The Pessoptimist Nation*, Oxford University Press.

142. The state is powerful and can override popular memories rather more easily than in Europe where national pasts exemplify more of a contested consensus between elites and masses.
143. Callahan 2010 p. 38.
144. Callahan 2010 pp. 64–70.
145. Callahan 2010 takes this idea from Raymond Williams.
146. Callahan 2010 p. 195.
147. Recently discussed by Benedict Anderson 2016 'Frameworks of Comparison' in *London Review of Books* 38.2, 21 January.
148. World Bank 1993 *The East Asian Miracle*, Oxford University Press.
149. See, for example, Gordon White ed. 1988 *Developmental States in East Asia*, London, Macmillan; R. Wade 2004 *Governing the Markets: Economic Theory and the Role of Government in East Asia*, Princeton University Press; C. Johnson 1995 *Japan: Who Governs?* New York, Norton; L. Weiss 1998 *The Myth of the Powerless State: Governing the Economy in a Global Era*, Cambridge, Polity.
150. Spence 2013 pp. 675–8.
151. Callahan 2010 pp. 195–204.
152. Callahan 2010 p. 217.

5. Contemporary China: domestic politics

The record of the economic and social reform of recent decades has propelled China to the front rank of states; the domestic economic record is without parallel, and the achievements of the period were celebrated internationally at the 2008 Beijing Olympics. However, change is never simple or straightforward and evident success has been accompanied by sometimes equally evident failures: headlong economic growth has been accompanied by sweeping social changes as ordinary people have had to adapt to shifting economic circumstances; it has been attended by severe environmental problems (widespread and severe pollution); it has been attended by extensive corruption in the machineries of the party-state (and thereafter more widely through the economy and society); and it has been attended by growing socio-economic inequality. The party-state leadership has declared that it will address some of these problems. The government of Hu Jintao and Wen Jiabao acknowledged the problems of rural China, and more recently President Xi Jinping's government[1] has stressed combating corruption, declarations have been made in respect of the environment and, more recently, moves have been made to strengthen the rule of law.

These are headline moves, but reform has been unfolding for many years, and this chapter turns to the record of accumulated success in reform and to the contemporary agendas of policy makers inside China.

CONTEMPORARY CHINA I: THE DEMANDS OF MODERNITY AND THE DEVELOPMENTAL STATE

The country continues to pursue economic reform and maintains high levels of economic growth, but policy makers also face difficulties. A number of these can be highlighted. First, the country is vast: it has 1.3 billion people, spread over a vast area with significant regional variations in patterns of living along with numerous local centres of economic and political power, and any instructions from policy makers in Beijing must both accommodate these differences and be transmitted down long, complex lines of party-state communication. Then, second, China's economic foundation is weak: following the inauguration of the reform policy the pace of economic development has been dramatic, but GDP per capita is still low and policy makers confront problems of over-investment in infrastructure, over-dependence on low-end manufactured exports and low levels of domestic consumption. And third, there are problems associated with inequality: economic growth in recent decades has created or accentuated inequality amongst the population, and there are disparities between regions, there are severe rural/urban disparities and there are increasingly sharp class distinctions within urban centres. Then, fourth, the problem of pollution: rapid economic growth has led to severe problems of environmental pollution in many cities. And, finally, fifth, the issue of the condition of the party-state machinery and its efficiency/effectiveness, otherwise 'state capacity' – one concern is with corruption, and Xi Jinping has launched a sweeping campaign targeting all levels of the apparatus, and whereas early commentary identified faction fighting, later commentary has dropped this claim amid new questions as to Xi's deeper objectives.

****

As noted in earlier chapters, the modern world of natural science based industrial capitalism was invented by accident in late medieval Europe: it is a dynamic system typified by internal and external advance, and it attained an apogee in the nineteenth century. At a macro level it took the form of a global system of state-empires, mostly European; however, as that system crumbled in the early twentieth century, it was replaced by an America-centred system, which stressed liberal markets and liberal finance, along with (an optional) liberal democracy. In recent decades the system has been celebrated in terms of the idea of globalization, where the idea points to a global level of integration; but this notion has attracted an alternate line of argument, again invoking the record of East Asia, where the detail reveals, it is claimed, not a process of global-ization, rather one of regionalization based around economic linkages; thereafter, other regions can be identified, most clearly, North America and Europe, perhaps then parts of the Global South.

In respect of the broad historical record of East Asia, four phases can be characterized: first, early trading contacts between local polities and incoming Europeans; second, the period of absorption of local polities into European-centred state-empires; third, a period of general crisis which saw warfare, collapse and the creation from a disintegrating state-empire territorial holdings of new states and nations; and then, fourth, the post-colonial and post-war phase dominated by the assiduous elite-sponsored pursuit of development and culminating, for the present, in an extensively integrated economic sphere, recognized as 'the East Asian region'.[2]

East Asia was home to long-established civilizations – in Southeast Asia, Indo-China, Northeast Asia and in the centre of the region, China – before the modern world, in the guise of European traders, made its appearance. These spheres were distinctive, locally coherent and linked by extensive trade networks.[3] European traders joined these flows of trade,[4] and in time they were joined by American and Japanese players. Traders in East Asia had a changing and deepening schedule of demands, and at first they sought locally produced craft goods in small quantities, but later, as their core economies changed, they sought the output of mines and plantations, much larger quantities of goods, and as their economic impact deepened so did their political demands. At first the trade was organized by the large, pre-modern companies of the Dutch, English and French. There were small factories serving a seasonal trade (sails/monsoon winds), later company-ordered quasi-colonies were developed and later still elaborate bureaucracies and armies buttressed the deepening demands of trade. This system, in turn, was superseded by core state control as formal colonial empires were organized with their cores/peripheries.

China was the goal for much of this expansion, and in time experienced a process of quasi-colonization. And in all these territories the justificatory ideology of empire was cast in economic and race terms; trade was deemed to be generally beneficial, and the colonized lands were home to less advanced or sometime great but now moribund civilizations, thus, China. Later, core theorists and policy makers also saw less advanced humans, and so leadership from the metropolitan cores was appropriate. But the exchange between incoming traders and local people was not entirely one-sided, for these empires could not have succeeded without local participation and local rulers; local traders and local people adjusted, producing a mix of winners and losers. The modern world was not simply transplanted ready-made into a new geographical location; rather, incoming traders and locals engaged in a drawn out exchange – exploitation, development and learning – with the result being the local creation of a novel variant form of the modern world in colonies and colonialism.

The Second World War marked the end of the European system of state-empires: the metropolitan core of the system collapsed into warfare; in the far-flung peripheral territories various nationalist groups made their voices heard; in East Asia, such responses were subsumed in the catastrophic processes of invasion and occupation by Imperial Japan; and local nationalist agitation continued (in collaboration with Japan in their conquered territories, in all other colonial territories and, of course, in a different fashion in China). During this period there were significant policy changes in the metropolitan centres as opinion moved away from empire in favour of independence; American officialdom was hostile towards the empires of the Europeans. In this period of upheaval local, nationalist-minded political groups took their chance and sought independent statehood. The dissolution of the system of state-empires was not a tidy process, and aspirant replacement elites had to settle matters amongst themselves and with out-going colonial elites. The business was made more difficult by the construction in the late 1940s of the machinery of the cold war, but, nonetheless, a number of new states took shape, invented nations, and variously pursued national development. However, in the immediate wake of the Pacific War, expectations amongst development theorists in regard to East Asia were pessimistic as the region was devastated by war and had relatively little by way of capital or industrial or manpower resources. The future seemed to be one of agriculturally based production plus thereafter a trade exchange with the developed countries for a limited stock of industrial goods. However, clearly, events took a quite different direction – the region began to develop; it did so in a number of discrete phases, starting with the recovery of Japan, until by the latter part of the century commentators were paying close attention.

A number of theories were advanced which purport to explain or elucidate (interpret) the post-war economic track record of the region:

- early growth theory cast matters in terms of the elite construction of effective nation states, and the expectation was that as decolonization ran its course replacement elites would embrace liberal markets and liberal-democratic forms;
- modernization theory inherited the above line and made it into an influential ideologically inflected package with the same mix of liberal markets plus liberal democracy, but now development was made easy and available in a desirable package in contrast to offers of socialism;
- state-socialist theories were available and typically stressed state-led industrial development, provisions of social services and ideas of people's democracy, and in China a variant form centred on the peasantry was created;
- neo-liberal theories offered an alternative to all the above noted in an aggressive celebration of the benefits of the putative free liberal

marketplace with a framework of law protecting property and contracts that would ensure a maximum benefit for all participants, and the system was confidently expected to embrace the global system, hence globalization;

● finally, a new debate began in the 1980s as reflection upon the actual historical experience of the countries of East Asia (over both their earlier shift into the modern world, especially in Northeast Asia, and their post-war record) issued in the view that the key to development was to be found in the role of the state, where an active, authoritative and interventionist state could best serve the goal of national development, and the view was summed in terms of the idea of the developmental state, and this was sometimes supplemented by related claims to a basket of 'Asian Values'.

The Developmental State – Japan

The Tokugawa Shogunate ruled Japan for several hundred years, and the culture was highly sophisticated, the agrarian economy advanced and the country was prosperous; however, in the mid-nineteenth century the authorities were unable to respond effectively to the demand of foreign traders: American in 1853 and a little later Russian in 1855. Elements of the elites organized a conservative revolution from above, the Meiji Restoration 1868, and sought to construct a modern state and thereafter to pursue development, and by the early twentieth century Meiji Japan was in the process of carving out an empire in Northeast Asia, as late development had been supplemented by the available foreign-relations model of empire.

The creation of an empire attracted the enmity of the USA, in particular when Japan expanded its operations in northern China and, a little later, engaged in outright war against that country. The Pacific War pitted the USA against the Japanese.[5] The war in China dragged on in stalemate. The war in the Pacific was won decisively by the USA, and the American occupation authorities introduced sweeping domestic reforms. From 1945 Japan was restricted to its original home islands;[6] however, the elite commitment to national development remained in place; post-war recovery was rapid and was analysed by scholars in terms of the notion of the developmental state.[7]

On the role of the state: after the war the country was mobilized for the pursuit of economic growth. The state machinery has been the vehicle for an alliance of elite bureaucrats, elite politicians and elite business, an iron triangle which collectively took responsibility for the family of Japanese people, who, in turn, affirmed the ideal of harmony.[8] The nature of the state has been debated, and one line of argument suggests it is weak (leaving a role for administrators)[9] whilst another stresses that the state is strong (again with administrators being key).[10] The issue is power: where does it lie? The ministries are powerful; there are numerous political parties; and ministries and parties link up with the corporate business world. The ensemble of players is committed to national development, hence the tag 'the developmental state', but it is not a liberal state as it intervenes in the marketplace, nor is it a state-socialist system as the market does play a significant role; rather, it is a novel solution to the issue of the relationship of state, society and marketplace.

Commentators have unpacked the way in which the market operates and identified two aspects: first, there is a dual economy comprising large conglomerates and a very large small firm sector which either supports the conglomerates or constitutes the retail sector; and the second aspect has been grasped in terms of the notion of relational contracting, that is, contracts are expected to be long term and such contracts are not simple legal agreements about buying and selling; rather, they imply long-term relations between their participants.[11] In this way Japan has crafted conglomerates with major international profiles and conjoined them with an adaptive and relatively closed domestic business world.

On the contribution of social norms, a number of lines of commentary have been advanced invoking the culture of the Japanese: some have identified a Confucian work ethic as a variant of Max Weber's Protestant ethic (but this is foolish[12]); other commentators have spoken of group-ism, where this is a kind of collective psychological characteristic, evidenced, for example, in company unions (also unhelpful[13]); there is a local literature dealing with the purported specialness of the Japanese, the Nihonjinron (again, unhelpful[14]); and finally, another opinion points to the social ideal of harmony.[15] Overall, it is better to see economics as the business not of marketplaces but rather the social production of liveli-hood; it is a social process and agents learn and, thereafter, read and react to given circumstances, that is, inherited ideas plus defeat plus occu-pation plus cold war created a business-dominated Japan, so ideas count, but how they count depends on local circumstances.

The Developmental State: Variant Forms

The four tigers offer variations on the theme of the developmental state. American policy and general influence also helped: first, by providing aid (financial, military and technical); second, by opening its markets (to the exports of these countries); third, by expanding the global market-place (into which the four tigers could expand by virtue of its own vigorous domestic economic growth). In South Korea and Taiwan there was cold war and state-led development, whilst Singapore and Hong Kong were successful trading cities.[16] The success of the four tigers attracted attention. There have been many debates about the reasons for their success.

There are a number of key factors:

- the role of the USA in providing aid and demanding reforms to domestic structures;
- the economic implications of American cold war military expend-itures in the region;[17]
- the role of the long post-Second World War economic boom (a benign economic environment within which elites could pursue national economic growth);
- the role of national elites in charge of competent state machineries (clear political projects coupled to effective bureaucracies);
- the contribution of the marketplace (structured competition);
- the nature of the developmental state (elites committed to national development).

The debate about the developmental state ran on through the 1980s and 1990s, and it confronted novel circumstances with the 1997 Asian Financial Crisis. Critics of the region were quick to speak of the perils of crony capitalism; others pointed out that the problems began with shifts in regional economic balances (devaluation of the yuan prior to 1997 and the liberalization policies of the Thai bureaucracy) and that those countries that stuck closest to the preference for an active state in pursuit of national development came out best, that is, their economies suffered relatively less damage.[18] Subsequent discussion has called attention to the necessity of these countries changing policy direction as rapid growth and catch-up gives way to highly developed or mature economic profiles; nonetheless, the region continues – overall – to be successful.

China: Quasi-colonialism, Revolution and Reform

It can be argued that China made three attempts to join the modern world after the slow collapse of the Qing Empire when subject to the quasi-colonial incursions of European and American traders, officials and military (Qing China was dismantled over the nineteenth century with the aid of a series of military incursions[19]). The first was the revolution of 1911 – linked to Sun Yat Sen and directed to the creation of a modern republic – failed and dissolved into warlordism followed by the regime of

Chiang Kai Shek. The second was the 1949 Revolution linked to Mao Zedong and oriented towards the goal of a communist system; the early record was ambiguous – reunification of the country, expulsion of foreigners, rapid economic growth plus failed reforms (such as the GLF) and social experiments (thus, the Cultural Revolution). And the third, current, attempt began with the 1978 reform programme associated with Deng Xiaoping, a local variant of the wider East Asian developmental state model, and these have been followed up to the present day, over nearly 40 years, with many shifts and changes.

The reform programme inaugurated by Deng was ambitious and its impact is undeniable; most commentators speak in terms of success, but there have been problems:

- corruption in the party-state machine – the party-state system is susceptible to problems caused by local cultural traditions (gift giving), private greed (officials using their positions for their own profit) and the relative absence of independent public oversight (a role played in Europe by the press and the wider public sphere). None of this is news; however, the anti-corruption drive initiated by Xi Jinping has revealed corruption on a massive scale for it is apparently endemic, and whilst individual instances are surprising (press/court reports on cases), some broader impacts are also surprising (thus, impacts on tourism to Macau and Hong Kong);
- a related lack of development in the rule of law as the law remains part of the wider administrative system and is thus open to local-level party-state interference;
- difficulties in relationships between the policy agendas of the centre and those of provincial- or city-level governments leading to mal-development in infrastructure, where there is duplication and poor standards and finance, where local budgets are overspent and thereafter bailed out by the centre (sometimes tagged 'soft-budgetary constraints'), coupled to great social inequality (data suggest that coastal areas have done much better than those inland and that there is inequality within urban areas);
- a related set of problems of rural–urban migration as inland areas are losing population to the cities, and whilst it is a familiar feature of the rapid development in China, these flows of people are measured in hundreds of millions;
- and finally, the whole 40-year period has led to severe environmental degradation, and urban pollution (air, land and water) is now a major problem in many Chinese cities.

China's policy makers continue with programmes of economic reform, but they also face difficulties. China has 1.3 billion people, its economic foundation is relatively weak, and although the pace of economic development is very fast, GDP per capita is still very low; there is serious rural–urban disparity along with unequal development amongst different regions in China.

CONTEMPORARY CHINA II: REFORM PROCESSES IN DOMESTIC SOCIETY AND POLITICS

The reform era has seen great changes in the economic organization of the country but, of course, these have immediate implications for society and politics. The resultant pattern of changes is complex, but the outlines of the various strands of policy making can be discerned.

Social Aspect – the Development of Social Policy

Social policy in China is developed in a specific political and socio-economic context. It is 'not regulated by welfare laws but by directives, decisions, circulars and proposals issued by the [State Council] and its ministries'.[20] It 'addressed problems that come as a result of industrialization and urbanization'.[21] Social policy making in China 'has been the exclusive prerogative of the Party-state leadership and the political elites'.[22]

The development of social policy can be divided into five stages: 1949–78, 1978–92, 1992–2003, 2003–13 and 2013–present.

The first stage: 1949–78
The PRC was formally established in October 1949 under the leadership of Mao Zedong. Until the end of 1978, China maintained a Soviet-style, centrally planned economy, which relied 'little on market dynamics and thoroughly rejected capitalist financial institutions and bourgeois business practices'.[23] Market forces played virtually no role in allocating resources and organizing economic activities.[24] Private ownership was abolished in order to eliminate inequality and exploitation.[25] Following the orthodox doctrines of Soviet-style Marxism–Leninism, the Chinese government emphasized the rapid development of a heavy industrial base.[26] The government 'aimed at achieving rapid industrialization by extracting agricultural surplus for capital accumulation in industries';[27] rural areas were utilized 'for cheap labour supply, and for cheap raw materials'.[28] And so full employment in the cities was seen as a 'fundamental

advantage of socialism'.[29] In the Mao period, the CCP strived to establish a social welfare system, which reflected the superiority of socialism, and it pushed for an egalitarian distribution of resources. The social welfare system in the cold war period was developed in 'the ideological and political contests between the capitalist and communist camps'.[30] It was used to show that 'the communist regime was performing better than its capitalist counterparts in securing a minimum living standard for its people'.[31] Maoist social policy was formulated to 'strengthen the government and social order ... [and] enhance fast industrialization'.[32] It had a dual nature that 'prioritized urban areas over rural areas',[33] because of low GDP and the financial weakness of the government.[34]

The key providers of welfare benefits were SOEs in urban areas and the people's communes in rural areas. In urban areas, welfare provision and employment were strongly tied together.[35] Comprehensive welfare benefits were 'distributed indiscriminately to employees as a means of supplementing the policy of low wages'.[36] Urban employees and those working in the state sectors enjoyed lifetime employment, which was referred to as the iron rice bowl. The government provided all kinds of welfare benefits, including health care, housing, education and social security, to employees through SOEs, and inevitably 'the state dictated the social life of the people and, in turn, the people came to rely on the state for their requirements'.[37] Hence, comprehensive welfare benefits were a political asset for the CCP, promising legitimacy and social stability.[38] In rural areas, all farmers were members of the people's commune, an economic organization which oversaw 'the multiplicity of rural activities'.[39] The commune 'guaranteed farmers' equal access to the collectively owned farmland, and thus guaranteed everyone a subsistence living'.[40] Besides, it was the so-called free supply system under which:

> half or more of the peasant's income was paid in the form of free food and welfare services ... [and to these] free supplies were added fixed cash wages ... [that were] generally administered as part of the seven guarantees pertaining to food, clothing, medical care, education, housing, childbirth, and marriage and funeral.[41]

But the system was a collective self-reliance system that was financed by the collective income of each individual commune.[42] The level of welfare provision in rural areas was low.

In sum, the socialist welfare system 'provided a basic social protection for both workers and farmers ... [however] the socialist welfare system suffered from the low productivity and backward economy'[43] and led to welfare dependency. The soaring welfare expenditures imposed heavy financial burden on SOEs and the government.

The second stage: 1978–92

Mao's successor, Deng Xiaoping, came to power in December 1978 and he 'inherited an inefficient and unbalanced urban industrial economy',[44] with a substantial rural–urban divide and serious social inequalities. An overemphasis on heavy industry and capital accumulation had led to 'slow growth in agricultural production accompanied by declining productivity'.[45] Deng was determined to implement economic reform in order to 'enhance the political legitimacy of the CCP',[46] and the 'egalitarian social policy … was an impediment to market reforms'.[47] Deng transformed the centrally planned economy and accelerated the process of modern development, as the importance of the Four Modernizations was emphasized (agriculture, industry, national defence, science and technology).[48] The primacy of economic growth and economic efficiency was also emphasized, and the pursuit of GDP became 'the central task of officials at all levels'.[49]

Mao-style egalitarianism was abandoned, with a belief that 'inequalities can provide the necessary incentives for higher productivity'.[50] The principle of 'to each according to his work' was implemented, representing 'a major departure from China's previous iron bowl policy',[51] and consequently reforms under Deng 'had widespread ramifications on the welfare system'.[52] The traditional socialist welfare model based on SOEs and people's communes was destroyed by the economic reforms.[53] Social policy had become subordinate to economic policy and 'was used as a tool to facilitate the state sector reform and promote economic growth'.[54] Social welfare was cut down in order to reduce labour costs,[55] and 'programmes such as pensions, housing, health care and education were gradually separated from the commercial activities of SOEs … [and] SOEs were no longer to provide generous packages of welfare and benefits to their employees'.[56] Instead, 'marketization became trendy in the main sectors of public services, such as education and health'.[57] The tradition of mutual assistance amongst family members, relatives and friends, and neighbours was raised in the Seventh Five-Year National Plan for Economic and Social Development (1986–90) in the 4th session of the 6th NPC in 1986.

In sum, economic construction was emphasized during Deng's era. The market-oriented economic reforms 'dismantled the state-led social welfare system'.[58] Such change was informed by 'neoliberal market ideology, which justified the retreat of the state from welfare provision and the pro-market shift in social policy orientation'.[59]

The third stage: 1993–2003

Deng's successor, Jiang Zemin, 'continued advancing China's economic reforms and adapting them to changing economic circumstances'[60] and 'set the country on a growth-at-all costs model during the 1990s … [leading to] widespread environmental destruction and growing social inequality'.[61] Economic reform during this period was to 'transform SOEs into modern business enterprises … [and create] autonomous competitors in an open economy'.[62] At this time, social policy was still subordinate to economic reform.

In September 1994, Premier Zhu Rongji mentioned, 'SOE reform must be supported by a social security system.'[63] The social security system was established by setting up various employment-related insurances, 'first in employment, healthcare, old age pension, work injury and maternal leave'.[64] Decentralization led to the central government delegating 'more and more of its welfare functions to local government authorities'.[65] Local governments were 'encouraged to experiment'[66] with different strategies. 'Health care, pension and unemployment had high priority and each underwent separate experimentations … [and maternity and work injury] were included in the trials in some places, but not in others.'[67] The standard of security for these insurances could only ensure a basic level of protection due to the lack of fiscal capacity.[68] The funding of these insurances mainly came from work units and employees. The central government only financed programmes related to social relief, resettlement and preferential treatment,[69] and so its role in welfare was mainly 'a regulator and enabler'.[70]

In September 1997, Jiang Zemin's report to the 15th Party Congress highlighted the importance of building a social security system. The report stated that old-age pension and medical insurance systems should be implemented by combining individual savings accounts and social pooling funds, and the unemployment insurance and social relief systems should be improved in order to provide the basic social security. In 1998, the Ministry of Social Security was established by the State Council to 'centralize the management of the social security'.[71] In sum, the new social security system was 'set up for people employed somewhere, not for persons outside the labour market … [and so employment is] a precondition for receiving social benefits'.[72] The pairing of individual savings accounts with social pooling funds indicates that the source of funding had moved from the public sphere to employers and employees. Social welfare benefits were no longer an entitlement but required employers and employees to share financial responsibilities through insurance contributions. The welfare system has become more localized and diversified.[73]

The fourth stage: 2003–13

In 2003, the outbreak of the severe acute respiratory syndrome (SARS) 'made China's new generation of leadership aware of the importance of social development and social construction'.[74] Jiang's successor, Hu Jintao, adopted the concept of building a harmonious society as the new direction of social policy in China, and the state's focus 'changed from economic growth to balanced comprehensive development and from efficiency to fairness'.[75] When addressing a high-level party seminar in 2007, Hu 'instructed the country's leading officials and party cadres to place building a harmonious society at the top of their agenda'.[76] In October 2007, Hu's report to the 17th Party Congress stated that all the people should 'enjoy their rights to education, employment, medical and old-age care, and housing, so as to build a harmonious society'.[77] Hence, it was important to accelerate 'the establishment of a social security system covering both urban and rural residents and guarantee their basic living conditions'.[78] In Hu's view, the backbone of a sound social security system was basic medical care, basic old-age pension and subsistence allowance, supplemented by commercial insurance and charity.[79] In 2012, Hu's Report to the 18th Party Congress stated that emphasis should be put on making the social security system more equitable and sustainable.[80]

During Hu's era, the idea of putting people first was adopted as a guiding principle when formulating social policy: improving people's livelihood or improving people's wellbeing had become the core work of the central government. First, in terms of health care, the government implemented the New Rural Cooperative Medical System in 2003. The Basic Medical Insurance that was originally implemented to cover urban employees in 1998 was extended to cover rural residents in 2007. Critical Illness Insurance for Urban and Rural Residents was implemented in 2012 to insure urban and rural residents against catastrophic health expenditures. The government strived to expand medical coverage so as to achieve the goal of basic health care protection with wide population coverage. Second, in the aspect of education, the government emphasized equal access to education. It amended the Law on Compulsory Education in 2006, which outlined 'the responsibilities of central and local governments in financing rural schools'.[81] It implemented free nine-year compulsory education for all rural students in 2007 and extended it to the whole country in 2008. 'Since the fall semester of 2007, the central government has provided rural students across the country with free textbooks.'[82] In 2012, it spent 13.44 billion yuan on textbooks for 130 million rural students enrolled in nine-year compulsory education.[83] Third, in the aspect of housing, the central government urged the local governments to increase land supply and capital investment in the building of cheap rental housing for low-income earners in urban areas. In 2006, the Government Work Report states that a sound, cheap rental housing system would be established. In 2010, the central government fully implemented the shantytown redevelopment to improve the living conditions of shantytowns in state-owned mining and forest areas. And fourth, in the aspect of old-age pension the government established a three-tiered old-age pension system by extending the coverage from urban employees in the 1990s to rural residents in 2009 and urban residents in 2011, and so it basically achieved basic protection and wide coverage when implementing the old-age pension; but the protection level was still too low.

The fifth stage: 2013–present

In March 2013, Hu Jintao's successor, Xi Jinping, came to power. Xi put forward the ideas of the China dream, which had the twin goals of rejuvenating the Chinese nation and improving the wellbeing of people. To rejuvenate the nation needs to let people enjoy better medical care, better education, a greater degree of social security, higher incomes, more stable employment, more comfortable living conditions and a better environment. In terms of health care, Xi strived to solve the problem of 'being difficult and expensive to see a doctor' and achieve the goal that everyone can enjoy the basic medical care by 2020.[84] In terms of education, Xi said that education was important for rejuvenating the nation and the prosperity of nation.[85] He strived to establish a knowledge society through education for all and life-long education.[86] In terms of housing, Xi mentioned that the government would 'increase the supply of land for homes and spend more on affordable housing projects'.[87] It would be 'mainly responsible for the supply of affordable housing while market forces [would] govern the supply of other types of housing'.[88] In the aspect of old-age pension, Xi strived to establish a fair and unified pension scheme for rural and urban residents before the year 2020. Similar to Hu, Xi Jinping put people first when formulating social policy.

Underprivileged Groups in China

Since the Hu-Wen era, the government has strived to put people first when formulating social policies. Nevertheless, there are still two under-privileged groups that suffer from poor health, insufficient emotional support and financial inadequacy in China nowadays. They are elderly 'empty nesters' and 'left-behind' children in rural China, who are victims under rapid economic development. Rapid economic development leads to rapid urbanization and an increase in social mobility. People who live in rural areas look for job opportunities in urban areas. They left the elderly and the children behind. As a result, these two special social groups in rural China have created lots of social problems, which reshape the roles of family, government and community.

The elderly empty nesters
China faces the problem of rapid population ageing, and according to MCA the total number of people aged 60 or above surpassed 200 million in 2013.[89] The problem of a growing elderly population is followed by the problem of growing elderly 'empty nesters' in rural and urban China. Empty nesters refers to old people who are left behind by their children to live alone and have no relatives living nearby to look after or accompany them. Their children are tied up in their work and rarely visit them or help them financially. Most of the elderly empty nesters live in rural areas, with their children looking for better prospects in bigger cities or working in cities. Children nowadays are departing from the Chinese tradition of living under the same roof with their parents, which is the essential part of filial piety. Being the main breadwinners, children usually go to other cities to work without bringing their parents with them because of high living costs and parents' unwillingness to leave their own home.

The one-child generation faces the work–life conflict, having difficulties in handling work and taking care of their ageing parents at the same time due to job stress and busy schedules. Family reunions are rare. Children only come home once a year during the Lunar New Year. Ageing parents who are deprived of care from their children struggle to make a living on their own and become increasingly vulnerable. They 'have to accept the undesirable empty-nest situations passively'[90] and face the problems of 'financial inadequacy, lack of physical care and insufficient emotional support'.[91] According to the *China Report of the Development on Ageing Cause* (2014), elderly empty nesters in China account for half of the total elderly population, and the number is expected to reach 70 per cent in future. At present, the elderly empty nesters add up to 100 million, and more than 40 million of them are in rural areas.[92] However, there is inadequate care for the elderly in society. At present, there are only 45,000 senior nursing homes to accommodate about 4.3 million people, which is far from enough when compared with the total number of elderly people.[93] 'Only about a third of them are in the rural areas, home to 60 per cent of the nation's aging population.'[94] Besides, senior care centres funded by the government are not enough to meet the growing demand, whilst 'privately run senior care centres have very small profit margins and little room for business expansion'[95] because of the 'lack of preferential policies and government support'.[96]

In order to improve the situation of elderly empty nesters, local governments implement different measures. For example, the Yanbian Prefecture government built residential courtyards for the elderly in rural villages to entertain themselves, renovated telephones, which let the elderly contact community workers by pressing one button, and introduced yellow ribbons for the elderly to tie on their windows when they are in need of help.[97] In Fusui of Chongzuo City, Guangxi, the government sets up senior care associations in villages which provide medical care and entertainment rooms for the elderly.[98] In Xiamen, local government pays for 'local nursing centres to provide professional services at home for seniors who are struggling with poverty, disability or who are over 100 years old'.[99] It is undeniable that the Chinese government has to play a greater role in improving the care of the elderly and complementing family support. But the Chinese government is still struggling to find effective solutions to solve the problem of elderly 'empty nesters'. After all, what the elderly 'empty nesters' need most is love and care from their children.

Left-behind children

The notion of 'left-behind children' refers to rural children that are left unattended by their parents who are migrant workers working in cities throughout the year. According to the All-China Women's Federation (ACWF), there were about 61 million left-behind children in rural areas in 2013,[100] which accounted for about 38 per cent of rural children and about 22 per cent of the total child population in China.[101] They 'mainly live in Sichuan, Henan, Anhui, Hunan, Chongqing and other labour-exporting provinces in central and western China'.[102] About a third of left-behind children are under the guardianship of their grandparents,[103] who are already too old and 'lack the energy or resources to emotionally engage with such children'.[104] Meanwhile, about 53 per cent of left-behind children are left by both parents.[105] They are forced to fend for themselves. Parents become the most familiar strangers to them. 'The number of preschool left-behind children increased by 7.57 million (47 per cent) since 2005.'[106]

Due to the absence of parents, left-behind children face three main problems. First, they are underprivileged children lacking parent–child emotional interactions, 'family closeness, security, protection and educational opportunities'.[107] In January 2014 a study, which surveyed more than 1,500 migrant workers in the Pearl River Delta, found that more than 82 per cent of parents with left-behind children 'consider themselves

as inadequate parents'[108] because of 'insufficient time and communication with their children, as well as inability to provide them with
appropriate guidance and quality education'.[109] Second, left-behind children are likely to suffer from developmental difficulties, and emotional
and psychological problems.[110] Released in 2012, the first report on the
health of left-behind children in rural China found that about 30 per cent
of left-behind children felt lonely and helpless whilst about 26 per cent
found it painful to be separated from their parents and 15 per cent felt
abandoned.[111] Third, left-behind children are susceptible to abuse, abduc-
tion, violence, molestation and child trafficking. 'Recent years have seen
an increasing number of left-behind children suffering from death by
drowning, poisoning, traffic accidents or fire incidents.'[112]

In recent years, different agents have been making efforts to improve
the lives of left-behind children. For example, the government trains
some barefoot social workers in 50 cities to identify the needs of
left-behind children and provide the children with care and practical
support.[113] At local level, a middle school in Yuanzhou District in
Guyuan City, Ningxia sets up a counselling room to help more than 900
students who are left-behind children solve their psychological problems.[114] In Guiyang Province, 800 nurseries are established in schools for
left-behind children to solve their psychological problems.[115] In Yiongxiu
County, Jiangxi Province, a care station has been established for left-
behind children to have 'video chat with their parents, receive safety
education, and seek psychological counselling'.[116] In 2014, Baofeng
County government in Henan Province invested over 100,000 yuan
(US$16,170) in local schools in order to provide day-care services for
more than 1,000 left-behind children during the summer holiday.[117] In
Henan, 138 Left-behind Children's Homes have been established to look
after rural left-behind children and let children have free telephone calls
and video chats with parents.[118] Besides, children's homes for left-behind
children have been established by many women federations to 'provide
life care, homework guidance and mental comfort'.[119]

However, whilst assistance from different parties helps improve the
situation of left-behind children, the problem of parents separating from
their rural children due to working in cities is a social problem that
cannot be easily solved. After all, video chats and phone calls cannot
replace a real-life relationship, and parents have an irreplaceable role to
play in child development. In the long run, the government needs to
consider creating more job opportunities in rural areas so that parents do
not need to work far away from home. And for companies that hire
parents with left-behind children, they are encouraged to implement
family-friendly policies in the workplace, including flexible working

arrangements, job sharing, family-related responsibilities paid leave, flexible emergency leave and financial support such as housing subsidies.

Changing Social Policy: Retrospect

To conclude, social policy in China is developed in a specific political and socio-economic context. Since the opening of China, social policy has been experiencing dramatic changes. Mao's cradle-to-grave social policy was replaced by Deng's market-oriented social policy. During Jiang's era, various employment-related insurances were set up to support the SOE reforms. During the Hu-Wen era, social policy became more people-oriented and emphasis was put on expanding the coverage of social insurances. When it comes to Xi's era, social policy is regarded as a tool to rejuvenate the nation. The change of political leadership provides a policy window for the change of social policy. Although the social policy over the past decade has been formulated to improve the livelihood of people, many social problems and social inequalities caused by rapid economic development still exist. In particular, the widening gap between the rich and the poor has become the price to pay for fast economic growth and has made China become a more unequal country. The problem of population ageing requires the central government to increase its spending on social policy and formulate a social policy that can achieve sustainability and equity in the long run.

Domestic Politics 1: the CCP, Changing Character and Goals

A number of issues can be discussed: (i) government–citizen relationship, that is, governance capacity; (ii) citizen use of the Internet to expose the malpractice of government officials (mass media also make use of the Internet to expose the malpractice of government officials); (iii) the movement towards universal health coverage, which still has difficulties; (iv) how to facilitate education equality and increase the quality of citizens; (v) arguments for reform of domestic politics; and (vi) the legal aspect, that is, how to make the legal system more comprehensive.

Theories of the Chinese state

China entered the modern world via a long experience of quasi-colonial rule, Republican Revolution, civil war, inter-state war and, finally, the establishment of the PRC. The core legacy of the party-state is that of the revolutionary acquisition of power in a war-ravaged sub-continent, that is, China. The key to the future lies within the elite circles and policy community centred on Beijing and organized via the double bureaucracy of the party-state system. The party remains the key locus of political life. It has around 80 million members and it has reformed.[120] There is also an arena of public debate (regional and local press plus Internet) and numerous signs of local popular dissatisfaction.[121] There have been drives against pervasive corruption, and the anti-corruption drive has been emphasized by Xi Jinping, and there has been a noticeable stress on nationalism, which finds expression in the official media and social media and is often hostile towards the USA and typically virulently anti-Japanese.[122]

As noted earlier, there are some standard available labels for the political system and they are listed by Flemming Christiansen and Shirin Rai:[123] first, totalitarian (the system is controlled by one ideologically motivated repressive party); second, factionalism and clientelism (the system is dominated by an elite but beset by continual manoeuvring for position and advantage); third, complex bureaucracy (the system is essentially bureaucratic and decisions are taken inside the system and handed down); and fourth, the culturalist approach (appeals to the cultural resources of the Chinese common practices of hierarchy and obedience).

However, the first of these can be dismissed as it belongs to cold war bloc-think, the second may have been accurate during the post-revolutionary period dominated by Mao Zedong when the future line of development of the country was unclear, and the last noted must carry some weight as humans are social animals, they dwell in communities, shaped by rules handed down. Yet for present purposes, it is the third line that is the most appropriate line of commentary: the party-state system is best conceived as a double bureaucracy and the CCP is the dominant element. The party-state works via a double bureaucracy that runs throughout the People's Republic. It is a vast and nominally unitary organization:

- the party elite is reported to number around 2,500;[124]
- the party has an elaborate hierarchical structure, it is reported to have a membership of some 80 million and it reaches down through a hierarchy of administrative levels producing around 825,000[125] committees of one sort or another, national, provincial, prefectural, municipality, township and village;
- the state runs the other side of the double bureaucracy with the State Council, NPC, Supreme People's Court and Central Military Commission, plus the civil service and provincial and local government, so in total around 7–8 million personnel.

The sum total of the activities of the machinery of the party-state has been recently summed up in terms of the notion of an 'organizational emperor';[126] the system can be read in terms of institutions and culture, so it is top-down but it does adjust, and lately, politically it has drawn in more participants, and commentators speak of a new middle class, and of 'civil society'.

Zheng[127] notes that civil society has grown since reforms began. There is a generational-cum-class element at work, that is, the growth of the middle class, but civil society is controlled and shaped by the state; yet civil society and market consumption offer individuals a way of acting outside party-state specified politics, that is, as individualistic consumers in a material realm. The reforms have permitted some diversity in patterns of life and this is reflected in the realm of ideas. A sequence of broad debates can be identified: (i) liberalism in the 1980s – along with market reforms and economic growth there was talk of political reform but this comes to a halt in the 1989 Tiananmen Square episode; (ii) nationalism from the 1990s – the elite stress nationalism and this is ongoing and often aimed at Japan and, thereafter, the West in general; (iii) New Left from the 1990s – sections of the elite respond to the negatives of headlong growth and stress the role of the state in tackling inequality, and they support Bo Xilai and the 'Chongqing model' whilst key elite figures resist and favour the 'Guangdong model'; (iv) cultural renaissance from the 2000s – the elite encourage the rediscovery of traditional China in order to further celebrate the 'China model', and whilst many join in this debate, there is no consensus as to its substance or purpose.

Finally, Zheng[128] adds one further issue, federalism. The relationship between peripheral players (provinces, cities and so on) and the core in Beijing has been debated since Sun Yat Sen. It revolves around the issue of centralization versus decentralization and thus the shifting balance of power between the cores and the peripheries. The post-Deng reforms implied greater power for the provinces, as economic development produces differentiation, but post-1989 the core has reasserted itself, and now there are complex ongoing power games, and whilst the core is not losing, the peripheries are not winning, and so it is a sort of de facto federalism.

However, that said, the reformed party-state is not oriented towards the goal of liberal democracy, and critical voices and novel social groups are absorbed as the inherited and unitary system adjusts.

Domestic Politics 2: Popular Understandings and Activities, the Internet

The internal dynamics of the party-state system have recently had to find ways of dealing with Internet-based communication. The use of computers and mobile phones is extensive throughout China, and the interaction between this digital realm and the machineries of the party-state system is fluid; thus, extensive criticisms of the party-state are made online as are criticisms of foreign powers, but, contrariwise, the state machinery is home to a large number of Internet censors and the leadership stress that the Internet sphere – like others – is subject to domestic law.[129]

Digital communication/Internet sovereignty in China
Advances in information technology have inevitably facilitated the exchange of information and ideas and enhanced interactions amongst people. The Internet enables citizens to easily and quickly access information, share information and voice opinions, and allows organizing that was unprecedented and unimaginable in the past.[130] China has the largest Internet user base in the world. According to *The 36th Statistical Report on Internet Development in China*, China's netizen population had reached 668 million and the number of people who accessed the Internet via mobile devices totalled 594 million by June 2015.[131] Netizens in China make use of the online social networking portal, online chat rooms or micro-blogging sites to express their opinions, discuss current affairs, expose wrongdoings by local officials and mobilize people to join protests. For example, Sina Weibo, which is loosely modelled on Twitter, is a popular social networking platform in China. Nowadays, the general public in China 'are remarkably less dependent on traditional news media and find new ways to satisfy their information and entertainment appetite'.[132] Realizing that the Internet was developing rapidly and the number of Internet users was increasing drastically in China, the Political Bureau of the CPC Central Committee in 2007 'held a session to discuss the development and administration of the new media'.[133]

E-government development in China
Electronic government (e-government) refers to the delivery of government information and services through information and communication technology (ICT), in particular the Internet, to the general public and other government agencies. In China, promoting the use of ICT is referred to with the term informatization or *Xinxihua* in Chinese, which was first enunciated by former Chinese leader Deng Xiaoping in 1984 for

facilitating economic development and modernization.[134] And 'The pre-occupation with informatization began with a series of "Golden Projects" launched in 1993.'[135] The Golden Projects aimed to create a communication network that connected all the provinces and major cities throughout the nation, foster the sharing of economic information and data exchange, and promote electronic banking.[136] In January 1999, the implementation of the Government Online Project (GOP) 'marked the entry of China's governmental informatization into the Internet'.[137] The GOP aimed to 'interconnect government agencies, make government documents and databases available online and allow the public to transact with the government online'.[138]

In August 2002, the General Office of the CPC Central Committee and the General Office of the State Council jointly issued *Guiding Opinions of the National Informatization Leading Group on the Development of E-government in China* (hereafter the 2002 Guiding Opinions), which stated that the development of e-government would be the main driver for economic growth and social development.[139] According to the 2002 Guiding Opinions, the goal of e-government development was to establish a standardized, secure and reliable e-government network platform with comprehensive functions in order to improve and strengthen the management capacity, decision-making capacity, risk management capacity and capacity for public service delivery of government departments and bureaus.[140] In 2006, the General Office of the CPC Central Committee and the General Office of the State Council jointly issued *National Informatization Development Strategy (2006–2020)*, which emphasized the strategic importance of developing e-government in fostering the development of informatization. It strived to improve the quantity and quality of public service online, provide more citizen-oriented e-government services and strengthen the overall regulation of e-government.[141]

The 2012 United Nations E-government Survey, which assessed the e-government development status of the 193 United Nations (UN) Member States, showed that China ranked 78 in the E-government Development Index (EGDI).[142] EGDI was 'a composite indicator measuring the willingness and capacity of national administrations to use information and communication technology to deliver public services'.[143] China belonged to middle-scoring countries in the 2012 E-government Survey. But the UN argued that China had made progress in e-government: 'China has enhanced the quality of its government portal by providing comprehensive information, more integrated services across different sectors, and greater interactions between government officials and citizens.'[144]

In the 2014 UN E-government Survey, China raised its ranking to 70th in the EGDI.[145] But China lagged far behind the Republic of Korea, Singapore and Japan, which respectively ranked 1, 3 and 6 in the EGDI.[146] The excellent achievement of the Republic of Korea, Singapore and Japan was attributed to their developed economies; developed Information Technology (IT) infrastructure; and high IT literacy rate.[147] The 2014 Survey showed that China still had much to do to move to the upper level of e-government.

Digital communication under the Hu-Wen administration

Commentators argue that digital 'communication changed how states relate to their citizens'.[148] Even authoritarian regimes like China cannot be immune from this digital revolution. The Internet affects the day-to-day operations of government and has become a useful channel for Chinese leaders and government officials to solicit public opinions. They can interact with citizens more easily. In 2003, former Foreign Minister Li Zhaoxing had a two-hour online chat with netizens or Internet users concerning China's foreign policy.[149] In January 2007, former Chinese President Hu Jintao urged members of the Political Bureau of the CPC Central Committee 'to improve their Internet literacy and use the Internet well so as to improve the art of leadership'.[150] In June 2008, Hu Jintao had his first live online chat with netizens via the website of *People's Daily*, which is a major news portal in China.[151] It was the first time in Chinese history that the top leader interacted with netizens online. Netizens greeted Hu with a flood of questions, ranging from corruption, Sino-Taiwanese relations and price hikes.[152] When having the online chat with netizens, Hu said that 'the Internet is a major channel to gather opinion and wisdom from the public'.[153]

In February 2009, former premier Wen Jiabao had his first online chat with netizens, which was jointly hosted by the central government website and the Xinhua News Agency website and answered questions related to the economy, real estate prices, education, employment and health care.[154] When having a two-hour online chat with netizens, Wen said that people 'have the right to criticize government policy and government also needs to be open and democratic in its policy-making'.[155] Besides, municipal governments, local legislature and the Legislative Affairs Office of the State Council made use of their official websites to collect public opinions on government projects and draft laws or regulations. For example, the Legislative Affairs Office of the State Council in 2007 'collected opinions on seven sets of draft regulations and received 16,888 opinions from more than 9,000 people'[156] through an information management system established on its official website.

In 2010, China ranked 32 in the E-participation Index in the UN E-government Survey.[157] The UN praised the Chinese government for being 'active in soliciting comments through online channels for consideration in decision-making'.[158] It recognized that Chinese top leaders did a good job in promoting e-participation in China. The 2010 UN E-government Survey praised that:[159]

> The emerging trend of e-participation in China has been given a boost by top leaders, among them Premier Wen Jiabao who has held online chat sessions with the aim of soliciting ideas that could inform Government policy in advance of the annual meeting of the National People's Congress.

According to the 2014 UN E-government Survey, China was one of the top 50 performers in e-participation.[160] The report showed that the Chinese government had made a great effort to increase their outreach to citizens and foster civic engagement in policy making. Nevertheless, the new cyber security policy implemented under the leadership of Xi Jinping indicated that in reality the input of citizens in policy making might in fact be very limited.

Stricter Internet control and the idea of Internet sovereignty under Xi Jinping

Since Xi came to power in March 2013, he has imposed stricter Internet controls and accelerated Internet censorship to a whole new level in China. He emphasizes the concept of Internet sovereignty, which refers to the right and ultimate power of a country to regulate and censor all electronic content transmitted within its national border. In fact, the concept of Internet sovereignty was first rolled out in a 2010 White Paper called *The Internet in China*, which was published by the State Council Information Office. The 2010 White Paper declared that: 'Within Chinese territory the Internet is under the jurisdiction of Chinese sovereignty. The Internet sovereignty of China should be respected and protected.'[161]

But the concept of Internet sovereignty was resurrected by Xi after Edward Snowden's revelations that the USA had been hacking into Chinese computer networks since 2009. Xi repeatedly reiterated the importance of respecting a nation's Internet sovereignty in public. When giving a speech to Brazil's National Congress in July 2014, Xi stressed that 'information technology of one country must not be used to violate Internet sovereignty of other countries ... [and that] ... a country cannot pursue its own Internet security at the price of threatening the security of other countries.'[162]

In November 2014, Xi stressed in China's first World Internet Conference that China was willing to join hands with other countries to 'respect Internet sovereignty, uphold Internet security and safeguard peace, security, openness and cooperation of the cyberspace.'[163] The official remarks made by Xi indicated that respecting Internet sovereignty was a shared responsibility amongst countries, and it was something that a responsible power should do and required international cooperation. It shows that China is 'seeking to shape global norms of internet governance'[164] by promoting the concept of Internet sovereignty that 'favours the authority of a nation-state over its netizens'.[165] Local media interpreted that the concept of Internet sovereignty endorsed by Xi carried two meanings: 'Internally, each country had the right to independently and autonomously develop, regulate and manage its domestic Internet issues ... [and] externally, each country had the right to defend its Internet from outside intrusion or attack.'[166]

Blocking the use of Virtual Private Networks (VPNs) was the recent action taken by the Chinese government to protect its Internet sovereignty, and an example of the stricter Internet control that have caused huge controversies and dismay at home and abroad. In January 2015, the Chinese government widely blocked the use of VPNs in order to prohibit Internet users from visiting overseas websites by circumventing the firewall system. As a result, Internet users could not freely access popular websites and services like Google, Facebook, Twitter, YouTube and news portals in the USA. The Chinese government did not give a clear explanation for such a move, but said that new measures were needed following the Internet development. It was believed that the real reasons for the government blocking VPNs were preserving China's Internet sovereignty, forbidding Internet users to read politically sensitive issues that would undermine the rule of the CCP, and fostering the business of Chinese Internet companies like Alibaba, Tencent and Baidu. However, VPN blocking came with a price. The immediate effect was that VPN blocking limited what the local population could read and discuss online. It brought inconvenience to students and scholars who needed to access foreign literature and those who wanted to stay tuned into the rest of the world. It also brought inconvenience to domestic and foreign companies doing business in China, foreign residents and investors who wanted to contact friends and clients overseas. In the long run, VPN blocking will have negative implications for the exchange of ideas and information. It will also stifle innovation and jeopardize economic development and growth.

Another measure introduced by the Chinese government was the real-name registration system. In February 2015, the Cyberspace

Administration of China promulgated *The Internet Users' Account Names Management Regulations* (hereafter the 2015 Internet Regulation), which came into effect on 1 March 2015. According to the 2015 Internet Regulation, users of blogs, microblogs, instant-messaging services, online discussion forums, news comment sections and related services were required to register accounts using their real names.[167] Besides, users were required to agree to seven bottom lines before being allowed to use a given service, which included 'respect the law, the socialist system, national interests, civil rights, public order, social morality and information authenticity'.[168] They were forbidden to have usernames that harmed national unity or national security, involved national secrets, incited ethnic hatred or discrimination, promoted terror, violence, gambling and pornography, or defamed others. Chinese Internet service providers were responsible for enforcing the 2015 Internet Regulation and verifying the identity of Internet users. The real-name registration policy was regarded as a measure to limit freedom of speech online and prevented anonymous Internet users from spreading rumours that were deemed unsuitable, objectionable or offensive to the Chinese government.

Transforming China into a 'cyber power'

At present, President Xi Jinping is ambitious to transform China into a cyber power through the dual approach of developing IT and safeguarding cyber security.[169] Being the chairman of China's new Central Internet Security and Informatization Leading Group, Xi emphasized that 'Internet security and informatization is a major strategic issue concerning a country's security and development as well as people's life and work.'[170] He pointed out that cyber security and informatization were like 'two wings of a bird and two wheels of an engine'.[171] For this reason, these two aspects should be advanced simultaneously. Xi said that 'without cyber security, there will be no national security; without informatization, there will be no modernization'.[172] Hence, the Central Internet Security and Informatization Leading Group is designed to lead, coordinate and oversee issues related to cyber security and informatization amongst different sectors, and 'formulate national strategies, development plans and major policies for cyber security and informatization'.[173]

International freedom versus international security

Commentators note that governments are 'struggling to adapt to the new digital landscape'.[174] There is definitely a trade-off between Internet freedom and Internet security as there 'is no such thing as the perfect Internet security system'.[175] Internet penetration and the number of Internet users have drastically increased over time. 'The security threat is constantly changing'[176] and requires the government to make long-term and unremitting efforts to address the issue. In a strong authoritarian regime like China, Internet security will always remain at the top of the political agenda. For the Chinese government, sovereignty is an evolving concept.[177] The Chinese government extends national sovereignty to cyberspace and hence wants to extend sovereign control into cyberspace. It is well aware of the deep and negative implications that cybercrimes, hacking and cyber warfare can bring to the nation, especially when 'states currently exploit cyberspace as a means of gaining a strategic and military advantage over another state'.[178] It believes that 'content sent through cyberspace holds significance in the "real" world'.[179] For this reason, the Chinese government will exert more control on the Internet and continue to keep Internet security threats in check. To sacrifice freedom for the sake of security is deemed reasonable in the eye of the government if the attempt to limit individual freedom can in turn protect national interests.

CONCLUSION: THE PARTY-STATE IN THE TWENTY-FIRST CENTURY

An historical institutionalist analysis directs attention to the particular logic of the state in the modern world. The state is an organizational membrane managing trans-state flows and ordering the domestic sphere: first, it is the machinery that serves to order domestic relationships of power, it is not neutral, it is the framework of public political activity (parliaments, judiciaries, parties, public spheres and so on); and second, it is the machinery that serves to enable the ruling elite to read and react to enfolding global structures of power, determine courses of action, formulate policy and to appropriately discipline the populations subject to their control.

Cast in these terms, there is no single model of a state rather each extant state within the modern world is constituted (domestically) by the historical aggregation of competencies and associated schemes of legitimation, and (internationally) by its relationships with other states. Seen this way, each state is a variant form of the machineries necessary to constitute and lodge discrete polities within the complex modern world, and seen this way it is futile to begin with a general model – American or European or, indeed, Asian – and thereafter try to fit it to specific local circumstances; rather, it is better to begin with the particular local logic, and thereafter an intellectually accumulative strategy of comparison could be pursued.

On this one comment/suggestion:[180]

> It has been historically impossible, and is impossible now, for a state based in China to rule with the consent of the governed, since there are no institutions through which individuals or the public en masse can grant consent. But ruling with the toleration of governed was manifestly the practice of the Qing. Attempts to radically alter that compact ... have all been defeated ... It is not democracy, it cannot emulate democracy, and it seems unclear whether it can lead to democracy. Neither is it despotism ... It is a field of political negotiation ...

The party-state is a system of political exchanges that has brought prosperity to many citizens. However, it is limited in its functioning (endemic corruption, no independent critical voices), it is limited in its ambitions (thus top-down politics and policy making) and confronts major problems (economic restructuring, inequality and environmental pollution). It is also limited in its legitimacy (evidenced in increasingly strident nationalism). Yet, if matters are cast in terms of the history of the country, the party-state serves 1.3 billion people, and over the last 70 years it has – in the main – served them reasonably well.

NOTES

1. See Kerry Brown 2014 *The New Emperors: Power and the Princelings in China*, London, I.B. Tauris.
2. See the early text by Gordon White ed. 1988 *Developmental States in East Asia*, London, Macmillan, but official recognition came with the World Bank 1993 *The East Asian Miracle*, Oxford University Press.
3. See Amitav Acharya 2000 *The Quest for Identity: The International Relations of Southeast Asia*, Oxford University Press.
4. See A.G. Frank 1998 *Re-Orient: Global Economy in the Asian Age*, University of California.
5. See Max Hastings 2008 *Retribution: The Battle for Japan*, New York, Alfred Knopf.
6. See John Dower 1999 *Embracing Defeat: Japan in the Aftermath of World War II*, London, Allen Lane.
7. On the historical development trajectory of Japan, see Barrington Moore Jr. 1966 *The Social Origins of Dictatorship and Democracy*, Boston, Beacon Press; on the politics, see Chalmers Johnson 1995 *Japan: Who Governs?* New York, Norton.
8. John Clammer 1997 *Contemporary Urban Japan*, Oxford, Blackwell.
9. K. van Wolferen 1989 *The Enigma of Japanese Power*, London, Macmillan.
10. Johnson 1995 calls the country a new Venice, that is, an oligarchic trading polity.
11. Ron Dore 1986 *Flexible Rigidities*, Stanford University Press; Ron Dore 1987 *Taking Japan Seriously*, Stanford University Press.
12. Weber was interested in showing ideas count, not in identifying Protestantism as the causal factor in the rise of capitalism, and Confucian hierarchies place merchants low in the scheme of things.
13. Rejected by Clammer 1997.
14. K. Yoshino 1992 *Cultural Nationalism in Contemporary Japan*, London, Routledge.

15. Clammer 1997.
16. Bruce Cummings 1997 *Korea's Place in the Sun: A Modern History*, New York, Norton; Robert Wade 1990 *Governing the Market*, Princeton University Press; Carl A. Trocki 2006 *Singapore: Wealth, Power and the Culture of Control*, London, Routledge; Chiu, S. and Lui, T.L. 2009 *Hong Kong: Becoming a Chinese Global City*, London, Routledge.
17. Richard Stubbs 2005 *Rethinking Asia's Economic Miracle: The Political Economy of War, Prosperity and Crisis*, London, Palgrave.
18. L. Weiss 1998 *The Myth of the Powerless State*, Cornell University Press.
19. R. Bickers 2011 *The Scramble for China: Foreign Devils in the Qing Empire 1832–1914*, London, Allen Lane.
20. Chan, Chak Kwan, Ngok, King-lun and Phillips, David 2008 *Social Policy in China: Development and Well-being*, Bristol, UK, Policy, p. 9.
21. Li, Peilin 2010 'Thirty Years of Reform and Changes of Social Policies' in Li Qiang ed. *Thirty Years of Reform and Social Changes in China*, Leiden, Brill, p. 453.
22. Zheng, Yongnian and Huang, Yanjie 2013 'Political Dynamics of Social Policy Reform in China' in Litao Zhao ed. *China's Social Development and Policy: Into the New Stage?* New York, Routledge, p. 161.
23. Wong, R. Bin 1997 *China Transformed: Historical Change and the Limits of European Experience*, Cornell University Press, p. 67.
24. Wong 1997; C. Tisdell 2009 'Economic Reform and Openness in China: China's Development Policies in the Last 30 Years' in *Economic Analysis and Policy* 39.2.
25. Mok, Ka-ho 2005 'Governing through Governance: Changing Social Policy Paradigms in the Post-Mao People's Republic of China' in J. Jabes ed. *The Role of Public Administration in Alleviating Poverty and Improving Governance*, Asia Development Bank, Online. <http://unpan1.un.org/intradoc/groups/public/documents/unpan/unpan025047. pdf> (accessed 22 October 2014), p. 401.
26. P.P. Jones and T.T. Poleman 1962 'Communes and the Agricultural Crisis in Communist China' in *Food Research Institute Studies* 3.1, p. 5.
27. Yang, Dennis and Fang, Cai 2000 The Political Economy of China's Rural-Urban Divide, Online. <http://iple.cass.cn/upload/2012/06/d20120601171201684.pdf> (accessed 22 October 2014); Yang and Fang 2000 p. 11.
28. Wang, Feng 2010 'Boundaries of Inequality: Perceptions of Distributive Justice among Urbanites, Migrants, and Peasants' in M.K. Whyte ed. *One Country, Two Societies: Rural–Urban Inequality in Contemporary China*, Harvard University Press, pp. 219–40; Wang 2010 p. 221.
29. Li, Peilin 2010 'Thirty Years of Reform and Changes of Social Policies' in Li Qiang ed. *Thirty Years of Reform and Social Changes in China*, Boston, MA, Brill, pp. 453–92; Li 2010 p. 461.
30. Guan, Xinping 2005 'China's Social Policy: Reform and Development in the Context of Marketization and Globalization' in Huck-ju Kwon ed. *Transforming the Developmental Welfare State in East Asia*, New York, Palgrave, pp. 231–56; Guan 2005 p. 232.
31. Guan 2005 p. 232.
32. Li 2010 p. 457.
33. Li 2010 p. 457.
34. Guan 2005 p. 233.
35. Guan 2005 p. 232.
36. J.C.B. Leung 1994 'Dismantling the "Iron Rice Bowl": Welfare Reforms in the People's Republic of China' in *Journal of Social Policy* 23.3, pp. 341–61; Leung 1994 p. 343.
37. Mok 2005 p. 402.
38. Leung 1994 p. 344.
39. Jones and Poleman 1962 p. 6.
40. Guan 2005 p. 232.
41. Jones and Poleman 1962 p. 8.
42. Leung 1994 p. 345.

43. Ngok, King-Lun 2014 'Bringing the State Back in: The Development of Chinese Social Policy in China in the Hu-Wen Era' in Ka Ho Mok and Maggie K.W. Lau eds. *Managing Social Change and Social Policy in Greater China: Welfare Regimes in Transition*, London, Routledge, pp. 96–110; Ngok 2014 p. 97.
44. M. Meisner 1996 *The Deng Xiaoping Era: An Inquiry into the Fate of Chinese Socialism, 1978–1994*, New York, Hill and Wang, p. 201.
45. Meisner 1996 p. 204.
46. Chan et al. 2008 p. 29.
47. J.C.B Leung 1998 'The Transformation of Social Welfare Policy: The Restructuring of the "Iron Rice Bowl"' in Joseph Y.S. Cheng ed. *China in the Post-Deng Era*, The Chinese University of Hong Kong Press, pp. 617–44; Leung 1998 p. 618.
48. Tisdell 2009 pp. 275–6.
49. Ngok, King-Lun and Zhu, Yapeng 2010 'In Search of Harmonious Society in China: A Social Policy Response' in K.H. Mok and Y.W. Ku eds. *Social Cohesion in Greater China: Challenges for Social Policy and Governance*, Singapore, World Scientific, pp. 69–94; Ngok and Zhu 2010 p. 72.
50. Leung 1998 p. 621.
51. Tisdell 2009 p. 276.
52. Leung 1998 p. 620.
53. Chan et al. 2008 p. 27.
54. Ngok, K.L. 2013 'Shaping Social Policy in the Reform Era in China' in Izuhara, M. eds. *Handbook on East Asian Social Policy*, Cheltenham, UK and Northampton, MA, Edward Elgar, p. 105.
55. Mok 2005 p. 403.
56. Ngok 2014 p. 98.
57. Ngok 2013 p. 108.
58. Ngok 2013 p. 109.
59. Ngok 2013 p. 109.
60. Tisdell 2009 p. 280.
61. MacKinnon 2011.
62. Chan et al. 2008 p. 34.
63. Zhu, R. 2013 *Zhu Rongji on the Record: The Road to Reform, 1991–1997*, Washington, DC, Brookings Institution Press, p. 256.
64. Zheng and Huang 2013 p. 163.
65. Chan et al. 2008 p. 55.
66. Leung 1998 p. 624.
67. Thelle, H. 2004 *Better to Rely on Ourselves: Changing Social Rights in Urban China since 1979*, Copenhagen, NIAS Press, p. 167.
68. Zhu 2013 p. 257.
69. Li 2010 p. 466.
70. Leung 1998 p. 630.
71. Li 2010 p. 466.
72. Thelle 2004 p. 184.
73. Chan et al. 2008 p. 55.
74. Ngok, King-Lun and Zhu, Yapeng 2010 p. 69.
75. Li 2010 p. 484.
76. China Daily 2007 September 29 Harmonious Society, Online. <http://english.peopledaily.com.cn/90002/92169/92211/6274603.html> (accessed 30 October 2014).
77. Hu, Jintao 2007 Report to the Seventeenth National Congress of the Communist Party of China on Oct. 15, 2007, Online. <http://www.china.org.cn/english/congress/229611.htm> (accessed 30 October 2014).
78. Hu 2007.
79. Hu 2007.
80. Hu, Jintao 2012 Full Texts of Hu Jintao's Report at 18th Party Congress, Online. <http://english.cntv.cn/20121118/100129.shtml> (accessed 30 October 2014).

81. Rong, Jiaojiao 2012 China Strives for Free Compulsory Education for All. Xinhua News October 5, Online. <http://news.xinhuanet.com/english/2006-10/05/content_5169944. htm> (accessed 31 October 2014).

82. People's Daily 2012 September 25 Almost Billion Yuan Added to Textbook Budget This Year, Online. <http://english.people.com.cn>.

83. People's Daily 2012.

84. Wu, Lejun 2012 Xi Jinping Met With WHO Director-General (Chinese version), People's Daily July 21, Online. <http://politics.people.com.cn/n/2012/0721/c1024-18566794.html> (accessed 5 November 2014).

85. Beijing Normal University 2014 Chairman Xi Jinping Called on the Nation's Teacher to Be a Party & People-Satisfied Teacher, Online. <http://english.bnu.edu.cn/2014-09-09> (accessed 5 November 2014).

86. Xinhua News 2013 September 26 Xi Jinping: China Will Work Hard to Promote Education for All and Life-long Education (Chinese version), Online. <http://news. xinhuanet.com>.

87. South China Morning Post 2013 October 30 China to Boost Availability of Affordable Homes, Says Xi Jinping, Online. <www.scmp.com>.

88. South China Morning Post 2013 October 30.

89. China News 2013 November 5 Ministry of Civil Affairs: Ageing Population Grows Quickly, Ageing Population Reaches 200 Million This Year (Chinese), Online. <www-.chinanews.com> (accessed 26 September 2014).

90. Xinhua News 2012 October 1 China Focus: Long Holiday Plagues Single White Collars, Online. <http://news.xinhuanet.com> (accessed 26 September 2014).

91. Xinhua News 2003 October 8 23.4 Million Empty Nesters Struggle to Live Alone, Online. <http://news.xinhuanet.com> (accessed 26 September 2014).

92. Xinhua News 2013 February 7 China Legislates to Maintain Spring Festival Tradition, Online. <http://news.xinhuanet.com> (accessed 26 September 2014).

93. Xinhua News 2013 October 11 Xinhua Insight: Aging China Faces Elder Neglect, Online. <http://news.xinhuanet.com> (accessed 26 September 2014).

94. Xinhua News 2013 October 11.

95. Xinhua News 2012 October 22 Xinhua Insight: Graying China in Dire Need of Senior Care, Online. <http://news.xinhuanet.com> (accessed 26 September 2014).

96. Xinhua News 2012 October 22.

97. Xinhua News 2014 April 23 Around China: Yellow Ribbons Tied by China's Empty Nesters, Online. <http://news.xinhuanet.com> (accessed 26 September 2014).

98. Xinhua News 2013 October 11 Xinhua Insight: Aging China Faces Elder Neglect, Online. <http://news.xinhuanet.com> (accessed 26 September 2014).

99. Xinhua News 2011 October 27 China Explores In-home Nursing As Population Pressure Grows, Online. <http://news.xinhuanet.com> (accessed 26 September 2014).

100. All-China Women's Federation 2013 December 18 SE China Establishes Care Station for Left-behind Children, Online. <www.womenofchina.cn> (accessed 28 September 2014).

101. All-China Women's Federation 2013 December 18 SE China Establishes Care Station for Left-behind Children, Online. <www.womenofchina.cn> (accessed 28 September 2014).

102. All-China Women's Federation 2014 March 12 NPC Deputy Urges More Care for Left-behind Children, Online. <www.womenofchina.cn> (accessed 28 September 2014).

103. All-China Women's Federation 2014 March 12 NPC Deputy Urges More Care for Left-behind Children, Online. <www.womenofchina.cn> (accessed 28 September 2014).

104. All-China Women's Federation 2014 June 4 Spotlight on Mental Health of Left-behind Children, Online. <www.womenofchina.cn> (accessed 28 September 2014).

105. All-China Women's Federation 2013 August 11 China's Left-behind Children Face Multiple Challenges, Online. <www.womenofchina.cn> (accessed 28 September 2014).

106. All-China Women's Federation 2014 March 12 NPC Deputy Urges More Care for Left-behind Children, Online. <www.womenofchina.cn> (accessed 28 September 2014).

107. Xinhua News 2014 April 14 Guizhou to Build 800 Nurseries for 'Left-behind' Children, Online. <http://news.xinhuanet.com> (accessed 26 September 2014).

108. All-China Women's Federation 2014 January 12 China: 80% of Migrant-worker Parents with 'Left-behind' Children Feel Inadequate, Online. <www.womenofchina.cn> (accessed 28 September 2014).

109. All-China Women's Federation 2014 January 12 China: 80% of Migrant-worker Parents with 'Left-behind' Children Feel Inadequate, Online. <www.womenofchina.cn> (accessed 28 September 2014).

110. In May 2014, the report released at the 21st International Federation for Psychotherapy (IFP) World Congress of Psychotherapy in Shanghai shows that over 50 per cent of 300 'left-behind' children in rural China surveyed suffer from behavioural and emotional disorders. In particular, depression and paranoia are prevalent amongst boys aged between 12 and 16. The experts call for the provision of medical counselling for these children.

111. All-China Women's Federation 2012 July 27 30% Chinese Left-behind Children Feel Helpless, Online <www.womenofchina.cn> (accessed 28 September 2014).

112. All-China Women's Federation 2013 December 18 SE China Establishes Care Station for Left-behind Children, Online. <www.womenofchina.cn> (accessed 28 September 2014).

113. All-China Women's Federation 2014 June 2 China Trains Social Workers to Help Left-behind Children, Online. <www.womenofchina.cn> (accessed 28 September 2014).

114. Xinhua News 2014 April 17 School in Ningxia Sets Up Counseling Room for Left-behind Children, Online. <http://news.xinhuanet.com> (accessed 26 September 2014).

115. Xinhua News 2014 April 14 Guizhou to Build 800 Nurseries for 'Left-behind' Children, Online <http://news.xinhuanet.com> (accessed 26 September 2014).

116. All-China Women's Federation 2013 December 18 SE China Establishes Care Station for Left-behind Children, Online. <www.womenofchina.cn> (accessed 28 September 2014).

117. All-China Women's Federation 2014 July 30 Henan Provides Day-Care Services to 'Left-behind' Children, Online. <www.womenofchina.cn> (accessed 28 September 2014).

118. All-China Women's Federation 2014 March 26 Henan to Construct 'Left-behind Children's Home', Online. <www.womenofchina.cn> (accessed 28 September 2014).

119. All-China Women's Federation 2014 March 12 NPC Deputy Urges More Care for Left-behind Children, Online. <www.womenofchina.cn> (accessed 28 September 2014).

120. D. Shambaugh 2008 *China's Communist Party: Atrophy and Adaptation*, University of California Press.

121. K. O'Brien and L. Li 2006 *Rightful Resistance in Rural China*, Cambridge University Press.

122. C.R. Hughes 2006 *Chinese Nationalism in the Global Era*, London, Routledge.

123. F. Christiansen and S. Rai 1996 *Chinese Politics and Society: An Introduction*, Hemel Hempstead, UK, Prentice Hall.

124. Cited in Brown 2014 p. 20.

125. R. McGregor 2012 *The Party: The Secret World of China's Communist Rulers*, London, Penguin, p.xi.

126. Zheng, Yongnian 2010 *The Chinese Communist Party as Organizational Emperor: Culture, Reproduction and Transformation*, London, Routledge.

127. Zheng 2014 see chapters 5 and 7.

128. Zheng 2014 see chapter 8.

129. A point made explicitly by Xi Jinping at the Wuzhen Conference, December 2015; reported in *The Guardian* December 16 2015.

130. S.B. Edwards III and D. Santos eds. 2015 *Revolutionizing the Interaction between State and Citizens through Digital Communications*, Hershey, IGI Global, p.xv.

131. The China Internet Network Information Centre 2015 The 36th Statistical Report on Internet Development in China (Chinese version), Online. <http://www.cnnic.cn/hlwfzyj/hlwxzbg/hlwtjbg/201507/P020150723549500667087.pdf> (accessed 29 July 2015), p. 1.

132. People's Daily 2008 June 20 President Hu Promises Divergent Voices Be Heard Online, Online. <http://en.people.cn/90001/90776/90785/6434293.html> (accessed 30 July 2015).

133. Xinhuanet 2007 November 2 Internet Becomes Important Channel for Chinese Public's Political Participation, Online. <http://news.xinhuanet.com/english/2007-11/02/content_6998791.htm> (accessed 30 July 2015).

134. Luk, Sabrina Ching Yuen 2013 'E-government in China: Opportunities and Challenges for the Transformation of Governance in the Information Age' in Bin Wu, Shujie Yao and Jian Chen eds. *China's Development and Harmonization: Towards a Balance with Nature, Society and the International Community*, New York, Routledge Curzon, p. 194.

135. K. Harford 2003 'West Lake Wired: Shaping Hangzhou's Information Age' in Chin-Chuan Lee ed. *Chinese Media, Global Contexts*, New York, Routledge Curzon, p. 173.

136. Tai, Zixue 2006 *The Internet in China: Cyberspace and Civil Society*, New York, Routledge, p. 125.

137. Good Governance International Corp. 2013 The China E-government Development Index Report 2013: Experiences in Hangzhou Municipality, Zhejiang Province, Online.<http://goodgovintl.org/dev/wp-content/uploads/2013/12/CEDI-REPORT-Part-One-ENGLISH.pdf> (accessed 2 August 2015), p. 23.

138. Luk 2013 p. 194.

139. The General Office of the CPC Central Committee and the General Office of the State Council 2002 Guiding Opinions of the National Informatization Leading Group on the Development of E-government in China (Chinese version), Online. <http://xzjc.zunyi.gov.cn/ch7625/ch7626/2011/04/27/content_2011180423.shtml> (accessed 2 August 2015).

140. The General Office of the CPC Central Committee and the General Office of the State Council 2002.

141. The General Office of the CPC Central Committee and the General Office of the State Council 2006 National Informatization Development Strategy (2006–2020) (Chinese version), Online. <http://www.cast.org.cn/n35081/n38213/n38259/10300409.html> (accessed 2 August 2015).

142. The United Nations 2012 The United Nations E-government Survey 2012: E-government for the People, Online. <http://unpan3.un.org/egovkb/en-us/Reports/UN-E-Government-Survey-2012> (accessed 2 August 2015), p. 12.

143. The United Nations 2012 p. 119.

144. The United Nations 2012 p. 25.

145. The United Nations 2014 United Nations E-government Survey 2014: E-government for the Future We Want, Online. <http://unpan3.un.org/egovkb/en-us/Reports/UN-E-Government-Survey-2014> (accessed 2 August 2015), p. 200.

146. The United Nations 2014 p. 15.

147. The United Nations 2014 p. 27.

148. Edwards III and Santos 2015 p.xv.

149. Xinhua News Agency 2004 March 3 Cyber Chat Topics Cover A to Z, Online. <http://www.china.org.cn/english/2004/Mar/89125.htm> (accessed 30 July 2015).

150. Xinhuanet 2009 March 2 Chinese Lawmakers to Talk with Netizens during 'Two Sessions', Online. <http://news.xinhuanet.com/english/2009-03/02/content_10929819.htm> (accessed 30 July 2015).

151. China Daily 2008 June 20 Chinese President Takes Part in Online Chat, Online. <http://www.chinadaily.com.cn/china/2008-06/20/content_6781790.htm> (accessed 30 July 2015).

152. Xinhuanet 2008 June 20 Chinese President Holds First Web Chat with Citizens, Online. <http://news.xinhuanet.com/english/2008-06/20/content_8406447.htm> (accessed 30 July 2015).

153. Xinhuanet 2008 June 20.

154. Xinhuanet 2009a February 28 Premier Wen Talks Online with Netizens, Online. <http://news.xinhuanet.com/english/2009-02/28/content_10917460.htm> (accessed 30 July 2015).

155. Xinhuanet 2009b February 28 People Have Right to Criticize Gov't, Says Chinese Premier Wen, Online. <http://news.xinhuanet.com/english/2009-02/28/content_10917646.htm> (accessed 30 July 2015).

156. Xinhuanet 2008 February 22 China's State Council to Use Internet for Public Opinion, Online. <http://news.xinhuanet.com/english/2008-02/22/content_7651001.htm> (accessed 30 July 2015).

157. The United Nations 2010 The United Nations E-government Survey 2010: Leveraging E-government at a Time of Financial and Economic Crisis, Online. <http://unpan3.un.org/egovkb/en-us/Reports/UN-E-Government-Survey-2010> (accessed 2 August 2015), p. 124.

158. The United Nations 2010 p. 89.

159. The United Nations 2010 p. 89.

160. The United Nations 2014 p. 65.

161. The State Council Information Office 2010 The Internet in China, Online. <http://news.xinhuanet.com/english2010/china/2010-06/08/c_13339232.htm> (accessed 31 July 2015).

162. Wu, Jiao and Zhao, Shengnan 2014 Xi: Respect Cyber Sovereignty, Online. <http://usa.chinadaily.com.cn/epaper/2014-07/17/content_17818027.htm> (accessed 1 August 2015).

163. Sina News 2014 November 19 Xi Jinping: Respect Internet Sovereignty, Maintain Internet Security (Chinese version), Online. <http://news.sina.com.cn/2014-11-19/093431169770.shtml> (accessed 1 August 2015).

164. T. Stevens 2015 China's Ban on Virtual Private Networks, Online. <http://thesigers.com/analysis/2015/3/11/chinas-ban-on-virtual-private-networks> (accessed 1 August 2015).

165. Jiang, Min 2013 China's 'Internet Sovereignty', Online. <http://www.fairobserver.com/politics/chinas-internet-sovereignty/> (accessed 1 August 2015).

166. Lan, Min 2014 Internet Governance and Respect Internet Sovereignty (Chinese version), Online. <http://gb.cri.cn/42071/2014/11/26/882s4780005.htm> (accessed 1 August 2015).

167. Cyberspace Administration of China 2015 The Internet Users' Account Names Management Regulations (Chinese version), Online. <http://www.cac.gov.cn/2015-02/04/c_1114246561.htm> (accessed 1 August 2015).

168. Cyberspace Administration of China 2015.

169. Xinhuanet 2014 February 27 Xi Jinping: Transforming China from a 'Big Cyber Country' into a 'Cyber Power' (Chinese version), Online. <http://thediplomat.com/2014/02/xi-jinping-leads-chinas-new-internet-security-group/> (accessed 30 July 2015).

170. Shannon Tiezzi 2014 Xi Jinping Leads China's New Internet Security Group, Online. <http://thediplomat.com/2014/02/xi-jinping-leads-chinas-new-internet-security-group/> (accessed 30 July 2015).

171. Xinhuanet 2014 February 27.

172. Xinhuanet 2014 February 27.

173. Xinhuanet 2014 February 27.

174. Edwards III and Santos 2015 p.xviii.

175. Bloomsbury 2009 *Business Essential*, A & C Black Publishers Ltd, p. 275.

176. Bloomsbury 2009 p. 275.

177. Adam Segal 2013 Cyberspace Cannot Live without Sovereignty, Says Lu Wei, Online. <http://blogs.cfr.org/asia/2013/12/10/cyberspace-cannot-live-without-sovereignty-says-lu-wei/#cid=soc-twitter-at-blogs-cyberspace_cannot_live_without-121013> (accessed 1 August 2015).

178. P. Franzese 2009 'Sovereignty in Cyberspace: Can It Exist?' in *Air Force Law Review* 64, p. 14.

179. Franzese 2009 p. 14.

180. P.K. Crossley 2010 *The Wobbling Pivot: China since 1800*, Chichester, UK, Wiley-Blackwell, p. 272.

6. Contemporary China: international politics

East Asia entered the modern world through the long, disruptive experience of absorption, formal or informal, into the expanding state-empire systems of the Europeans, plus later the Americans and Japanese. These state-empire systems reached an apogee in the years before the European Great War, but thereafter the conflicts amongst the core countries of empire spilled over and drew in distant colonial holdings. The impacts of war, later depression and the Second World War, fatally undermined these systems; local agents took their chance and state-empire systems dissolved into the contemporary pattern of sovereign nation states.

These intermingled processes of dissolution and reconstitution have produced an international political pattern which comprises three major players, along with a host of variously positioned smaller players, allies or otherwise of one or other power. In East Asia today there are three key players, the USA, Japan and China. There are significant secondary players, South Korea and Taiwan, along with the Association of Southeast Asian Nations (ASEAN) countries. And there are distinctive contemporary issues including legacies of decolonization, legacies of cold war and the effects of decades of economic success upon patterns of relationships within the region and between the region and the wider global system. Most recently, there have been changes in country interactions following the end of the cold war and, most especially, the rise of China.

Commentators argue that 2008 marked the symbolic emergence of the PRC onto the international political stage, and the rhetoric of the government revolves around the notion of peaceful rising, but foreigners are sceptical, and most Western commentators tend to the view that the Beijing elite reads the international world in realist terms, that is, in terms of simple power relations. It may be true, or it may simply be a projection, an approach ascribed to Beijing generated simply by the basic assumptions of mainstream international relations theory. Unsurprisingly, in contrast, writers in China often present a positive view, that is, that official declarations in respect of 'peaceful rising' do in fact grasp the truth of these matters. It could be added that these exchanges, most especially when expressed in the mass media, often have an ideological tinge, hence arguments on behalf of Washington confront arguments on behalf of Beijing. Such debates have their own utility. However, in contrast to both lines of commentary, in this text we have embraced an approach grounded in historical institutionalism supplemented by culture critical work – hence institutions, agents and ideas – and this points to an agenda centred on the historical trajectory of the Chinese elite's dealings with neighbours, allies and enemies.

INTERNATIONAL RELATIONS IN EAST ASIA: IDENTIFYING THE ISSUES

Cast in substantive terms (and drawing on the insights of both historians[1] and development theorists[2]), following the collapse of the system of state-empires the elites of the new states and nations faced significant domestic problems in creating states, building nations and, thereafter, pursuing development, and after that equally challenging international problems of managing the demands of the international system, which offered further problems for the new governments of countries within the region. Unpacking these a little in respect of international politics produces a simple agenda of problems/issues: building states, accommo- dating regional problems and later dealing with unfolding questions of regional prosperity.

So, first, most immediately, as state-empires dissolved, aspirant replacement elites had to stake their claim to territory and build states, thus there were local issues of borders, basic law, citizenship, official languages, the status of minorities and so on. Plus there was the routine business of international politics, involving diplomatic recognition and the apparatus of international relations and cooperations, as elites lodged their states within the international system of states – in retrospect, straightforward, at the time, anything but simple.

Thereafter, second, there were regional issues relating to the cold war concerns of outside powers. Local states had outward-oriented alliance linkages with the USA and the USSR (trade links, aid links and military links); local states could become involved in proxy wars (notably Korea and Vietnam); local states could combine as part of the Non-Aligned Movement (embracing elements of the Global South) or, more restrict- edly, as ASEAN (covering Southeast Asia); and local states could also find that they were subject to the demands of larger powers (in regard to terrorism or trade in weapons or drugs or other goods).

Then, third, newer regional/global issues have emerged relating to the increasing importance of East Asian countries within the wider global system; thus the role of Japan or, more recently, China, as both are significant economic powers, and the growth of an element of integration within East Asia itself – hence 'the East Asian region'.

****

Once the process of dissolution and reconstruction had run at least its preliminary course, the region became home to a number of new nation states, but in the late 1940s and 1950s there were many international political difficulties – the disruptions of the end of the Chinese Civil War, the Korean War and the overarching division of the region into two hostile blocs – at which point, intellectually, scholars in international relations theory began to make a contribution to unpacking the logics of unfolding events.

Mainstream[3] international relations theory developed in the wake of the 1914–18 Great War in Europe. There have been a number of shifts in thinking within this tradition: a sequence of theories (from idealism to realism), a sequence of locales (from Europe to the USA) and a sequence of epistemes (from philosophical/critical to scientistic). The upshot is that American work dominates the core of the discipline and lays claim to scientific status.[4] Communities of non-American scholars are obliged to respond: either embrace the core and work within its frameworks or alternatively look to local, intellectual/moral resources and ground a distinct approach in these materials. In this vein some scholars have called for a dialogue between Chinese and European scholars, where both tend, presently, to look to the USA.[5]

The central preoccupation of mainstream work is with the nature and management of human conflict. There are three main lines of contemporary theory. First, realism/neo-realism, which sees the global system as anarchical: states assert their own power through the state/military in competition with others and a rough balance of power might be achieved but a hegemonic power can ensure system stability. It is the dominant position within international relations theory and has been heavily criticized as it radically oversimplifies and is implausibly positivistic. So, the first line of analysis invites us to look at relations of power (primarily military). Second, neo-liberalism sees the global system as extensively organized through both state/military power relations and through market trading relationships. The system may lack an overarching source of authority, but there are many agreements and rules on state and market power that help to create international order. It is a supplementary position in international relations theory and is seen as usefully calling attention to economic interlinkages. It has been criticized as too sanguine about the development of the global capitalist system (economic interests can create conflict as well as build cooperation) and rather blasé about conflict (there are conflicts and the military does have a clear, continuing role). So, the second line of analysis invites us to look at relations of economics (trade and trans-national production). And third, constructivism, which insists that the international system is a social/cultural system, and like other social/cultural systems, it is a construct. It has no final grounding, state/military relations depend on perceptions in respect of the power and intentions of prospective enemies and market relations depend on routine interactions based, finally, on nothing more than subjective agreements about what is and what is not worth trading/having; and so the current international system is thus radically contingent. The approach has been criticized/dismissed by mainstream international relations theorists as hopelessly vague, and critics say that proponents cannot formulate clear testable hypotheses, but in reply adherents claim that once free of the illusory goal of a natural science style status, all social science looks vague, and it is not a problem. So, interpretive work gets at the ways in which people think, and international relations are a species of social relationship.

The third noted approach of social constructivism invites us to look at how policy makers view the world, as understanding and action are always bounded by given circumstances and the demands of particular audiences. As noted this text is based in historical institutionalism and culture criticism; other approaches can be envisaged, and in Latin America local scholars starting during the upheavals of the Second World War created an approach to reading their own circumstances that culminated in what became known as dependency theory. In a similar fashion scholars in China have long been concerned with the exchange of those ideas that are part and parcel of the modern world with those lodged within the broad cultural traditions of China itself. It is an area of reflection that begins in the late nineteenth century with the debates around self-strengthening, has been pursued down the decades and now reprised in discussions of a 'Chinese international relations theory'.

Nele Noesselt[6] argues that China's rise to a global power has provoked discussion. Some Western commentators have deployed mainstream ideas. Some Chinese scholars have used the same intellectual resources. And some Chinese scholars have looked for a 'Chinese approach to international relations theory', and this last noted concern is not simply abstract theorizing, it engages with policy making in China and reacts to outside characterizations of China.

Two intellectual sources can be identified, including a Sinicized Marxism and a new current reading of Confucianism, and these streams have merged and found expression in notions of harmonious society and peaceful rising, and these, in turn, interact with imported ideas of international relations theory, in particular realism. So the mix is subtle, and the party-state affirms an official view of the world informed by Sinicized Marxism and scholars work within and with reference to this frame. Hu Jintao re-emphasized the importance of Marx in 2004.

In addition to this stream of enquiry, other scholars have turned to Confucianism, an indigenous tradition. Yan Xuetong and the 'Tsinghua group' have looked to take ideas from this tradition, identifying three ways of ruling: kingship, hegemony and tyranny. The former resonates with the party-state's self-presentation as an alternative to the expansionary power of empire. Others pick up the idea of China as a 'civilization state', an alternative to competitive, Westphalia-type states. These are utopian-style arguments and they pick up a long tradition amongst Chinese scholars: formally, description and exhortation in light of an ideal, and, substantively, discussions from the late nineteenth century Self-Strengthening Movement; that is, they work differently from mainstream international relations theory (with its affirmation of notion/status of science). However, these domestic debates are not all of a piece and there are many strands and differences of emphasis. In all, the notion of a Chinese approach targets two audiences: first, domestic, celebrating the distinctive nature of the history, polity and approach to international politics of China; second, international, seeking to defuse threat perceptions via the celebration of soft power, the ideal of harmony.

It may be read as another variant of the idea of Asian Values or the Asian Model – attempts to step outside foreign imposed intellectual categories. One comparator might be dependency theory as this was a local attempt to theorize the historical development experience of Latin America. It was home grown; thereafter, it attracted the attention of others outside Latin America. In this vein, Victoria Tin-bor Hui[7] considers recent Chinese scholarship, notes that many are concerned to reject the idea that the country's foreign policy is realist, and then goes on to note the tendency to conflate the history of ideas with history per se and suggests that a Chinese alternative to mainstream international relations will require local scholars to look carefully at the history as declarations about peaceful rising are not enough.

Returning to mainstream work, it is clear that the three lines noted are not mutually exclusive, and each can help a scholarly understanding of the international relations of the countries in East Asia. In this text with its focus upon institutions, agents and ideas, all three lines might be used, but the centre of intellectual gravity would be the last noted, as social relations constitute and shape human interactions.

KEY PLAYERS IN EAST ASIA: TRAJECTORIES, CONCERNS AND INTERACTIONS

As noted, in the years since the end of the Pacific War three countries have played major roles in the international politics of East Asia: China, America and Japan. A number of issues can be identified around the exchanges between the elites of these three countries, both geo-strategic (military, diplomatic expressed as alliances) and, lately, geo-economic (trade, trade treaties, rule-making institutional centres). Thereafter, a multiplicity of issues and arguments can be identified and pursued.[8]

The USA: Key Power over the Last Fifty Years

The USA was deeply involved in the shift to the modern world in East Asia.[9] The country had links with Japan, China and the Philippines, and its merchants and missionaries cast their nets wider still. It had links throughout the region. In the nineteenth and early twentieth centuries the USA was one amongst a number of great powers that jostled for position, making and unmaking treaties and competing for areas of interest within China. But it was the conflicts between Japan and China that first destabilized the region and then precipitated its wholesale reordering: the Pacific War was the catalyst.

The Pacific War fatally undermined the state-empires of the Europeans, and they did not long survive the end of the war; the same fate befell Japan's empire in Northeast Asia. The victorious allies stripped the Japanese of all the territories accumulated during their period of expansion. Numerous new nation states were formed. And, crucially, the Chinese Civil War was settled in favour of the Communist Party as the PLA swept aside the armies of the nationalists;[10] American reaction was wholly negative, and a cold war division was superimposed on the region.

The USA emerged as the region's dominant economic, military and political power; in the early post-war years one key policy was containment, and it informed the creation of the various mechanisms of the cold war (a mix of economic, political and diplomatic strategies) which were deployed in Europe and in East Asia. The cold war saw two major wars in the region: Korea and Vietnam (plus parts of Laos and Cambodia). The cold war saw a number of local rebellions read in cold war terms: the

Philippines (Huk Rebellion); Malaya (Emergency); and Indonesia (1965 Coup). The cold war also fixed in place a number of other conflicts: the Northern Islands (Japan/USSR); and the issue of the status of Taiwan (ROC/PRC). However, more positively, the cold war assisted the rapid economic growth of the region[11] as the USA sought to aid nations within its sphere of control. These developments led international relations theorists to draw a distinction between geo-strategy (with its focus on the military balance) and geo-economics (with a focus on economic relationships); the latter way of thinking found expression in numerous regional trade bodies, and for a period the military took something of a back seat in policy making.

The end of the cold war saw Washington reconsidering its overall stance. There were a number of important factors: (i) it remained the dominant military power in the region; (ii) it was no longer the dominant economy; (iii) but it had extensive trade and financial links to the region; (iv) Japan was now militarily strong/more independent minded; (v) South Korea was less inclined to follow the US line in regard to the Korean Peninsula; (vi) Taiwan was increasingly inclined to affirm its status as a country; (vii) China was the major rising power; (viii) Australia, New Zealand and Singapore were regional allies; and (ix) the region was home to significant Muslim populations with some relatively low-level, probably locally generated, insurgency activity. Today, in the early years of the second decade of the twenty-first century, the agenda has changed somewhat but the USA remains the dominant power in the Pacific; however, it is no longer unchallenged, and smaller nations must now adjust to the big-power exchanges of the USA with China. The American view of the future has found expression in the 'Pivot to Asia', which has seen naval units shifted from the Atlantic to the Pacific, and it has also found expression in the pursuit of a regional trade deal, the TPP.

So the key issues more recently include: first, how to reconfigure alliances in order to meet the challenge of the rising power of China, with trade bodies embodying liberal trade rules (WTO, Asia-Pacific Economic Cooperation (APEC) and TPP) and military reconfigurations (pivoting to East Asia, encouraging Japanese involvement and responding appropriately to the issues of the South China Sea); second, how to manage problems in North Asia, that is, assisting neighbouring countries in managing the regime in North Korea; third, how to manage the ongoing Taiwan issue, where de facto independence is presently managed by de jure ambiguity; and, more recently, fourth, how to deal with radical Islamist groups in the region as local issues (e.g. Thailand's Southern Provinces or Malaysia's institutionalized communalism) show signs of some linkages to the violence of groups in the Middle East and parts of South Asia.

Japan: Established Power

The military defeat of Imperial Japan in the summer of 1945 was followed by an Allied occupation, and the key players during this time were the Americans. General MacArthur headed the SCAP adminis- tration and SCAP reworked the Japanese state, its military and its politicians, and consequently shaped the post-war trajectory of Japan. The 1951 peace and security treaties bound Japan to the USA. The Japanese economy recovered quickly, giving rise to the notion of the developmental state, but the country continued to be a military and diplomatic subordinate to the USA. However, the evident success of the Japanese economy coupled to the stresses and strains experienced during the 1960s and 1970s by the USA slowly remade this relationship. Militarily, the USA was the unchallenged alliance leader, but economic- ally this was less clear cut and a signal event was the 1985 Plaza Accord whereby the yen was re-valued, opening the way to the creation of Japan centred production networks throughout East Asia, and, in turn, the economic success opened the way for Japanese diplomatic efforts. In the last few years of the twentieth century the Japanese government sought membership of the UN Security Council (unsuccessfully), and today, in the second decade of the twenty-first century, the Japanese government is being encouraged by their key ally to play a greater role in regional security. All these tangled debates about economic, military and diplo- matic power continue, and they draw in domestic, regional and inter- national contributors.

The military relationship between the USA and Japan had a cold war origin, and the end of the cold war, which was clear in Europe but less obviously marked in East Asia, meant the relationship became less immediately important, but the political dynamic of the region has moved on, and the key issue now reanimating the relationship is the rise of China. So currently the issue for the two allies is accommodating the rise of China, plus there is one further issue to deal with, that is, the inward looking, eccentric regime of North Korea, in principle easier, a matter of simple containment.

Looking at the economic, political and military rise of China, the USA has encouraged Japan to upgrade its military profile, and there are two aspects to note: domestic political debates around revisions to the law governing the use of the Self Defence Forces and, in the background, quiet conversations about possible revisions to the 'Peace Constitution'.

In regard to the use of the navy and other resources, military planners have considered sea-lane defence and out of area support missions, and changes in domestic law seem to pave the way for Japanese forces to directly assist American forces. In this vein, more recently, there have been low-level exchanges with China around the Senkaku/Daiyou Islands as both China and Japan claim sovereignty over these uninhabited rocky islands; their position is significant, not merely as local resources, but as part of the First Island Chain that Beijing sees as curbing its naval aspirations.

However, in all this, there are domestic problems with upgrading the military. First, Japan has a strong peace movement which centres on the experience of the cities of Hiroshima and Nagasaki, and it has encouraged a deeper understanding of the role of Japanese forces during the wars in the region (e.g. comfort women, germ warfare experiments, slave labour and the like). One aspect of Japanese self-identity is given not merely by the experience of nuclear attack but also by the 70 years of peaceful development (plus extensive Official Development Assistance[12]) that has followed, so that Japanese self-understanding affirms the notion of a peaceful country.[13] And second, many American bases are located in the Ryukyu Island Chain, where they are opposed by the locals. However, third, the Peace Constitution is opposed by nationalists and groups in the Liberal Democratic Party, and history textbooks are an arena of ritual domestic/international conflict; the visits of senior politicians to the Yasakuni Shrine are also problematical, and critics (foreign and domestic) claim that the Japanese elite has not acknowledged nor made recompense for the aggressive wars waged in East Asia by earlier generations.

The military growth plus nationalists plus unsettled matters of memory from the Pacific War make the Japanese position in East Asia problematical;[14] at the same time, Japanese aid has flowed to East Asia in vast quantities. Japanese trade and foreign direct investment have followed and made a major contribution to the present wealth of the entire region, including China. Japanese relationships vary with different parts of East Asia. In general, Japan's links with ASEAN countries are relatively good, supported by lots of aid, trade and foreign direct investment. Most Japanese aid is directed towards East Asia and after the Asian Financial Crisis Japan made further aid available to East Asia. It also organized the Chiang Mai Agreement 1999 for 'currency swop' arrangements as a way of protecting countries against forex speculators. However, Japan's links with its Northeast Asia neighbours are poor, in particular with China. The history of relationships in the modern period is poor, including a series of wars. Japan and China are both now significant military powers, both strong economic powers and, they both have extensive economic links, and as the role of the USA comparatively declines, the relationship between these two powers assumes a greater prominence.

More generally, Japan is a global economic power. It has a large aid budget (although most is focused on East Asia), makes major contributions of money/diplomatic effort to the UN and has supported peace-making in Cambodia. The UN has been a major arena for Japanese diplomatic activity; it has been a route back to respectability within the international community and with the episode of military expansion now some 70 years in the past, for the Japanese government the key issues more recently include: first, how to revise the Peace Constitution so that the country's significant armed forces can be given a wider remit; second, whether or not to build nuclear weapons, where at present the country is sometimes described as a 'virtual nuclear power'; and third, how to manage the tensions that suffuse Northeast Asia – in particular the triangle of links between China, South Korea and Japan, where the memories of warfare are an enduring irritant.

China: Rising Power

More than a few commentators have noted the historical examples of the difficulties established powers can have with rapidly rising new powers, and the late nineteenth and early twentieth centuries in Europe are often cited, when an energetic Imperial Germany clashed with the established global empire of the British and a naval building competition ensued, followed by war. The upshot was that local European and global balances were upset, and a new stable global political configuration was established only in 1945. The superficially apparent lesson has been deployed in respect of the relationship of America and China, and some commentators have seen conflict as more or less inevitable.

These matters can be cast in terms of a simple political narrative. First, in 1949 the PRC faced demands analogous to those of the newly decolonized area, that is, order, security and development; the government of Mao settled domestic problems of order, they settled international borders, they adopted a low profile in international affairs and joined the Non-Aligned Movement. Membership of the UN was blocked by that organization recognizing, at the behest of the Americans, the Taiwan based ROC. This diplomatic situation changed following the Sino-US rapprochement, and in 1971 the PRC replaced ROC in the UN. Then, second, in the latter years of Mao's leadership the domestic political system was mired in the confusion of the Cultural Revolution and Mao's 1976 death was followed by a brief interregnum as the CCP closed down the advocates of radical leftism but affirmed the work of Mao in the 'two whatever stance', a period of elite drift/reordering. Then, third, Deng Xiaoping emerged as the key figure amongst the leadership, and in 1978 a reform programme was inaugurated; the PRC slowly recovered from the excesses of the Cultural Revolution and the economy grew; it is a familiar story. Thereafter, the country became more engaged with the international community, more of a player in global politics; however, the 1989 Tiananmen Square demonstrations damaged this process, and thereafter there was slow recovery, further economic advances and, in time, the resumption of active diplomatic linkages.

As domestic reforms continued and as the economy burgeoned, the turn of the century has seen further economic and political integration within the global system. The recovery of the country both domestically and internationally was celebrated in the 2008 Beijing Olympics. At the present time, in the early twenty-first century, China continues to integrate into the international community, and there is a debate amongst Chinese commentators as to how the international political aspects of this trajectory should be grasped: an appeal to mainstream international relations or the construction of a domestically rooted way of understanding, a Chinese international relations.

The reform programme inaugurated by Deng might be tagged 'a conservative revolution from above', rather like the Meiji Restoration, as the party-state elite has looked backwards in order to plot a route to the future;[15] two strands of thinking are available, thus invoking the past and characterizing the desired future.

The party-state elites are assiduous in invoking the past. Looking to the past, to the national past, one aspect of Chinese elite thinking in respect of international relations is captured in the notion of the 'century of humiliation'. It posits the partial dismemberment of a long-established civilization at the hands of rapacious foreigners, it notes continuing foreign interference during the twentieth century and it celebrates the role of the CCP in helping China to stand on its feet once again. A subsidiary element of this overarching tale looks to the behaviour of the USA, first as the source of one more group of foreign traders, then as key allies to the KMT, then as a direct military threat during the Korean War and, thereafter, up to the present day, as a mixture of cold war opponent, occasional diplomatic ally against the USSR and, as evidencing in their contemporary domestic economy, a highly desirable standard of life.

Looking to the past in terms of collective memory, there are links with the above, but they are not coterminous. Citizen intellectuals in civil society[16] offer a number of readings of the past. Turning to the resources of tradition, as China, like Europe, has a written history of some 2,500 years, opens up ideas from Confucianism: ideas of 'All under Heaven', 'Great Harmony' and the 'Kingly Way'.[17] Invoking these ideas can illuminate the present of Chinese people and identify routes to the future. It is a vocabulary distinct from imported Western ideas. It is also, again like Europe, a rich and varied tradition; there are no simple ideas ready to translate easily into policy practice, so the result is debate, but built around the idea that China has the intellectual/moral resources to plot its own future.

Looking to the future, the national past in future orientation functions to read the past so as to illuminate the present and the future as it points to an essential race-nation nature. So for current Chinese elite, reading the past points to a process of recovery: at the start of the modern era China was a major power, and the current trajectory of China can be understood as a process of recovery of that position, and this could be unpacked as 'peaceful rising'. It could also be unpacked in commentary as a 'patriarchal nationalism' in the service of a 'right wing authoritarian party state'.[18] The nature of Beijing's involvement with the international system is not straightforward, and opening up is clearly a multi-aspect process: cooperation, conflicts and – one might guess – mutual incomprehension, as players talk past each other.

Beijing's relations with the USA are uneasy, and whilst there is much trade there is also much mistrust. Trade volumes are not in balance and financial flows are problematical. The American arms budget is very large, and there are bases adjacent to the Chinese coast. The Chinese arms budget is much smaller but growing, and it is subject to well informed but hypocritical American questioning, official and media. One arena of debate involves the First and Second Island chains, another the South China Sea. Commentators argue that Beijing's concerns are to assert a measure of naval control over these areas, and the American government has signalled that it will fulfil security treaty obligations to its allies in the region in the event of aggression from China and has adopted a strategy of 'pivoting to Asia', so Japan is once again a crucial ally. Here again, Beijing's relations with Japan are also awkward. There is diplomatic competition for influence within East Asian political networks. There is ongoing maritime confrontation over the sovereignty of disputed islands, and the issue of war/memory routinely emerges as the Chinese government plays the nationalist card domestically and provokes a response from the Japanese right wing. But against these diplomatic problems, there are trade linkages, tourist travel and student exchanges. All these remain strong.

On a wider scale the situation is varied. There are further regional problems; thus managing relations with Taiwan, where there is much trade plus measured nationalist bluster along with a distinctive ritual diplomatic status competition. There is the task of managing relations with a divided Korea, in particular distancing from the North and building better relations with the South. Here there are many awkward issues: the North's nominal socialism versus the South's evident economic success; claims from North and South Korea that the Korea/China border remains contestable – it was settled in 1909 by the Japanese colonial administration, a regime whose legitimacy would not be accepted by current governments. Recent research work in China suggested the Koguryo was a vassal state of the Chinese empire, that is, in effect, historically a part of China, a claim impacting the identity of Koreans, North and South.[19] Thereafter, moving further afield, China has growing links with the ASEAN member countries of Southeast Asia. These have been good in the past but are more in question today; in particular, there are problems in respect of multiple claims to the economic rights to large areas of the South China Sea. Chinese expansionism by building facts on the ground via occupying and upgrading reefs and islets has provoked a reaction, drawing in America and seeing local naval resources enhanced. And then, further afield, relations with the European Union are good. These exchanges centre on trade, and there are no diplomatic/military anxieties or tensions. Finally, China is deepening relations with Africa, where its presence is disturbing diplomatic taken-for-granted relations, and it has a growing presence in Latin America. But all these linkages are, in sum, what would be expected of a significant global economic player.

The key issues for Chinese policy makers include: first, managing the relationship with the USA; second, upgrading and reorienting the military (from low-tech to modern high-tech) from a multiple role focus (security and nation building) to a professional focus (security and war fighting); third, dealing with Taiwan; fourth, deepening positive links with South Korea and Japan (where nationalism continues to generate public disquiet); and fifth, continuing to raise the profile of the country on the global stage, where the country now has links with Africa and Latin America, and has recently offered a policy of rebuilding the Silk Road ('One Belt, One Road') supporting it with the formation of the AIIB.

Regional Institutions: Ordering Interaction, Contesting Rules

The elites of the countries in East Asia must read and react to changing circumstances, and one aspect has been the construction of regional organizations. East Asia is home to a multiplicity of organizations, some involving extra-regional powers, others informed by local agendas; and here, as elsewhere, the exchanges between various agents over the design of organizations can be awkward. A further anxiety now centres on accommodating an emergent China[20] but these are often the anxieties of outsiders, and another way of coming at the last noted issue is to recall the nature of the pre-colonial, Sino-centric tribute system and ask whether any of these ideas have run through into the present – concerns for culture, hierarchy and reciprocity.[21]

Regions are not simply given by geography. The idea of a region is a way of grasping sets of relationships between agents: power, trade and mutual perceptions.[22] Regions are social constructions. They are ways in which agents can make sense of a set of geographically bounded relationships, speaking, for example, of an 'economic region' or a 'political region' or a 'cultural region'. In the context of international politics the relevant agents are to be found amongst the political elites, in the administrative machineries of the state and within the public sphere, and debates between these players will produce ideas of regions. Such ideas will thereafter be pursued in conversations with other groups of players and, in the contest of international politics, those from other states.

Where state-to-state conversations in respect of order are successful, this produces formal organizations. Some early organizations were concerned with security and military questions (Southeast Asia Treaty Organization, US/Japan Security Agreement, US/South Korea Security Agreement, US/Taiwan Security Agreement, USSR/PRC, PRC/North Korea) and in the cold war period governments were preoccupied with geo-strategy. More recently, there are organizations like ASEAN,[23] ASEAN plus 3 and the East Asian Submit (EAS). These are inevitably differently constituted,[24] and they are always provisional: subject to reform, adjustment and neglect depending on the ever shifting concerns of the involved players. In respect of the core concerns of realists – industrial/military power – the key organizational expression of power relations is to be found in the links that the USA has with its various allies in the region, pre-eminently Japan, thereafter South Korea and Taiwan, with other countries in Southeast Asia and Australasia also variously linked.

In the recent period, economic interlinkages – the concern of liberals – are many: informal networks (migrants or informal sector finance or criminal fraternities); corporate networks (regional production networks); plus state-sponsored links (regional free trade agreements, regional development bodies, such as Asian Development Bank (ADB) or Mekong River Commission or Singapore–Johor–Riau Growth Triangle, or specialist regional agreements, such as Chiang Mai Agreement). All these feed into the creation of economic interlinkages, thus recently, the new Silk Road,[25] and also competition between major players[26] around the rules of the game, thus APEC, The Asia–Europe Meeting (ASEM) and the AIIB.

The development trajectory of post-war East Asia has been shaped by the sets of ideas which political agents have used to make sense of their situations. Some of this finds expression in organizations: domestically, the familiar repertoire of flags, parades and anthems; internationally, a concern for what is now tagged 'soft power' via cultural activities, for example, acknowledged by ASEAN's Socio-cultural Community or by China's Confucius Institutes, and so on.

Asian regionalism can be seen to be the result of complex exchanges: domestic (within local countries), regional (between local countries) and global (between local countries and the major power centres, in particular the USA and the European Union). The upshot has been a particular concern for sovereignty, cast in terms of the idea of non-intervention, and a preference for consultative and consensus-building formal exchanges, along with a reluctance to go for legally based formal organizations. Acharya[27] argues that a distinctive and successful type of regionalism has been developed. A key preoccupation has been with sovereignty and non-intervention, and this has expressed anxieties about former colonial powers and current great powers (with their cold war competition), and a looser worry about revolutionary groups (in particular, those inspired by or linked to the CCP). The member states avoided formal bodies and so embraced the idea of process diplomacy, the business of continuing consultations. They avoided formal collective defence organizations (such as the North Atlantic Treaty Organization, NATO) and so embraced the looser idea of security cooperation. And looking to the future, they turned their thinking to their common problem of development, hence the idea of developmental regionalism.

So, to reiterate, regions are not simple givens, they are made as local elites read and react to enfolding circumstances, and the key is the slow creation of dense networks of interlinkages built around the business of livelihood, together with the elite concern for ordering these exchanges, thus the slow shift from acknowledging regionalization to embracing regionalism to the collective creation of a region.[28] But in contrast, say, to the European Union, there have been relatively modest advances. Webber[29] notes that after the 1997 crisis many commentators spoke of greater integration, but in the event it has not happened; instead, there are lots of bi-lateral and mini-lateral trade deals, and so for Webber the region is too dispersed to come together.

CHINA AND INTERNATIONAL RELATIONS: ANXIETIES/REASSURANCES

Since 2008 China has assumed a higher profile in global politics, American, European and other commentators have taken note and responses vary. Those who are pessimistic/alarmist see China as a rising power that will almost inevitably clash with other powers, in particular, the relatively declining USA. Meanwhile, those who are optimistic/ forward looking see China as an engine for the global economy and consequently a marketplace for exporters, hence the interest of foreign governments in securing trade or investment links with China. Some, however, see China as both given and problematic, thus neighbours look to the economic/political weight of China and must, perforce, adjust.

Here, two sets of reflections: first, some familiar ways in which commentators report that the Chinese elite understand themselves; and second, some familiar ways in which commentators note problems with the rise of China.

China: Rise or Rejuvenation?

The rise of China has heightened international concerns. Since the launch of the reform and opening-up policies in 1978, China has experienced remarkable economic growth and become a modern nation. The 2008 Global Financial Crisis hit the Western countries the hardest. The crisis also hit China hard. But China's economy rebounded quickly due to the government's direct and indirect stimulus measures to increase household consumption and investment. It has remained the largest contributor to global economic growth. At present, China is the world's largest manu- facturing economy and largest exporter of goods. It is the second largest trading partner of the European Union and has become the largest trading partner of ASEAN since 2009. According to the figures of IMF, China overtook the USA to become the largest economy in the world in December 2014. China's growing economic and political power seems to emerge as a challenge to the USA, the incumbent dominant power that is now in relative decline. The Obama administration's 'return-to-Asia' strategy indicates the USA's effort to strengthen relations with its existing allies and security partnerships in the region in order to secure and even advance its interests whilst counterbalancing the growing power and assertiveness of China in the region. The rise of China is also perceived as a threat to other Western nations because China's adoption of illiberal capitalism demonstrates that the Western-style liberal democracy is not the only model for successful national development.

Throughout history, major powers such as the USA, Britain, Germany and Japan engaged in outward expansion and imperialism after going through rapid industrialization and economic growth.[30] The interests of rising powers usually clash with that of established powers. Whilst established powers want to defend the current international order from which they continue to benefit, rising powers 'feel constrained or even cheated by the status quo and struggle against it to take what they think is rightfully theirs'.[31] Some commentators have noted that it is rare to 'have rising powers risen without sparking a major war that reshaped the international system to reflect new realities of power'.[32] Besides, China's communist ideology, its violation of human rights and denial of civil and political liberties do not fit with the presently dominant Western-style democracy. Thus the growing anxiety amongst some commentators that the rise of China would constitute a threat to peace and international security.

The Chinese government wants to break the iron law of seeking hegemony after becoming strong, but this requires strong political will and concrete actions, and people at home and abroad have different interpretations about a rising China. Whilst people abroad regard China's remarkable economic achievements as China's rise, people at home, in particular the Chinese leaders, regard China's remarkable economic achievements as national rejuvenation. In other words, the Chinese leaders and their people regard China's achievements as 'returning to the position of regional pre-eminence that it once held'[33] after experiencing a century of oppression and the horrors of war. Whether it is China's rise or rejuvenation, it is very clear that China has become an indispensable player in the global economy and on many international issues, and every strategic move of China can have a profound impact on the world, especially when China has made considerable contributions to the maintenance of world prosperity.

In response to the fear and scepticism of other nations about the rise of China, Chinese leaders have reiterated on many occasions that China does not have any hegemonic ambitions to dominate or challenge the current world order and will stay firmly on the path of peaceful development. In fact, China's commitment to pursue peaceful development can be traced back to 7 May 1978, when Deng Xiaoping first expressed in his speech that China 'shall never seek hegemony'.[34] In 1984 Deng reiterated, in his talk titled *We Must Safeguard World Peace and Ensure Domestic Development* that 'China will never seek hegemony or bully others'.[35] Articulated in 1990, Deng's famous 24-Character Admonition, which emphasized coping with affairs calmly and never claiming leadership,[36] directed foreign policy towards avoiding confrontation in international affairs so that the nation could focus on domestic development. Peace and development became the central tenant of the Chinese foreign policy afterwards. Deng's successor, Jiang Zemin, emphasized the essence of seeking harmony but not uniformity in the conduct of foreign relations: 'Harmony promotes co-existence and co-prosperity; whereas differences foster mutual complementation and mutual support.'[37] In other words, China respected the diversity of the world and would not impose its ideology and social system on other countries.[38] When Hu Jintao became the third generation leader, he advanced the idea of peace and development by calling for people of all countries to build a harmonious world of lasting peace and common prosperity. He said in the UN Summit that all countries 'must abandon the Cold War mentality, [and] cultivate a new security concept featuring mutual trust, mutual benefit, equality and cooperation'.[39]

It has been argued that the notion of building a harmonious world shows that 'China has broadened its concern from domestic development to taking into account both internal and external affairs.'[40] Further, realizing that countries had become more interdependent and interconnected, President Xi Jinping thought that countries were 'all equal members of the international community with equal rights to participate in regional and international affairs'.[41] The notions of equal members and equal rights indicate that Xi did not favour hegemonism and power politics in all forms. Xi proposed a new diplomatic strategy of building a community of common destiny that seeks win-win cooperation and common development in political, economic, cultural, security and many other fields. He encouraged mutual learning amongst different nations and upheld the principles of amity, mutual benefit and inclusiveness that helped China promote friendship and partnership with its neighbouring countries.

Commentators report that there are two main reasons why Deng Xiaoping and subsequent Chinese leaders adopted harmony-oriented diplomacy. First, it is said that the concept of harmony is traditional Chinese wisdom derived from Confucian philosophy. 'Harmony is the most cherished ethical and social ideal in Chinese culture ... [It is] an active process in which heterogeneous elements are brought into a mutually balancing, cooperatively enhancing, and often commonly benefiting relationship.'[42] The adoption of harmony-oriented policy helps project China as a strong but benign and trustworthy power. The use of non-violent and non-confrontational means to resolve disputes and conflicts can 'minimize damage to others' interests while pursuing one's own interests through mutual adjustment – i.e., live and let live'.[43] Second, it is thought that China's advocacy of harmony reflects its expectation that other countries will respond with similar gestures, as from a pragmatic perspective, 'China's development needs cooperation from other countries',[44] so a stable and peaceful international environment can be conducive to China's continued rise.

Indeed, many global challenges such as natural disasters, financial crises, the spread of contagious diseases and terrorism require joint actions that go beyond the boundaries of any one state's sovereignty. However, many states find it difficult to agree on their respective responsibilities and obligations on a wide range of international issues. In the case of climate change, for example, developed and developing countries disagree on who was most responsible for tackling climate change. In 2014, President Obama criticized China as a global free rider for the past three decades and pressured China to assume more global responsibilities.

Commentators report that for President Xi and his administration, China is willing to be a responsible power, and it will be more active in fulfilling the role of a responsible power regarding regional and international affairs. But three points should be highlighted. First, a distinction should be drawn between a hegemonic power and a responsible power. When giving his keynote speech at the Boao Forum, Xi[45] agreed that a big country should shoulder greater responsibilities for regional and world peace and development. But he was 'opposed to [a big country] seeking greater monopoly over regional and world affairs'.[46] Second, the notion of responsibility should be separated from domestic politics:[47] 'Acting as a responsible power does not give others a license for international interferences with China's human rights practice' or other internal affairs or sovereignty.[48] And third, the levels of international responsibility a country undertakes should be commensurate with its strengths and development stage. And on this point, Premier Li Keqiang pointed out in the meeting of the National Leading Group on Climate Change, Energy Conservation and Emissions Reduction that China, as a major responsible country, was 'willing to undertake international obligations commensurate with its national conditions, development stage and real capacity'.[49] From a sceptical perspective, Chinese scholars and officials thought that 'talk of China assuming more responsibility was a trap into which they should not fall because it would simply slow their growth'.[50] Besides, talk of China assuming more responsibility was used as an excuse by Western countries to shirk the responsibilities they should have borne. For example, industrialized nations, which were responsible for historical emissions of greenhouse gases, argued that emission cuts should be based on current levels, whilst emerging economies with growing emissions of greenhouse gas argued that 'emission cuts should be based on the accumulation of greenhouse gases in the atmosphere'.[51]

Meanwhile, the Chinese leaders thought that facilitating peaceful co-prosperity and coexistence was one of the important tasks China should accomplish as a responsible power. The 'One Belt, One Road' initiative, which establishes new routes linking Asian, European and African continents and their adjacent seas, is expected to enhance connectivity, economic exchange and trade ties through building the transportation infrastructure together. The 'One Belt, One Road' initiative aspires to build 'a community of shared interests, destiny and responsibility featuring mutual political trust, economic integration and cultural inclusiveness'.[52] The establishment of the China-led AIIB, which has 57 countries joining as prospective founding members, 'marks the beginning of Beijing's intention to accelerate its deeper integration into the world economy'.[53] It is expected that the AIIB can help meet Asia's infrastructure-financing needs whilst facilitating regional economic cooperation and integration and sustainable economic growth in the long run. These two economic projects may over time bring indirect diplomatic and security benefits to China.

China: Contemporary Debates about International Relations

As might be expected, contemporary debates amongst mainstream commentators cover a range of issues, but whilst the materials of historical institutionalism and culture criticism offer ways of reading the overall trajectory of development and identifying something of the logic of the system, they do not help order the more ad hoc collection of issues that find their way into debates. Three broad areas of debate can be identified – settling borders, organizing economies and engaging with audiences – and within each arena of debate many smaller passing issues could be pursued.

Settling borders
Some debates are holdovers from the past.

First, there is the question of the status of Tibet. In the nineteenth century, as the British and others weakened, the Qing and their relationship with Tibet altered, and the latter moved towards a species of independent statehood; but later, when the PRC was formed, re-establishing an acceptable relationship with Tibet was a concern for Beijing, and the PLA moved in and took control. Later, a revolt followed, with the spiritual leader of the territory fleeing to India. There is now a

Tibetan diasporic community with a base in India, and the status of the territory has become a domestic issue (local protests around ethnicity, religion and pressures of inward migration of Han Chinese) and a diplomatic issue as various countries intermittently press the case of the Tibetans.

Second, there is the question of the status of Taiwan. The island was for many centuries home to Polynesian peoples; later, it was part of the Portuguese sphere of influence, then a base for a Ming Chinese warlord. The Qing asserted some control in 1683 and cross-strait inward migration began, and so the island became a province in 1885. The First Sino-Japanese War 1894–95 saw the island ceded to Japan as a part of their empire in Northeast Asia and then after the defeat of Japan in 1945 it was occupied by Nationalist China, and it became their base after their 1949 defeat. The ROC was a cold war protectorate of the USA and was accorded diplomatic recognition, but its status was changed in 1971 when USA recognized Beijing. The situation now is anomalous, for whilst Taiwan is de facto an independent state, sovereignty is claimed by Beijing. Relations between China and Taiwan have been uneasy for decades – Taiwan has left its exiled KMT status behind and is a functioning liberal democracy and Beijing has in the past been bellicose in its rhetoric towards the island but in recent decades has preferred to grow trade relations. The current diplomatic situation is governed by the 'one China, two interpretations' stance acknowledged by Taipei and Beijing, and other countries are obliged to dance around the issue.

And third, there is the matter of links with North Korea. Chinese involvement in the Korean War has been read as a proxy war between the newly formed PRC and a virulently anti-communist USA. The war was facilitated by outsiders, with the division of the peninsula and the promotion of local allies, but was initiated by mutually hostile Korean groups. Outsiders were subsequently drawn in. For the PRC the territory of North Korea remains a nominal socialist ally, but the nature of the regime is such that its future is in doubt, and the consequences of a breakdown of order in North Korea worries both Beijing and Seoul.

Some debates mix holdovers from the past with key contemporary concerns.

First, the status of Xinjiang, which was a remote area of the Qing Empire, with the border contested between the Qing and Czarist Empire. Again, as with Tibet, after 1949 Beijing moved to reassert its control. Today the territory is controlled by and is formally a constituent part of China. Yet the indigenous population has a quite different form of life and culture. At the present time, inward migration by Han Chinese meets local Uighur protests, sometimes violent. However, the territory is now a key area in the newly mooted new Silk Road, as it holds valuable resources and sits astride lines of communication with Central Asia and, thence, Russia and Europe.

Second, there is the issue of historical memories of the Second Sino-Japanese War, where matters are routinely racked up from a matter of memory to a diplomatic-cum-nationalist shouting match. The diplomatic aspect takes the form of apology diplomacy whilst the nationalist aspect takes the form of politicians and functionaries signalling to available masses that they can make hostile demonstrations. The tactic is used quite blatantly by the Chinese side and deployed more circumspectly by sections of Japanese elite/popular opinion. The issue runs into contemporary politics, both domestic and international.

Some issues are relatively new.

First, there is the question of the development of Hong Kong and Macau. Both have the status of a Special Administrative Region (SAR), with the former transferred from the colonial authority of Britain in 1997 and the latter transferred from the colonial authority of Portugal in 1999. The latter colony had long been used to a strong connection with China, and so retrocession was unproblematic; however, Hong Kong had sustained its separateness, and from the 1960s onwards the local population had come to think of themselves as Hong Kong people, that is, distinct from mainlanders. The subsequent trajectory of the Hong Kong SAR has been beset with political tensions, both local and between sections of the local population and Beijing.[54]

And second, there is the ongoing issue of control of the South China Sea. This area is home to significant fisheries and perhaps oil and gas reserves, and it is also a strategic area for the passage of shipping, both commercial and naval. The government of China has laid claim to more or less the entire area, and the interests of other littoral states have been disregarded, as have the stipulations of the Law of the Sea.[55] The elite in Beijing have refused to discuss matters with ASEAN and are clearly working to divide the members and thus block any united stance. The elite in Beijing have also deployed force (in the past there have been naval clashes and recently action has been pursued in the guise of reclamation work and the construction of military bases in various places in the area). Beijing's activities are part and parcel of its naval build-up and part and parcel of its self-understanding as a great power;[56] unfortunately, it has stoked a regional arms race and drawn back in the American military.[57]

Organizing economies

A second group of issues relate to new economic activities, for as the Chinese economy has developed over the last few decades, it now serves networks around the globe. First, there are debates about the Silk Road[58] (or 'One Belt, One Road'), a proposal from Beijing to build infrastructure around Asia by creating both sea and overland routes to Europe. Both elements of the idea imply extensive infrastructure developments plus new patterns of diplomatic relations. The projected increased flows of trade imply disturbances to status quo arrangements, as, for example, the Chinese companies build ports and naval facilities in the Indian Ocean, or Chinese traders operate in Central Asian republics, and so both related ideas are ambitious. And both imply extensive infrastructure development in roads, railways, airports, ports, pipelines and so on. Second, there are debates about Chinese involvement in Africa, where Chinese firms have invested in primary products such as minerals and land and where some associated inward migration of traders to Africa has followed creating, in places, local problems of adjustment. And some Western security commentators have worries about the future. Then, third, there are debates about renminbi internationalization – Beijing wishes the currency to be used for international trade and this requires the provision of banking systems outside China and implies a more liberal market style governance of the currency. And fourth, there are debates about the TPP[59] (whose current membership excludes China) and AIIB, where China is in competition with the USA over the rules of international trade. The AIIB will be headquartered in Beijing, and it has attracted European support.

Engaging with audiences

A third group of issues relates to the notion of soft power. China has both raised its profile within the global system and paid attention to how it is represented to the variety of audiences available, that is, elite, corporate and popular. The Beijing Olympics of 2008 were used as a kind of coming-out party for China, and the games presented a favourable image of the country to a global audience. Subsequently, cast in more overtly ideological terms, first, there is the idea of the China dream; here there are Beijing sponsored speculations about the future of China; these are utopian in flavour,[60] often invoking Chinese classical philosophy and Confucianism and showing a preference for harmony and order. And then, second, there is the related idea of peaceful rising or peaceful development, which is Beijing's presentation of its projected line of development, cast in reassuring terms for foreign audiences (one example of the country's engagement with the global community is found in the rising numbers of Confucius Institutes).

****

These three areas encompass a multiplicity of more restricted specialist concerns, but at a general level, however, it is clear that these will have to be slowly worked through as China more thoroughly embeds its economy and polity within the extant world system.

CONCLUSION: INTERNATIONAL RELATIONS OF EAST ASIA

European and American expansion in the period 1600–1900 overthrew existing East Asian polities and created empires and the political form of the colony. They were distinctive and had equally distinctive justificatory theories (revolving around the putative superiority and responsibilities of the colonial rulers), and slowly some metropolitan political ideas and systems were transferred to colonial territories. When the Pacific War disturbed global political patterns, local elites took their chance, and they affirmed goals of nationalism and statehood and took power. East Asian colonial empires dissolved into a series of modern nation states. The new nation states faced similar problems: from the legacies of dissolving foreign empires new elites had to create states and nations and the cold war complicated these tasks; then, once in power, elites had to pursue economic development. The countries show common domestic political characteristics: a tendency to top-down politics and the use of the institutional mechanisms of a developmental state oriented towards the goal of national development.

Trade within the region is growing and has encouraged linkages; the end of the cold war has encouraged deeper linkages; and economic links plus political relaxation has encouraged a sense that the region has its own identity and future. A number of regional organizations have developed, including ASEAN, APEC, ASEM, and whilst all are ostensibly concerned with economics, all have served to foster political dialogue. Yet political change is still mostly slow. The key project has been national development, and controlling disorder and managing change are central to political life.

The major power in East Asia since 1945 has been the USA, and Japan has been a subordinate ally, but changes are visible. Now China is an emerging power. The USA has made a 'pivot to Asia', and Japan is taking a more prominent role. So a number of questions are generated: how to grasp the changing relationship between the USA and Japan; how to grasp the changing relationship between Japan and China; and, crucially, how to grasp the changing relationship between China and the USA.

NOTES

1. On the dissolution of the British sphere, C. Bayly and T. Harper 2007 *Forgotten Armies: The Fall of British Asia 1941–45*, London, Allen Lane.
2. Usefully bridging the gap between development theory and international relations, see Susan Strange 1988 *States and Markets*, London, Pinter.
3. See C. Hay 2002 *Political Analysis: A Critical Introduction*, London, Palgrave.
4. A critical comment on this is offered by Benedict Anderson 2016 'Frameworks of Comparison' in *London Review of Books* 38.2, January 21.
5. P.M. Kristensen 2015 'International Relations in China and Europe: The Case for Interregional Dialogue in a Hegemonic Discipline' in *The Pacific Review* 28.2.
6. N. Noesselt 2015 'Revisiting Debate on Constructing a Theory of International Relations with Chinese Characteristics' in *The China Quarterly*, June.
7. Victoria Tin-bor Hui 2012 'History and Thought in China's Traditions' in *Journal of Chinese Political Science* 17; Hui cites a 1996 paper by A.I. Johnston arguing that China is hard realist, printed in P. Katzenstein ed. 1996 *The Culture of National Security*, Columbia University Press.
8. A conventional mainstream overview is given by M. Yahuda 2011 3rd ed. *The International Politics of the Asia Pacific*, London, Routledge; an interpretive line is available in the work of A. Acharya 2000 *The Quest for Identity: International Relations of Southeast Asia*, Oxford University Press; and for rhetorically engaged material celebrating Asia, see K. Mahbubani 2008 *The New Asian Hemisphere*, New York, Public Affairs; K. Mahbubani 2013 *The Great Convergence*, New York, Public Affairs.
9. B. Cummings 1999 *Parallax Visions: Making Sense of American–East Asian Relations at the End of the Century*, Durham, Duke University Press.
10. The standard story is of PLA competence versus KMT incompetence (and worse), but Mitter and Moore suggest that this maybe understates the contribution of the nationalist forces, see R. Mitter and A.W. Moore 2011 'China in World War II, 1937–45' in *Modern Asian Studies* 45.2.
11. On the contribution of war, see R. Stubbs 2005 *Rethinking Asia's Economic Miracle*, London, Palgrave; on regions, see for example, M. Beeson 2014 *Regionalism and Globalization in East Asia*, London, Palgrave; and the issue of regions has been widely debated, see M. Beeson and R. Stubbs eds. 2012 *Routledge Handbook of Asian Regionalism*, London, Routledge.
12. R.J. Orr 1990 *The Emergence of Japan's Foreign Aid Power*, New York, Columbia; B.M. Koppel and R.J. Orr eds. 1993 *Japan's Foreign Aid: Power and Policy in a New Era*, Boulder, Westview; P. Katzenstein and T. Shirashi eds. 1997 *Network Power: Japan and Asia*, Cornell University Press; P. Katzenstein 2005 *A World of Regions: Asia and Europe in the American Imperium*, Cornell University Press.
13. On this see K. Gustafsson 2015 'Identity and Recognition: Remembering and Forgetting the Post-war in Sino-Japanese relations' in *The Pacific Review* 28.1 argues that identity is part of international politics in which case Beijing's habit of stopping history in 1945 and disregarding the following 70 years acts to dismiss a crucial aspect of Japanese self-understandings, their claims to a peaceful status over the post-war period.

14. A simple argument illustrative of criticism of the Japanese elite is made by I. Buruma 1994 *The Wages of Guilt: Memories of War in Germany and Japan*, London, Jonathan Cape. For more detail, see also P.W. Preston 2010 *National Pasts in Europe and East Asia*, London, Routledge.
15. B. Moore Jr. 1966 *Social Origins of Dictatorship and Democracy*, Boston, Beacon Press.
16. W.A. Callahan 2013 *China Dreams: 20 Visions of the Future*, Oxford University Press, p. 3.
17. All under Heaven (tianxia) – Chinese civilization, embracing all; Great Harmony (datong) – a global community or a future organic unity of all; Kingly Way (wangdao) – a benevolent authority (and a stable order).
18. W.A. Callahan 2010 *China: The Pessoptimist Nation*, Oxford University Press, p. 204; one oddity for outside commentators is the Beijing elite's invocation of Singapore as a model, that is, clean, honest and successful. It is a highly selective tale and the mis-reading of Singapore is surprising, see S. Ortmann and M.R. Thompson 2014 'China's Obsession with Singapore: Learning Authoritarian Modernity' in *The Pacific Review* 27.3.
19. C. Wirth 2015 'Power and Stability in the China – Japan – South Korea Regional Security Complex' in *The Pacific Review* 26.4, pp. 560–1 argues that the combination of bi-lateral hostilities creates a tri-lateral measure of stability as the status quo is routinely reaffirmed.
20. G. Rozman 2012 'East Asian Regionalism' in M. Beeson and R. Stubbs eds. *Routledge Handbook of Asian Regionalism*, London, Routledge.
21. David Kang 2012 'East Asia when China was at the Centre' in Beeson and Stubbs eds. 2012.
22. Mainstream international relations theory offers various takes on regions and in some debates the European Union is the favoured referent – for a note see F. Soderbaum 2012 'Theories of Regionalism' in Beeson and Stubbs eds. 2012.
23. There is a vast literature on ASEAN and its various extensions; for an overview, see A. Acharya 2000 *The Quest for Identity: International Relations of Southeast Asia*, Oxford University Press; A. Acharya 2010 *Whose Ideas Matter: Agency and Power in Asian Regionalism*, Singapore, ISEAS.
24. Acharya 2010; see also E. Frost 2009 'Whose Ideas Matter: Agency and Power in Asian Regionalism' in *Contemporary Southeast Asia* 33.3, which reviews Acharya's work and notes the idea of 'constitutive localization', that is, the local use of ideas, which opens the way to seeing the nature and success of the 'ASEAN way'; see also A. Ba 2009 *(Re)Negotiating East and Southeast Asia: Region, Regionalism and the Association of Southeast Asian Nations*, Stanford University Press (reviewed by D. Nair 2011 in *Contemporary Southeast Asia* 33.1).
25. P.B. Rana 2013 'Connectivity in Asia: Reviving the Old Silk Road?' in *RSIS Commentary* 6 June 2013 writes about regional and sub-regional connectivity, noting that there are many proposed plans.
26. Gilbert Rozman 2012 'East Asian Regionalism' in M. Beeson and R Stubbs eds. *Routledge Handbook of Asian Regionalism*, London, Routledge points to the competition between China and the USA, cast in liberal terms, open versus closed regionalism.
27. Acharya 2010 see chapters 3 and 4.
28. The classic text, so to say, comes from the World Bank 1993 *The East Asian Miracle: Economic Growth and Public Policy*, Oxford University Press.
29. D. Webber 2010 'The Regional Integration That Didn't Happen: Cooperation without Integration in Early Twentieth Century East Asia' in *Pacific Review* 23.3.
30. S.P. Huntington 2011 *The Clash of Civilization and the Remaking of World Order*, New York, Simon & Schuster, p. 229.
31. Aaron L. Friedberg 2011 Hegemony with Chinese Characteristics, Online. <http://users.clas.ufl.edu/zselden/coursereading2011/friedberg.pdf> (accessed 4 July 2015), p. 18.
32. R. Kagan 2005 'The Illusion of "Managing" China' in *The Washington Post*, May 15 2005.
33. Friedberg 2011 p. 20.
34. Deng Xiaoping 1978 May 7 Realize the Four Modernizations and Never Seek Hegemony, Online. <https://dengxiaopingworks.wordpress.com/2013/02/25/realize-the-four-modernizations-and-never-seek-hegemony/> (accessed 4 July 2015).

35. Deng Xiaoping 1984 May 29 We Must Safeguard World Peace and Ensure Domestic Development, Online. <http://en.people.cn/dengxp/vol3/text/c1200.html> (accessed 4 July 2015).
36. Deng Xiaoping's '24-Character' guideline: 'Observe calmly; secure our position; cope with affairs calmly; hide our capacities and bide our time; be good at maintaining a low profile; and never claim leadership.'
37. Jiang, Zemin 2002 October 24 Speech by President Jiang Zemin at George Bush Presidential Library, Online. <http://no.china-embassy.org/eng/dtxw/t110222.htm> (accessed 4 July 2015).
38. Permanent Mission of the People's Republic of China to the United Nations 2003 China's Independent Foreign Policy of Peace, Online. <http://www.china-un.org/eng/gyzg/wjzc/t40387.htm> (accessed 4 July 2015).
39. Hu, Jintao 2005 Build towards a Harmonious World of Lasting Peace and Common Prosperity, Online. <http://www.un.org/webcast/summit2005/statements15/china050915 eng.pdf> (accessed 4 July 2015).
40. Su, Hao 2008 Harmonious World: The Conceived International Order in Framework of China's Foreign Affairs, Online. <http://www.nids.go.jp/english/publication/joint_research/series3/pdf/3-2.pdf> (accessed 4 July 2015), p. 30.
41. Xi, Jinping 2015 Towards a Community of Common Destiny and a New Future for Asia, Online. <http://english.boaoforum.org/hynew/19353.jhtml> (accessed 4 July 2015), p. 1.
42. Li, Chenyang 2014 *The Confucian Philosophy of Harmony*, New York, Routledge, p. 1.
43. Cheng, Jason 2012 'Challenges for China's Harmonious Diplomacy' in H. Lai and Y. Lu eds. *China's Soft Power and International Relations*, p. 121.
44. Su 2008 p. 30.
45. Xi 2015.
46. Xi 2015.
47. Deng, Yong 2015 'China: The Post-Responsible Power' in *The Washington Quarterly* 37.4, p. 121.
48. Deng 2015 p. 121.
49. China Daily 2015 June 13 Li Stresses Importance to Increase Efforts in Response to Climate Change, Online. <http://www.chinadaily.com.cn/china/2015-06/13/content_20989 851.htm> (accessed 5 July 2015).
50. F. Ching 2015 China Accepts US Challenge of Greater Responsibility, Online. <http://www.ejinsight.com/20150421-china-accepts-us-challenge-greater-reponsibility/> (accessed 5 July 2015).
51. R. Donald 2013 The UN Climate Talks Have a Responsibility Problem, Online. <http://www.carbonbrief.org/blog/2013/11/warsaw-climate-talks-solving-the-responsibility-problem/> (accessed 5 July 2015).
52. Ministry of Foreign Affairs 2015 Accelerating Building of the Belt and Road, Forging China–Afghanistan Community of Common Destiny, Online. <http://www.fmprc.gov.cn/mfa_eng/wjb_663304/zwjg_665342/zwbd_665378/t1255410.shtml> (accessed 5 July 2015).
53. Zhao, G. 2015 'Let's Not Get Carried Away; Asian Infrastructure Investment Bank Faces Many Hurdles' in *South China Morning Post*, April 30, Online. <http://www.scmp.com/comment/insight-opinion/article/1781746/lets-not-get-carried-away-asian-infrastructure-investment> (accessed 5 July 2015).
54. P.W. Preston 2016 *The Politics of Hong Kong China Relations*, Cheltenham, UK and Northampton, MA, Edward Elgar.
55. *Financial Times* 30 October 2015 reported that the Permanent Court of Arbitration in The Hague which deals with cases related to the United Nations Convention on the Law of the Sea (UNCLOS) agreed to hear the complaint of the government of the Philippines against China's nine dash line.
56. *Economist* 2015 'Who Rules the Waves' October 17.
57. At which point it might be said that the PLAN behaviour is inept however if Beijing's strategy is longer term then the gamble is that slowly building up a naval presence will squeeze out the Americans – see IISS *Comments* 2015 (21.4) 'China's Land Reclamation

in the South China Sea', IISS *Comments* 2014 (20.9) 'Chinese Vision Drives East Asian Détente', IISS *Comments* 2014 (20.9) 'US Navy Seeks to Maintain Supremacy', IISS *Comments* 2014 (20.4) 'Philippines China Dispute: A Sign of Regional Shifts'.

58. C. Clover and L. Hornby 2015 'China's Great Game: Road to a New Empire' in *Financial Times* October 12; see also T. Mitchell 2015 'China's Great Game: New Frontier, Old Foes' in *Financial Times* October 13.

59. A. Capling and J. Ravenhill 2011 'Multilateralising Regionalism: What Role for the Trans-Pacific Partnership Agreement' in *The Pacific Review* 24.5.

60. See Callahan 2013.

7. Afterword: the logic of Chinese politics

This book had its occasion in the authors' reactions to post-2008 commentary on China when two strands of overlapping discussion seemed to have taken root, with neither entirely convincing. On the one hand there was commentary in the English-language (primarily, Western- or Washington-oriented) media which seemed to mix overstated anxieties about China (numbers of population, growth rates in the economy, the size of financial reserves, rising military spending plus claims made in Beijing to great power status) with parallel over-generous admiration (both actual, in regard to the uplifting of hundreds of millions from poverty, and opportunistic, in regard to its marketplace, a target for foreign companies). And then, on the other hand, there is material available in Chinese and English which asserts the re-emergence of China as a great power, and here some of these arguments are cast in aggressive nationalist terms; often taking 1931–45 Japan and the Japanese as objects of definition; some of the arguments are cast in terms of resisting American hegemony, in particular in the Western Pacific, others are cast in broad historical terms, with claims to an implicitly unbroken history of many thousands of years, whilst some are cast in softer terms, with talk of peaceful rising and the re-establishment of the Silk Road, a trading network of general benefit. But neither of these internally diverse lines of commentary carry much conviction, and in place of such work, both the sceptical and the enthusiastic, this book has been concerned to uncover something of the underlying logic of Chinese politics: we have not asked whether China was about to collapse or make businessmen rich or take over global leadership, but, rather, how it worked; what was the animating logic of the political system in China.

The approach adopted in this book is fundamentally interpretive/ critical. It is rooted in historical institutionalism along with culture critical analysis, and this approach directs attention to agents, their ideas and the institutional machineries that they construct and thereafter inhabit. These materials can be used to illuminate present sets of circumstances, and they can also be used to track change down through time as local elites read and respond to the ever shifting international and domestic demands of the modern world. This last noted entails a further set of intellectual commitments as the notion of the shift to the modern world points to the dynamic of the natural science based industrial capitalist form of life that underpins the diverse pattern of nation states that comprise the global political system. So the contemporary pattern is contingent, political arrangements are fluid, and there is no clear end point in view.

The substantive story offered in this text adopts the strategy of historical institutionalism and acknowledges the notion of the shift to the modern world. It thereby calls attention to the dynamics of the unfolding shift to the modern world in China, to the shifting international contexts and domestic arrangements within which local political agents had to act, and to the goals that they pursued (successfully or otherwise). The multiple exchanges of the Chinese elites and the wider population with the intrusive and disruptive demands of the modern world can be characterized in terms of a number of discrete historical phases – overall a process of collapse, warfare and recovery.

In the nineteenth century the Qing Dynasty was confronted with the agents of the available modernity – rapacious, violent traders from Europe[1] – and initially their demands were not understood as they were read as one more group of unruly traders, perhaps simply pirates; in the event, at the time of the earliest contacts, their impact was marginal as the empire was large and had its own domestic problems. However, over time, the incoming groups undermined the Qing. The process was long drawn out; thus the British seized Hong Kong in 1844 but the Qing elite did not step down from power until 1911. In the intervening period, some sixty-odd years, there were extensive debates – domestic and foreign – in respect of the condition of China. For outsiders, China was a mix of exotic high culture (the arts that Europeans in the late nineteenth century found so desirable and inspirational), recalcitrant elites (unable to run their country or meet steadily the requirements of foreign traders) and impoverished, possibly drug-addled masses (this last, of course, a case of blaming the victim). On the other hand, for local scholars and reform-minded officials, it was a time of experiment (Self-Strengthening Movement, the Hundred Days Reform) interspersed with rebellion (the Boxers) and progressive protest (New Culture Movement). It was also increasingly a period of insurrectionary plotting, and there were a number of failed insurrections until, in time, a protest aimed at issues of railway funding turned into a general rebellion and the Qing Empire was overthrown.

The makers of the revolution sought to build a variant form of republic, and they embraced ideas taken from Europe, America and

Japan; the last noted, at the time, a local example of quickly learning the lessons of modernity and joining the existing community of modern nation states or powers. However, they failed to achieve their goals: political manoeuvrings, assassinations, limited support, local anxieties and the residual powers of sometime agents of the now defunct Qing regime all combined to undermine the drive to build a republic. There was an attempt at a restoration of the monarchy, albeit with a new emperor, but the attempt failed with the putative emperor's death. And then there were only warlords, with a multiplicity of locally based groups – some 300 or so – centred on the control of the machineries of war, and many local wars were fought, some involving armies measured in hundreds of thousands.

The following decades were filled with warfare. The 1926 Northern Expedition launched by Chiang Kai Shek saw a measure of relief for the country from the depredations of the warlords; however, in the process of dealing with that problem, with a mixture of military campaigns and political co-options, Chiang created another when his KMT forces plus local groups attacked his nominal allies in the Communist Party in Shanghai. The upshot was civil war as the remnants of the party retreated to the countryside, where they were pursued by KMT forces. One aspect of this tale came to provide New China with one of its founding myths – the Long March – celebrated as an heroic accomplishment, but in reality a defeat. However, that said, the party survived, and an alliance of sorts with the KMT was forged following the Japanese invasion of China; further rounds of warfare followed, and in the course of a few years most of the country was occupied, with the KMT based in the far southwest in Chongqing and the CCP based in the remote north in Yan'an.

The Japanese invasion pushed back both the forces of the KMT and those of the CCP, but whilst the Japanese armies could win battles, they could not hold territory; China was too vast, the Japanese army too few in numbers and too weak. In 1941 the Japanese attack into Southeast Asia brought European and American forces into what was now a world war and a measure of cooperation between the KMT and CCP was sustained. But with the military defeat of the Japanese at the hands of the Americans, the drift towards renewed fighting was quick and clear. It was also supported by outside powers, as the Americans and Russians made weapons and material available to the two contending parties. After a pause, the civil war resumed. The KMT, with the help of the Americans, moved forces north, whilst the CCP was given access to captured Japanese weapons by the Russians, and the civil war resumed. The KMT forces were defeated and the residue retreated to Taiwan. In October 1949 the CCP proclaimed the establishment of the PRC.

The PRC utilized a party-state system of political organization: a double bureaucracy of party and state, with the former in the key role. In the early years of the PRC the politico-administrative system was led by Mao Zedong along with his close colleagues from the war years. The policy adopted looked to the construction of a socialist system, where the goal was informed by both the model of the USSR and Mao's belief in the vitality of the ordinary peasantry. In this period great success (order, stability and growth) was also attended by great failure, arguably forgivable (GLF) and clearly wholly unforgivable (Great Proletarian Cultural Revolution). The last noted political and cultural experiment came to an end with the death of Mao and the subsequent removal from office of his closest followers. And, after some confusion, a successor as paramount leader emerged: Deng Xiaoping.

In 1978 Deng introduced a series of reforms focused upon the economy, and these reforms were pursued slowly, against domestic opposition, at first in rural areas and later in urban areas. The crucial innovation was the opening up of a number of SEZs adjacent to established coastal cities, as these provided a bridgehead between the economy of a reforming China and the global system of internationalized liberal trading. The SEZs became economic production units for global supply chains, and as a result the Chinese economy began to advance rapidly. Economic changes of such magnitude required parallel changes in social organization, social welfare and personal expectations on the part of tens of millions of Chinese. The following years of headlong growth and wrenching social change saw the life chances of millions improved, but they also generated a number of severe problems such as inequality, corruption and pollution.

The reforms of Deng Xiaoping, and those leadership groups that have followed, have produced the China that is visible today, where economic growth has been concentrated in the cities in the west, in particular, those with access to the sea, whilst inland China has remained rural and comparatively poor. So development has been rapid and lop-sided, but this should be understood in the context of 30 years of headlong change; there has been great success and terrible failure (inequality, pervasive corruption and catastrophic pollution), but what is clear beyond doubt is that China has made its shift into the modern world and the elite are determined upon further advances in pursuit of the country's distinctive variant form of modernity.

THE MAIN ARGUMENTS OF THE TEXT

It is difficult to write in a brief fashion about a country like China as it has a long history, a large population, and its system of governance is distinctive and complex. In regard to setting up an enquiry, two broad lines of available political analysis present themselves: mainstream English-language political analysis, either somewhat anxious in tone, seeing security problems, or optimistic, opportunistically seeing trade possibilities; and their Chinese equivalents, cast in terms of forward-looking commentary and exhortation to recover the historically central role within the global system of the Chinese polity.

So, first, mainstream treatments of China, the anxious and the opportunistic. The former includes those cast in terms of totalitarianism or authoritarianism or the failings of the party-state and so on, and they are of limited or little use in grasping the logic of Chinese politics. Such mainstream work is coloured by a number of identifiable traits. It is intellectually rooted in the days of cold war (hence the familiar and implausible dualisms, for example, totalitarian versus democratic). It takes the model of the West in general, and the USA more particularly, entirely for granted, and this latent nationalism blocks any direct characterization of the logic of other systems; instead, they are described in terms of how they diverge from the taken for granted model. It evinces a preference for positivistic work, that is, data gathering plus generalization, and so enquiry is skewed towards that which can be quantified, and once again established quantitative reference standards can be invoked whether or not they have any relevance to the other culture in question (thus, all the indices on human rights, or democracy, or press freedom, and so on – in all cases the referent is the West in general or the USA more particularly). Thereafter, the later opportunistic counterpart to the familiar anxious line inverts the discussion and looks at the Chinese marketplace as a realm of opportunity for trade linkages, and so rather than fearing China, these commentators recommend its embrace, pointing to a potential customer base of some 1.3 billion, disregarding the wider consequences of the decades-long Chinese pursuit of export-led growth.

The second broad strand of work is produced by patriotic Chinese scholars: all those 'citizen intellectuals'[2] who 'worry about China'[3] and mix description with exhortation (that China 'should do X'), those who sketch out utopian prospects for the Chinese people in general (Chinese people 'should do X'), those who offer specimens of 'the China Dream' (anodyne description conjoined to utopian sentiment, thus 'China is rising peacefully and will work with all peoples').[4] These are similarly unhelpful. Davies[5] characterizes their work as typically positivistic, moralizing and nationalistic; again, such work is un-reflexive or un-critical.

Against such work, this text has embraced historical institutionalism and culture critical analysis. The approach has a number of characteristics, is distinctive and is turned to a distinct substantive concern. It places agents and institutions at the centre of the enquiry, and it takes political life to be a matter of ever unfolding contingencies (not an evolution towards some goal or other). Thereafter, the text has a substantive focus on the slow process of the social construction of contemporary Chinese politics – agents and institutions – in the unfolding shift to the modern world. And these theoretical machineries unpack into a particular substantive view, which, in the broadest terms, is that China's route to the modern world was mediated by a disruptive exchange with the then dominant European system of state-empires. A number of themes are present. First, that European traders were, in addition to their private motives, expressions of a vigorous form of life; that form of life was an early version of what was to become industrial capitalism, a relentlessly dynamic system, one in which, as Marx noted, 'all that is solid melts into air'. Second, that pre-contact Qing China was not in this sense modern as the system was a species of what in a European context would be tagged agrarian feudalism, and the political elite were conservative, that is, both serving and content with the status quo. Third, that the exchange between these two forms of life was asymmetric: arts and specialist goods flowed out of China to Europe, much to the benefit of the latter, and the rich ensemble of ideas, artefacts and social practices associated with industrial capitalism flowed from Europe into China, with ordinary people adjusting as best they may (prospering or not), whilst the elite were placed at a disadvantage and slowly undermined. And fourth, the process was disruptive to extant elite ideas but also offered a slew of new ideas, eventually prompting their domestic foes to organize their removal and later, after a chaotic violent interlude, reconstitute an independent polity and, thereafter, pursue a variant state-socialist path of development.

The Current Scene in China

The contemporary scene has been deeply marked by this historical development trajectory, and this is not surprising, as it merely replicates in local form the experience of every other polity making the shift into the modern world, where this entails that the cultural resources of the past are amended to accommodate the demands of modernity. In the case of China, cast in very general terms, there are two streams of ideas embraced by the elite, informing politics and policy and thereafter deployed to order and mobilize the wider society. The first of these comprises the cultural resources of an ancient civilization: the materials of a 'little tradition',[6] that is, patterns of domestic life, relationships amongst kin groups, attachments to place, and language communities; plus, thereafter, the materials of a 'great tradition', that is, fine arts, literature, religion and the like. In English-language commentary this ensemble of ideas and practice is often simply summed as Confucianism, then, in addition a second stream of influences, embraces the work of late nineteenth and early twentieth century European social theorists and comprises a cluster of ideas around the idea of states, races and nations, with a further cluster of ideas around democracy, nationalism and livelihood; a series of debates unfold that culminate in the mid-twentieth century in the embrace of a variant form of Marxism. This line of ideas and actions in turn runs through a number of discrete phases. Early on, Chinese communists sought to learn from the experience of European sister-parties; they sought an urban proletariat, an idea that came to an abrupt end in Shanghai. Thereafter as the party sought bases in rural areas, a species of peasant-based socialism was contrived, usually associated with Mao. Broadly successful during the early phases of building the PRC, it was superseded by a less state-centric form during the period of Deng Xiaoping and successors as a continuing official Marxism is supplemented (or displaced) by an admixture of ideas associated with the developmental state (from the experience of East Asia) and market liberalism (from the USA, the destination of many Chinese, both sojourners and migrants).

The upshot is a political realm that mixes inherited ideas from Confucianism (hierarchy, moral rightness, paternalism), Marxism (social class, class conflict and progress along with the pre-eminent role of the party) and the East Asian developmental state (the elite ordered pursuit of national development). All this amounts to the creative mixture of the resources of an ancient civilization and those of the modern world, and it produces a distinctive local realm of debate summed in recent years as 'Socialism with Chinese characteristics' and translated into practice in a variety of ways (the CCP boasts 80 million members but the population of the country is 1.3 billion) via the machinery of the party-state, the country's 'organizational emperor'.

Change continues and the country is in the process of ongoing domestic reform (economic, social and political). First, there are the reforms associated with Deng (and his immediate successors), that is, the Four Modernizations (agriculture, industry, science and defence), and these included (i) village level reforms (household responsibility system and TVEs); (ii) reforms to SOEs (reworked as profit and loss centres with power devolved to local management); (iii) SEZs (free trade areas, utilizing imported money and technology and local labour); and (iv) the start of reforms to the military, initiating a slow shift from inland-oriented, militia-type organizations to a modern war-fighting military. And there were related areas of reform with the earliest moves in regard to social welfare (now with economic and administrative decentralization less likely to run alongside work units) – education, health care, housing and social security.

Then there are the reforms associated with more recent governments. First, embracing the developmental state, the mix of state direction and market activity, with the whole ensemble being oriented towards national development. Second, economic reforms dealing with a range of problems: over-investment in infrastructure (the task of reigning in multiple provisions); prevalence of low-end manufacturing (task of moving up the value chain); low levels of domestic consumption (excess savings and thus a weak local market and lower standards of living than necessary); corruption in the party-state and business; along with catastrophic pollution. Here economic growth has been headlong, and policy makers have favoured growth now, clean up later, but this has now caught up with them and China has a catastrophic pollution problem (air, water and land). Third, there are related issues in general social policy, for example, health care reforms and old-age pensions. Then, fourth, there are some specific issues in social policy (elderly empty nesters, left-behind children, with both problems created by younger people migrating to the cities for work, plus the more subtle problems of single children who consequently lack siblings). And, thereafter, there are other reforms; thus digital communication has created a virtual online public sphere – with many voices – giving rise to party-state anxieties and attempts at control; there have been reforms to bureaucracy (e-government), and, lately, there has been a severe crackdown on corruption, along with restrictions to the public sphere, and, for CCP members a reassertion of the importance of Marxism and cadre discipline.

In the international political environment many commentators take the view that China is in the process of becoming a great power. Domestically, the intellectual resources informing politics and policy making oriented towards the wider global system once again involve the resources of inherited cultural tradition, the long-established local variant of Marxism, plus more recent imports of foreign ideas, in particular the materials of mainstream international relations theory. These resources are deployed to read the regional and global situation. The Beijing government is increasingly active in both areas, asserting its power within the region and calling attention to its status within the wider global sphere.

Beijing has been involved in a number of key exchanges in the region. First, there is the crucial relationship with the USA. Thus, the USA supported Nationalist China during the civil war, and the defeat of the nationalists was read into a nascent cold war division of East Asia, and this in turn was solidified by the Korean War (where American and Chinese military forces were directly engaged). Second, there is the difficult relationship with Japan. Here Japan's exchange with the modern world in the late nineteenth century saw them constructing not merely a modern economy and society but also an empire in Northeast Asia. This was constructed in part against the interests of the declining Qing Empire, and the slow disintegration of that empire encouraged deeper Japanese involvement, justified in terms of notions of Pan-Asian doctrines, until the relationship degenerated into open warfare. And third, China has mostly cordial relationships with members of ASEAN, although recently difficulties have arisen in connection with Chinese claims on the entirety of the South China Sea.

Beijing faces a number of key issues: the status of Tibet, the status of Taiwan, the status of Xinjiang, the condition of links with Hong Kong and Macau, the nature of its links to North Korea; it faces disputes over the South China Sea; and it must have a concern for embedding the country in formal global networks (UN, WTO, AIIB and the like). One recent initiative has been cast in terms of building a new Silk Road – linking China, through Asia, to Europe.

Commentators in Beijing now assert the country's claim to the status of great power and for a European audience this can have unfortunate resonances, redolent of the exchanges between European powers in the years leading up to the Great War; however, the elite in Beijing are at pains to soften their status claims with ideas of peaceful rising or the China Dream and, more broadly, with an idea of the appropriate recovery of status for the country, a process of picking up all the economic and political threads broken in the process of the long shift to the modern world.

FINAL COMMENTS

China entered the modern world via a long experience of quasi-colonial rule, and Europeans and later Americans and Japanese, riding the power of the cultural form of life of industrial capitalism, were the agents of sweeping change in China. From the early nineteenth century through to the opening years of the twentieth, the nature of Chinese politics – institutions and ideas – were shaped by the exchange with foreigners. The Qing elite was slow to react; later, they did make efforts to modernize, but it was too little, too late, and they were pushed aside. The earliest attempts at a coherent and effective response to the demands of the modern world came with a revolution provoked by disputes about funding railways. Now associated with the ideas and work of Sun Yat Sen, it was an attempt to build a modern republic. But this endeavour failed, and a period of warlord rule followed, which in turn gave way to civil war, with the domestic situation made infinitely more difficult by inter-state warfare against Japan. The domestic situation was not stabilized until 1949, when matters were brought under control with the establishment of the PRC. A new political settlement was put in place: foreign forces along with domestic enemies (elite and mass) were expelled or subordinated to the new regime, new institutional machineries and ways of understanding were put in place, and together they carried new domestic power relations and official ways of understanding, and these in turn informed development projects looking forward.

Contemporary China is ordered via a party-state system. It is the key institutional machinery of the Chinese polity, and it is best thought of as a double bureaucracy; the elements intermix at all levels and together all this produces a single countrywide hierarchical system. One line provides a career structure for aspirant politicians. An aspiring politician will work his or her way up this hierarchy, moving from appointment to appointment, and from an elite perspective this allows the identification of those who are particularly effective and can thus be recruited to high-level positions. The other complementary line provides a career structure for aspiring administrators, or civil servants, and it too is hierarchical and national. Administrators work their way up the hierarchy and established elite figures can identify recruits for high-level positions. The party and state bureaucracies are nominally separate, but in practice they interpenetrate at all levels. The party is the superior line of power. In this system both political cadres and administrators must work their way up their respective hierarchies; thereafter, of course, like any such system, family background and personal connections can aid upward movement.

This party-state system is the politico-administrative backbone of the Chinese polity, and the party elite in Beijing formally orders the system. Instructions are passed down. But, contrariwise, any demands for change originating from the top must necessarily be translated into practice by the lower levels of the party-state machineries, and drastic reforms are not easily accomplished as unwanted demands for reform are easily stymied. Nonetheless, the double bureaucracy is neither unresponsive nor static. It may be ordered top-down, but it does adjust, and so problems are identified and tackled. Political debate takes place within the relevant bureaucratic hierarchy. Dissent is not welcome, and whilst individual critics can be absorbed, organized criticism is not dealt with kindly, and open opposition is met with repression, whilst violence is met head-on. One recent commentator has characterized the party as an 'organizational emperor':[7] it lays claim to benign paternalistic concern; it does not welcome public questions as they impact its established self-understandings; however, such self-understandings open the system to traditional ways of engineering change, for if the emperor loses the mandate of heaven then rebellion is justified.

****

The party-state will change and adapt as it has in the past.[8] However, the goals built into the party apparatus do not point towards a European- or American-style liberal-democratic party system,[9] and cast in terms of the historical trajectory of the country there is no reason to suppose that it should; the party has been shaped by the shift to the modern world as that process unfolded in China, and whilst it has reformed internally, and reformed its involvement with wider society, it has not moved towards a European or American competitive party system. The party-state is the core of the Chinese political system. It will not change its core identity – reforms yes, accumulative, drawing in more people and slowly regularizing the procedures inherited from civil war and days of revolution, but the core machinery of the system is oriented towards continuity.[10]

The machinery is centred on Beijing and is organized via the double bureaucracy of the party-state system, animated by the machinery of the party and legitimated in terms which call attention both to extensive material advances and an emphatically articulated ideology of Chinese nationalism. The party remains the key locus of political life, and elite party circles and the associated policy community determine the overall line of policy. In recent years Xi Jinping has emphasized the role of the party and the related importance of the anti-corruption drive; plus there has been a stress on nationalism. Commentators[11] suggest that Xi Jinping's government is in a sense conservative, committed to the rule of the party, committed to its deepest ideas/beliefs, committed to the continuation of the party-state system and, most generally, committed to the continuing rise of China.

NOTES

1. R. Bickers 2011 *The Scramble for China: Foreign Devils in the Qing Empire 1832–1914*, London, Allen Lane; J. Lovell 2011 *The Opium Wars: Drugs, Dreams and the Making of China*, London, Picador.
2. W.A. Callahan 2013 *China Dreams: 20 Visions of the Future*, Oxford University Press.
3. G. Davies 2009 *Worrying about China: The Language of Chinese Critical Enquiry*, Harvard University Press.
4. Callahan 2013.
5. Davies 2009 – see chapter 1.
6. The ideas of little/great traditions come from an American anthropologist Robert Redfield. The former idea has proved to be influential – it called attention to the sets of ideas running through ordinary life.
7. Zheng, Y. 2010 *The Chinese Communist Party as Organizational Emperor: Culture, Reproduction and Transformation*, London, Routledge.
8. D. Shambaugh 2008 *China's Communist Party: Atrophy and Adaptation*, University of California Press notes the way the party responded to the unanticipated collapse of the USSR – it upgraded its performance; others would add that for its public it upgraded its nationalist rhetoric, see C.R. Hughes 2006 *Chinese Nationalism in the Global Era*, London, Routledge; Zhao, Suisheng 2004 *A Nation-State by Construction: Dynamics of Modern Chinese Nationalism*, Stanford University Press.
9. Zheng 2010 pp. 176–7.
10. Zheng 2010 pp. 176–7.
11. That is, Xi's reforms and nationalism are aimed at strengthening the party-state, not changing it (reports began to appear in the *Financial Times*, *Economist*, *South China Morning Post* and so on in mid-2015).

Bibliography

Acharya, A. 2000 *The Quest for Identity: International Relations of Southeast Asia*, Oxford University Press.

Acharya, A. 2010 *Whose Ideas Matter: Agency and Power in Asian Regionalism*, Singapore, ISEAS.

All-China Women's Federation 2012 July 27 30% Chinese Left-behind Children Feel Helpless, Online. <www.womenofchina.cn>.

All-China Women's Federation 2013 August 11 China's Left-behind Children Face Multiple Challenges, Online. <www.womenofchina.cn>.

All-China Women's Federation 2013 December 18 SE China Establishes Care Station for Left-behind Children, Online. <www.womenof china.cn>.

All-China Women's Federation 2014 January 12 China: 80% of Migrant-worker Parents with 'Left-behind' Children Feel Inadequate, Online. <www.womenofchina.cn>.

All-China Women's Federation 2014 March 12 NPC Deputy Urges More Care for Left-behind Children, Online. <www.womenofchina.cn>.

All-China Women's Federation 2014 March 26 Henan to Construct 'Left-behind Children's Home', Online. <www.womenofchina.cn>.

All-China Women's Federation 2014 June 2 China Trains Social Workers to Help Left-behind Children, Online. <www.womenofchina.cn>.

All-China Women's Federation 2014 June 4 Spotlight on Mental Health of Left-behind Children, Online. <www.womenofchina.cn>.

All-China Women's Federation 2014 July 30 Henan Provides Day-Care Services to 'Left-behind' Children, Online. <www.womenofchina.cn>.

Anderson, B. 2016 'Frameworks of Comparison' in *London Review of Books* 38.2 January 21.

Ash, R. 2002 'The Cultural Revolution as an Economic Phenomenon' in Draguhn, W. and Goodman, D.S.G. eds. *China's Communist Revolutions: Fifty Years of the People's Republic of China*, London, Routledge Curzon.

Ba, A. 2009 *(Re)Negotiating East and Southeast Asia: Region, Regionalism and the Association of Southeast Asian Nations*, Stanford University Press.

Ballard, J.G. 1988 *Empire of the Sun*, London, Grafton.

Ballard, J.G. 2008 *Miracles of Life: From Shanghai to Shepperton: An Autobiography*, London, Fourth Estate.

Barrett, D.P. and Shyu, L.N. eds. 2001 *Chinese Collaboration with Japan, 1932–1945: The Limits of Accommodation*, Stanford University Press.

Bayly, C. and Harper, T. 2007 *Forgotten Armies: The Fall of British Asia 1941–45*, London, Allen Lane.

Beeson, M. 2014 *Regionalism and Globalization in East Asia*, London, Palgrave.

Beeson, M. and Stubbs, R. eds. 2012 *Routledge Handbook of Asian Regionalism*, London, Routledge.

Beijing Normal University 2014 Chairman Xi Jinping Called on the Nation's Teacher to Be a Party & People-Satisfied Teacher, Online. <english.bnu.edu.cn/ 2014-09-09>.

Beyazit, A. 2014 'Human Rights Violations against Uyghur Turks in China' in *Human Rights Review* 4.8.

Bickers, R. 2011 *The Scramble for China: Foreign Devils in the Qing Empire 1832–1914*, London, Allen Lane.

Bloomsbury 2009 *Business Essential*, A & C Black Publishers Ltd.

Bregolat, E. 2015 *The Second Chinese Revolution*, New York, Palgrave.

Brook, T. 2005 *Collaboration: Japanese Agents and Local Elites in Wartime China*, Harvard University Press.

Brown, K. 2014 *The New Emperors: Power and the Princelings in China*, London, I.B. Tauris.

Bucknall, K.B. 1989 *China and the Open Door Policy*, Sydney, Allen & Unwin.

Buruma, I. 1994 *The Wages of Guilt: Memories of War in Germany and Japan*, London, Jonathan Cape.

Callahan, W.A. 2010 *China: The Pessoptimist Nation*, Oxford University Press.

Callahan, W.A. 2013 *China Dreams: 20 Visions of the Future*, Oxford University Press.

Cao, C. 2013 'Science Imperilled: Intellectuals and the Cultural Revolution' in Wei, C.N. and Brock, D.E. eds. *Mr. Science and Chairman Mao's Cultural Revolution: Science and Technology in Modern China*, Lanham, MD, Lexington Books.

Capling, A. and Ravenhill, J. 2011 'Multilateralising Regionalism: What Role for the Trans-Pacific Partnership Agreement' in *The Pacific Review* 24.5.

Carson, R.L. 1998 *Comparative Economic Systems: Transition and Capitalist Alternatives*, New York, M.E. Sharpe, Inc.

Chan, C.K., Ngok, K.L. and Phillips, D. 2008 *Social Policy in China: Development and Well-being*, Bristol, Policy Press.

Chan, K.M. 1995 'Education – Decentralization and the Market' in Wong, L. and Macpherson, S. eds. *Social Change and Social Policy in Contemporary China*, Aldershot, UK, Avebury.

Chen, J. 2001 *Mao's China and the Cold War*, University of North Carolina Press.

Chen, J. 2003 *The Path toward Sino-American Rapprochement 1969– 1972*, GHI Bulletin Supplement 1.

Chen, J. 2009 'A 60-year Review of Housing Development in China' (Chinese version), Working Paper of Centre for Housing Policy Studies, Fudan University, Online. <http://www.chps.fudan.edu.cn/cn/ content.asp?id=50>.

Chen, N.H.H. and Fu, T.H. 2009 'Older People's Income Security in China: The Challenges of Population Ageing' in Fu, T.H. and Hughes, R. eds. *Ageing in East Asia: Challenges and Policies for the Twenty-First Century*, New York, Routledge.

Cheng, J. 2012 'Challenges for China's Harmonious Diplomacy' in Lai, H. and Lu, Y. eds. *China's Soft Power and International Relations*, New York, Routledge.

China Daily 2007 September 29 Harmonious Society, Online. <http:// english.peopledaily.com.cn>.

China Daily 2008 June 20 Chinese President Takes Part in Online Chat, Online. <http://www.chinadaily.com.cn>.

China Daily 2015 June 13 Li Stresses Importance to Increase Efforts in Response to Climate Change, Online. <http://www.chinadaily. com.cn>.

China News 2013 November 5 Ministry of Civil Affairs: Ageing Population Grows Quickly, Ageing Population Reaches 200 Million This Year (Chinese version), Online. <www.chinanews.com>.

Ching, F. 2015 China Accepts US Challenge of Greater Responsibility, Online. <http://www.ejinsight.com>.

Chiu, S. and Lui, T.L. 2009 *Hong Kong: Becoming a Chinese Global City*, London, Routledge.

Chow, G.C. 2015 *China's Economic Transformation*, Chichester, UK, Wiley-Blackwell.

Christiansen, F. and Rai, S. 1996 *Chinese Politics and Society: An Introduction*, Hemel Hempstead, UK, Prentice Hall.

Clammer, J. 1997 *Contemporary Urban Japan*, Oxford, Blackwell.

Crossley, P.K. 2010 *The Wobbling Pivot: China since 1800*, Chichester, UK, Wiley-Blackwell.

Cummings, B. 1997 *Korea's Place in the Sun: A Modern History*, New York, Norton.

Cummings, B. 1999 *Parallax Visions: Making Sense of American–East Asian Relations at the End of the Century*, Duke University Press.

Cyberspace Administration of China 2015 The Internet Users' Account Names Management Regulations (Chinese version), Online. <http://www.cac.gov.cn>.

Datta, K.L. 2004 *Central Planning: A Case Study of China*, New Delhi, Concept Publishing.

Deng, X. 1977 'Respect Knowledge, Respect Trained Personnel', from *The Selected Works of Deng Xiaoping, Volume II (1975–1982)*, Online. <www.dengxiaopingworks.wordpress.com>.

Deng, X. 1978 May 7 Realize the Four Modernizations and Never Seek Hegemony, Online. <https://dengxiaopingworks.wordpress.com>.

Deng, X. 1984 May 29 We Must Safeguard World Peace and Ensure Domestic Development, Online. <http://en.people.cn>.

Deng, Y. 2015 'China: The Post-responsible Power' in *The Washington Quarterly* 37.4.

Dillon, M. 2015 *Deng Xiaoping: The Man Who Made Modern China*, London, I.B. Tauris.

Ding, C. 2009 *Shijie zhuyao yiliao baozhang zhidu moshi jixiao bijiao* (Comparative Studies on Major Health Insurance Systems around the World), Shanghai, Fudan University Press.

Donald, R. 2013 The UN Climate Talks Have a Responsibility Problem, Online. <http://www.carbonbrief.org>.

Dong, W. 2001 Health Care Reform in Urban China, Online. <www.munkschool.utoronto.ca>.

Dore, R. 1986 *Flexible Rigidities*, Stanford University Press.

Dore, R. 1987 *Taking Japan Seriously*, Stanford University Press.

Dower, J. 1999 *Embracing Defeat: Japan in the Aftermath of World War II*, London, Allen Lane.

Duckett, J. 2011 *The Chinese State's Retreat from Health: Policy and the Politics of Retrenchment*, New York, Routledge.

Edwards, S.B. III and Santos, D. eds. 2015 *Revolutionizing the Interaction between State and Citizens through Digital Communications*, Hershey, IGI Global.

Fenby, J. 2005 *Generalissimo: Chiang Kai Shek and the China He Lost*, London, The Free Press.

Frank, A.G. 1998 *Re-Orient: Global Economy in the Asian Age*, University of California.

Franzese, P. 2009 'Sovereignty in Cyberspace: Can It Exist?' in *Air Force Law Review* 64.

Friedberg, A.L. 2011 Hegemony with Chinese Characteristics, Online. <http://users.clas.ufl.edu/zselden/coursereading2011/friedberg.pdf>.

Frost, E. 2009 'Whose Ideas Matter: Agency and Power in Asian Regionalism' in *Contemporary Southeast Asia* 33.3.

Gao, J. 2004 *The Communist Takeover of Hangzhou: The Transformation of City and Cadre, 1949–1954*, University of Hawaii Press.

Genzberger, C. 1995 *China Business: The Portable Encyclopedia for Doing Business with China*, San Rafael, CA, World Trade Press.

Gerson, M.S. 2010 The Sino-Soviet Border Conflict: Deterrence, Escalation, and the Threat of Nuclear War in 1969, Online. <www.cna.org>.

Good Governance International Corp. 2013 The China E-government Development Index Report 2013: Experiences in Hangzhou Municipality, Zhejiang Province, Online. <http://goodgovintl.org>.

Grice, H. 2009 *Asian American Fiction, History and Life Writing: International Encounters*, London, Routledge.

Guan, X. 2005 'China's Social Policy: Reform and Development in the Context of Marketization and Globalization' in Kwon, H.J. ed. *Transforming the Developmental Welfare State in East Asia*, Basingstoke, UK, Palgrave Macmillan.

Gustafsson, K. 2015 'Identity and Recognition: Remembering and Forgetting the Post-war in Sino-Japanese Relations' in *The Pacific Review* 28.1.

Harford, K. 2003 'West Lake Wired: Shaping Hangzhou's Information Age' in Lee, C. ed. *Chinese Media, Global Contexts*, New York, Routledge Curzon.

Hastings, M. 2008 *Retribution: The Battle for Japan*, New York, Alfred Knopf.

Hay, C. 2002 *Political Analysis: A Critical Introduction*, London, Palgrave.

Hu, J. 2005 Build towards a Harmonious World of Lasting Peace and Common Prosperity, Online. <http://www.un.org>.

Hu, J. 2007 Report to the Seventeenth National Congress of the Communist Party of China on Oct. 15, 2007, Online. <http://www.china.org.cn>.

Hu, J. 2012 Full Texts of Hu Jintao's Report at 18th Party Congress, Online. <http://english.cntv.cn>.

Hu, S. 2012 'Russia and Cross-Taiwan Strait Relations' in Wei, G. ed. *China–Taiwan Relations in a Global Context: Taiwan's Foreign Policy and Relations*, New York, Routledge.

Hughes, C.R. 2006 *Chinese Nationalism in the Global Era*, London, Routledge.

Hui, V.T.B. 2012 'History and Thought in China's Traditions' in *Journal of Chinese Political Science* 17.

Huntington, S.P. 2011 *The Clash of Civilization and the Remaking of World Order*, New York, Simon & Schuster.

IISS *Comments* 2014 (20.9) 'Chinese Vision Drives East Asian Détente'.

IISS *Comments* 2014 (20.9) 'US Navy Seeks to Maintain Supremacy'.

IISS *Comments* 2014 (20.4) 'Philippines China Dispute: A Sign of Regional Shifts'.

IISS *Comments* 2015 (21.4) 'China's Land Reclamation in the South China Sea'.

Jiang, M. 2013 China's 'Internet Sovereignty', Online. <http://www.fairobserver.com/politics/chinas-internet-sovereignty/>.

Jiang, X. 2002 October 24 Speech by President Jiang Zemin at George Bush Presidential Library, Online. <http://no.china-embassy.org/eng/dtxw/t110222.htm>.

Johnson, C. 1995 *Japan: Who Governs?* New York, Norton.

Jones, P.P. and Poleman, T.T. 1962 'Communes and the Agricultural Crisis in Communist China' in *Food Research Institute Studies* 1.

Kagan, R. 2005 'The Illusion of "Managing" China' in *The Washington Post*, May 15.

Kang, D. 2012 'East Asia when China Was at the Centre' in Beeson, M. and Stubbs, R. eds. *Routledge Handbook of Asian Regionalism*, London, Routledge.

Katzenstein, P. 2005 *A World of Regions: Asia and Europe in the American Imperium*, Cornell University Press.

Katzenstein, P. and Shirashi, T. eds. 1997 *Network Power: Japan and Asia*, New York, Cornell University Press.

Khoo, N. 2005 'Realism Redux: Investigating the Causes and Effects of Sino-US Rapprochement' in *Cold War History* 5.4.

Kolko, G. 1968 *The Politics of War*, New York, Vintage.

Koppel, B.M. and Orr, R.J. eds. 1993 *Japan's Foreign Aid: Power and Policy in a New Era*, Boulder, CO, Westview.

Kraus, W. 1982 *Economic Development and Social Change in the People's Republic of China*, New York, Springer-Verlag.

Kristensen, P.M. 2015 'International Relations in China and Europe: The Case for Interregional Dialogue in a Hegemonic Discipline' in *The Pacific Review* 28.2.

Lan, M. 2014 Internet Governance and Respect Internet Sovereignty (Chinese version), Online. <http://gb.cri.cn/42071/2014/11/26/882s4780005.htm>.

Larus, E.F. 2012 *Politics and Society in Contemporary China*, Boulder, CO, Lynne Rienner.

Lee, C.K. and Yang, G. eds. 2007 *Re-envisioning the Chinese Revolution*, Stanford University Press.

Lee, P.N.S. 1995 'Housing Privatization with Chinese Characteristics' in Wong, L. and Macpherson, S. eds. *Social Change and Social Policy in Contemporary China*, Aldershot, UK, Avebury.

Leung, J.C.B. 1994 'Dismantling the "Iron Rice Bowl": Welfare Reforms in the People's Republic of China' in *Journal of Social Policy* 23.3.

Leung, J.C.B. 1998 'The Transformation of Social Welfare Policy: The Restructuring of the "Iron Rice Bowl"' in Cheng, J.Y.S. ed. *China in the Post-Deng Era*, Hong Kong, Chinese University Press.

Li, C. 2014 *The Confucian Philosophy of Harmony*, New York, Routledge.

Li, J.F. 2009 Social Insurance in Rural China Should Be Legalized (Chinese version), Online. <http://paper.people.com.cn>.

Li, P. 2010 'Thirty Years of Reform and Changes of Social Policies' in Li, Q. ed. *Thirty Years of Reform and Social Changes in China*, Leiden, Brill.

Li, Q. 2009 *Zhongguo quanmin yiliao baozhang shixian lujing yanjiu* (Pathway to Realizing Universal Health Insurance in China), Beijing, People's Publishing House.

Li, X. 2007 *A History of the Modern Chinese Army*, University Press of Kentucky.

Li, X. ed. 2012 *China at War: An Encyclopedia*, Santa Barbara, CA, ABC-CLO, LLC.

Lin, Z. and Zobisch, M.A. eds. 2006 *Resource Use and Agricultural Sustainability: Risk and Consequences of Intensive Cropping in China*, Kassel University Press.

Liou, T.K. 1998 *Managing Economic Reforms in Post-Mao China*, Westport, CT, Greenwood Publishing.

Lo, B. 2008 *Axis of Convenience: Moscow, Beijing, and the New Geopolitics*, Washington, DC, Brookings Institution Press.

Lovell, J. 2011 *The Opium War: Drugs, Dreams and the Making of China*, London, Picador.

Lu, X. 2004 *Rhetoric of the Chinese Cultural Revolution: The Impact on Chinese Thought, Culture, and Communication*, University of South Carolina Press.

Lu, Z. and Hong, F. 2014 *Sport and Nationalism in China*, New York, Routledge.

Luk, S.C.Y. 2013 'E-government in China: Opportunities and Challenges for the Transformation of Governance in the Information Age' in Wu, B., Yao, S. and Chen, J. eds. *China's Development and Harmonization: Towards a Balance with Nature, Society and the International Community*, New York, Routledge Curzon.

Luk, S.C.Y. 2014 *Health Insurance Reforms in Asia*, London, Routledge.

Macfarquhar, R. and Scheonhals, M. 2006 *Mao's Last Revolution*, Harvard University Press.

MacKinnon, M. 2011 Dead or Alive, Former Chinese Leader Zemin Subject of Censorship in China, Online. <http://www.theglobeand mail.com>.

Mahbubani, K. 2008 *The New Asian Hemisphere*, New York, Public Affairs.

Mahbubani, K. 2013 *The Great Convergence*, New York, Public Affairs.

Mark, C.K. 2012 *China and the World since 1945: An International History*, New York, Routledge.

Marti, M.E. 2002 *China and the Legacy of Deng Xiaoping: From Communist Revolution to Capitalist Evolution*, Washington, DC, Brassey's.

Meisner, M. 1996 *The Deng Xiaoping Era: An Inquiry into the Fate of Chinese Socialism, 1978–1994*, New York, Hill and Wang.

Ministry of Foreign Affairs 2015 Accelerating Building of the Belt and Road, Forging China–Afghanistan Community of Common Destiny, Online. <http://www.fmprc.gov.cn>.

Ministry of Health and Ministry of Finance 1984 Notification of Further Strengthening the Management of the Government Insurance Scheme (Chinese version), Online. <http://www.chinalawedu.com/falvfagui/fg22598/23676.shtml>.

Mitter, R. and Moore, A.W. 2011 'China in World War II, 1937–45' in *Modern Asian Studies* 45.2.

Mok, K. 2005 'Governing through Governance: Changing Social Policy Paradigms in the Post-Mao People's Republic of China' in Jabes, J. ed. *The Role of Public Administration in Alleviating Poverty and Improving Governance*, Asia Development Bank, Online. <http://unpan1.un.org/intradoc/groups/public/documents/unpan/unpan025047.pdf>.

Moore, B. Jr. 1966 *Social Origins of Dictatorship and Democracy*, Boston, MA, Beacon Press.

Ngok, K.L. 2013 'Shaping Social Policy in the Reform Era in China' in Izuhara, M. ed. *Handbook on East Asian Social Policy*, Cheltenham, UK and Northampton, MA, Edward Elgar.

Ngok, K.L. 2014 'Bringing the State Back in: The Development of Chinese Social Policy in China in the Hu-Wen Era' in Mok, K.H. and Lau, M.K.W. eds. *Managing Social Change and Social Policy in Greater China: Welfare Regimes in Transition*, London, Routledge.

Ngok, K.L. and Zhu, Y. 2010 'In Search of Harmonious Society in China: A Social Policy Response' in Mok, K.H. and Ku, Y.W. eds. *Social Cohesion in Greater China: Challenges for Social Policy and Governance*, Singapore, World Scientific.

Noesselt, N. 2015 'Revisiting Debate on Constructing a Theory of International Relations with Chinese Characteristics' in *The China Quarterly*, June.

O'Brien, K. and Li, L. 2006 *Rightful Resistance in Rural China*, Cambridge University Press.

Orr, R.J. 1990 *The Emergence of Japan's Foreign Aid Power*, New York, Columbia University Press.

Ortmann, S. and Thompson, M.R. 2014 'China's Obsession with Singapore: Learning Authoritarian Modernity' in *The Pacific Review* 27.3.

Pearson, V. 1995 'Health and Responsibility; But Whose?' in Wong, L. and Macpherson, S. eds. *Social Change and Social Policy in Contemporary China*, Aldershot, UK, Avebury.

Peattie, M., Drea, E. and van de Ven, H. eds. 2011 *The Battle for China: Essays on the Military History of the Sino-Japanese War of 1937–1945*, Stanford University Press.

People's Daily 2000 January 15 The First National Working Conference on Housing System Reform in 1988 Identified the Ideas of Housing Reform (Chinese version), Online. <http://www.people.com.cn>.

People's Daily 2008 June 20 President Hu Promises Divergent Voices Be Heard Online, Online. <http://en.people.cn>.

People's Daily 2010 April 30 Deng Xiaoping: Talks on the Construction Industry and Housing Issues (Chinese version), Online. <http://news.163.com>.

People's Daily 2012 September 25 Almost Billion Yuan Added to Textbook Budget This Year, Online. <http://english.people.com.cn>.

People's Republic of China 1986 Compulsory Education Law of the People's Republic of China (Chinese version), Online. <http://www.edu.cn>.

Permanent Mission of the People's Republic of China to the United Nations 2003 China's Independent Foreign Policy of Peace, Online. <http://www.china-un.org/eng/gyzg/wjzc/t40387.htm>.

Preston, P.W. 2010 *National Pasts in Europe and East Asia*, London, Routledge.

Preston, P.W. 2016 *The Politics of Hong Kong–China Relations*, Cheltenham, UK and Northampton, MA, Edward Elgar.

Prozumenschikov, M.Y. 1997 'The Sino-Indian Conflict, the Cuban Missile Crisis, and the Sino-Soviet Split, October 1962: New Evidence from the Russian Archives' in *Cold War International History Project Bulletin*, Issue 8–9.

Rana, P.B. 2013 'Connectivity in Asia: Reviving the Old Silk Road?' in *RSIS Commentary*, June 6.

Report to Central Committee June 1981 Resolution on Certain Questions in the History of Our Party since the Founding of the People's Republic of China, Online. <www.marxists.org>.

Robinson, T.W. 1994 'Chinese Foreign Policy from the 1940s to the 1990s' in Robinson, T.W. and Shambaugh, D. eds. *Chinese Foreign Policy: Theory and Practice*, Oxford, Clarendon Press.

Rong, J. 2012 China Strives for Free Compulsory Education for All, Xinhua News, October 5, Online. <http://news.xinhuanet.com>.

Rosen, S. 1985 'Recentralization, Decentralization, and Rationalization: Deng Xiaoping's Bifurcated Educational Policy' in *Modern China* 11.3.

Rozman, G. 2012 'East Asian Regionalism' in Beeson, M. and Stubbs, R. eds. *Routledge Handbook of East Asian Regionalism*, London, Routledge.

Saich, T. 2004 *Governance and Politics of China*, London, Palgrave.

Segal, A. 2013 Cyberspace Cannot Live without Sovereignty, Says Lu Wei, Online. <http://blogs.cfr.org>.

Shambaugh, D. 2008 *China's Communist Party: Atrophy and Adaptation*, University of California Press.

Share, M.B. 2007 *Where Empires Collided: Russian and Soviet Relations with Hong Kong, Taiwan, and Macau*, The Chinese University of Hong Kong Press.

Shen, Z. and Xia, Y. 2015 *Mao and the Sino-Soviet Partnership, 1945–1959: A New History*, Lanham, MD, Lexington Books.

Short, P. 2004 *Mao: A Life*, London, John Murray.

Sina News 2014 November 19 Xi Jinping: Respect Internet Sovereignty, Maintain Internet Security (Chinese version), Online. <http://news.sina.com.cn>.

South China Morning Post 2013 October 30 China to Boost Availability of Affordable Homes, Says Xi Jinping, Online. <www.scmp.com>.

Spence, J. 2001 Introduction to the Cultural Revolution, Online. <http://spice.standford.edu>.

Spence, J.D. 2013 *The Search for Modern China*, New York, Norton.

Spence, J. and Chin, A. 1996 *The Chinese Century: A Photographic History*, London, Harper.

Stevens, T. 2015 China's Ban on Virtual Private Networks, Online. <http://thesigers.com>.

Strange, S. 1988 *States and Markets*, London, Pinter.

Stubbs, R. 2005 *Rethinking Asia's Economic Miracle: The Political Economy of War, Prosperity and Crisis*, London, Palgrave.

Su, H. 2008 Harmonious World: The Conceived International Order in Framework of China's Foreign Affairs, Online. <http://www.nids.go.jp>.

Tai, Z. 2006 *The Internet in China: Cyberspace and Civil Society*, New York, Routledge.

Taylor, B., Chang, K. and Li, Q. 2003 *Industrial Relations in China*, Cheltenham, UK and Northampton, MA, Edward Elgar.

The Central Committee of the Communist Party of China 1985 Decision on the Reform of the Educational Structure (Chinese version), Online. <http://learning.sohu.com>.

The Central Committee of the Communist Party of China and the State Council 1980 Decision on Several Issues in Universalizing Primary Education (Chinese version), Online. <http://www.chinalawedu.com>.

The China Internet Network Information Centre 2015 The 36th Statistical Report on Internet Development in China (Chinese version), Online. <http://www.cnnic.cn>.

The General Office of the CPC Central Committee and the General Office of the State Council 2002 Guiding Opinions of the National Informatization Leading Group on the Development of E-government in China (Chinese version), Online. <http://xzjc.zunyi.gov.cn>.

The General Office of the CPC Central Committee and the General Office of the State Council 2006 National Informatization Development Strategy (2006–2020) (Chinese version), Online. <http://www.cast.org.cn>.

The Hainan Government 1991 Temporary Regulations on Medical Insurance for Employees (Chinese version), Online. <http://laws.66law.cn/law-79637.aspx>.

The Housing System Reform Leading Group of the State Council 1987 The Bulletin of Forum on the Pilot Reform on Urban Housing System (Chinese version), Online. <http://www.bjfang.com>.

The Housing System Reform Leading Group of the State Council 1991 Opinions on Implementing Urban Housing System Reform on Full Scale (Chinese version), Online. <http://www.110.com>.

The Ministry of Civil Affairs 1987 The Report on Exploring the Establishment of a Basic Social Security System in Rural China (Chinese version), Online. <http://www.law-lib.com>.

The Ministry of Civil Affairs 1991 Trail Implementation Plan on Rural Social Insurance Pension at the County Level (Chinese version), Online. <http://www.chinaacc.com>.

The State Council 1983 Ordinance on Managing Private Housing in Urban Areas (Chinese version), Online. <www.szhome.com>.

The State Council 1986 The Interim Regulations on Unemployment Insurance for Employees of State-owned Enterprises (Chinese version), Online. <http://www.law-lib.com>.

The State Council 1988 The Implementation Plan for a Gradual Housing System Reform in Cities and Towns (Chinese version), Online. <http://www.gdczt.gov.cn>.

The State Council 1991a Notification of the Continuation of Urban Housing System Reform in an Active and Stable Manner (Chinese version), Online. <http://www.law110.com>.

The State Council 1991b Decision on Reforming Old Age Insurance System for Enterprise Workers (Chinese version), Online. <http://3y.uu456.com>.

The State Council Information Office 2010 The Internet in China, Online. <http://news.xinhuanet.com>.

The United Nations 2010 The United Nations E-Government Survey 2010: Leveraging E-Government at a Time of Financial and Economic Crisis, Online. <http://unpan3.un.org>.

The United Nations 2012 The United Nations E-Government Survey 2012: E-Government for the People, Online. <http://unpan3.un.org>.

The United Nations 2014 United Nations E-Government Survey 2014: E-Government for the Future We Want, Online. <http://unpan3.un.org>.

Thelle, H. 2004 *Better to Rely on Ourselves: Changing Social Rights in Urban China since 1979*, Copenhagen, NIAS Press.

Tiezzi, S. 2014 Xi Jinping Leads China's New Internet Security Group, Online. <http://thediplomat.com>.

Tisdell, C. 2009 'Economic Reform and Openness in China: China's Development Policies in the Last 30 Years' in *Economic Analysis and Policy* 39.2.

Trocki, C. 1999 *Opium, Empire and the Global Political Economy: A Study of the Asian Opium Trade 1750–1950*, London, Routledge.

Trocki, C.A. 2006 *Singapore: Wealth, Power and the Culture of Control*, London, Routledge.

Tsai, K.S. 2007 *Capitalism without Democracy: The Private Sector in Contemporary China*, Cornell University Press.

van Wolferen, K. 1989 *The Enigma of Japanese Power*, London, Macmillan.

Veeck, G., Pannell, C.W., Smith, C.J. and Huang, Y. 2011 *China's Geography: Globalization and the Dynamic of Political, Economic, and Social Change*, Lanham, MD, Rowman & Littlefield.

Wade, R. 2004 *Governing the Markets: Economic Theory and the Role of Government in East Asia*, Princeton University Press.

Walder, A.G. 2015 *China under Mao: A Revolution Derailed*, Harvard University Press.

Wang, F. 2010 'Boundaries of Inequality: Perceptions of Distributive Justice among Urbanites, Migrants, and Peasants' in Whyte, M.K. ed. *One Country, Two Societies: Rural–Urban Inequality in Contemporary China*, Harvard University Press.

Webber, D. 2010 'The Regional Integration that Didn't Happen: Cooperation without Integration in Early Twentieth Century East Asia' in *The Pacific Review* 23.3.

Weiss, L. 1998 *The Myth of the Powerless State: Governing the Economy in a Global Era*, Cambridge, Polity.

White, G. ed. 1988 *Developmental States in East Asia*, London, Macmillan.

Whiting, A.S. 1995 'Chinese Nationalism and Foreign Policy after Deng' in *The China Quarterly* 142.

Wirth, C. 2015 'Power and Stability in the China–Japan–South Korea Regional Security Complex' in *The Pacific Review* 26.4.

Wong, R. Bin 1997 *China Transformed: Historical Change and the Limits of European Experience*, Cornell University Press.

World Bank 1993 *The East Asian Miracle: Economic Growth and Public Policy*, Oxford University Press.

Wu, J. and Zhao, S. 2014 Xi: Respect Cyber Sovereignty, Online. <http://usa.chinadaily.com.cn>.

Wu, L. 2012 Xi Jinping Met with WHO Director-General (Chinese version), People's Daily, July 21, Online. <http://politics.people.com.cn>.

Xi, J. 2015 Towards a Community of Common Destiny and a New Future for Asia, Online. <http://english.boaoforum.org>.

Xinhuanet 2007 November 2 Internet Becomes Important Channel for Chinese Public's Political Participation, Online. <http://news.xinhuanet.com>.

Xinhuanet 2008 February 22 China's State Council to Use Internet for Public Opinion, Online. <http://news.xinhuanet.com>.

Xinhuanet 2008 June 20 Chinese President Holds First Web Chat with Citizens, Online. <http://news.xinhuanet.com>.

Xinhuanet 2009a February 28 Premier Wen Talks Online with Netizens, Online. <http://news.xinhuanet.com>.

Xinhuanet 2009b February 28 People Have Right to Criticize Gov't, Says Chinese Premier Wen, Online. <http://news.xinhuanet.com>.

Xinhuanet 2009 March 2 Chinese Lawmakers to Talk with Netizens during 'Two Sessions', Online. <http://news.xinhuanet.com>.

Xinhuanet 2014 February 27 Xi Jinping: Transforming China from a 'Big Cyber Country' into a 'Cyber Power' (Chinese version), Online. <http://thediplomat.com>.

Xinhua News 2003 October 8 23.4 Million Empty Nesters Struggle to Live Alone, Online. <http://news.xinhuanet.com>.

Xinhua News 2004 March 3 Cyber Chat Topics Cover A to Z, Online. <http://www.china.org.cn>.

Xinhua News 2011 October 27 China Explores In-home Nursing as Population Pressure Grows, Online. <http://news.xinhuanet.com>.

Xinhua News 2012 October 1 China Focus: Long Holiday Plagues Single White Collars, Online. <http://news.xinhuanet.com>.

Xinhua News 2012 October 22 Xinhua Insight: Graying China in Dire Need of Senior Care, Online. <http://news.xinhuanet.com>.

Xinhua News 2013 February 7 China Legislates to Maintain Spring Festival Tradition, Online. <http://news.xinhuanet.com>.

Xinhua News 2013 September 26 Xi Jinping: China Will Work Hard to Promote Education for All and Life-long Education (Chinese version), Online. <http://news.xinhuanet.com>.

Xinhua News 2013 October 11 Xinhua Insight: Aging China Faces Elder Neglect, Online. <http://news.xinhuanet.com>.

Xinhua News 2014 March 3 A Historical Review of Housing System Reform in China (Chinese version), Online. <http://www.ce.cn>.

Xinhua News 2014 April 14 Guizhou to Build 800 Nurseries for 'Left-behind' Children, Online. <http://news.xinhuanet.com>.

Xinhua News 2014 April 17 School in Ningxia Sets Up Counseling Room for Left-behind Children, Online. <http://news.xinhuanet.com>.

Xinhua News 2014 April 23 Around China: Yellow Ribbons Tied by China's Empty Nesters, Online. <http://news.xinhuanet.com>.

Yahuda, M. 2011 3rd ed. *The International Politics of the Asia Pacific*, London, Routledge.

Yang, D. and Fang, C. 2000 The Political Economy of China's Rural–Urban Divide, Online. <http://iple.cass.cn/upload/2012/06/d20120601171201684.pdf>.

Yang, K. 2013 *Capitalists in Communist China*, New York, Palgrave.

Yang, Z. 2015 *Local Government and Politics in China: Challenges from Below*, New York, Routledge.

Yang, Z. and Chen, J. 2014 *Housing Affordability and Housing Policy in Urban China*, Berlin, Springer.

Ye, H. 2015 'Key-point Schools and Entry into Tertiary Education in China' in *Chinese Sociological Review* 47.2.

Yoshino, K. 1992 *Cultural Nationalism in Contemporary Japan*, London, Routledge.

Zhang, X. 2014 *Enterprise Management Control Systems in China*, Berlin, Springer.

Zhao, G. 2015 'Let's Not Get Carried Away; Asian Infrastructure Investment Bank Faces Many Hurdles' in *South China Morning Post*, April 30, Online. <http://www.scmp.com>.

Zheng, Y. 2010 *The Chinese Communist Party as Organizational Emperor: Culture, Reproduction and Transformation*, London, Routledge.

Zheng, Y. and Huang, Y. 2013 'Political Dynamics of Social Policy Reform in China' in Zhao, L. ed. *China's Social Development and Policy: Into the New Stage?* New York, Routledge.

Zhu, L. 2014 'China's Cold War Experience and Its New Security Concept' in Mastny, V. and Zhu, L. eds. *The Legacy of the Cold War: Perspectives on Security, Cooperation, and Conflict*, Lanham, MD, Lexington Books.

Zhu, R. 2013 *Zhu Rongji on the Record: The Road to Reform, 1991–1997*, Washington, DC, Brookings Institution Press.

Zu, Y. and Zhang, X. 2012 'Pension and Social Assistance: The Development of Income Security Policies for Old People in China' in Chen, S. and Powell, J.L. eds. *Ageing in China: Implications to Social Policy of a Changing Economic State*, New York, Springer.

Index